1956

1977

1963

200

1989

ST. LOUIS POST-DISPATCH
BERLIN WALL OPENS
Joyous Throngs Mob E. German Border

Getting On Base

The Vi-Jon Team and the American Dream

· · · · · ·

One Hundred Years and More with the Brunner Family

by

Edward A. Lemay

Our Purpose	**A Value Choice For A Better Life**
Our Mission	**"Go-To, Can-Do"**
Our Focus/Strategy	**On Time & Complete… "OTC"**
Our Method	• **Consistent Quality** • **Collaborative Teamwork** • **Continuous Improvement** • **Competitive Cost Advantage**
Our Character	• **Integrity** • **Honesty** • **Enthusiasm** • **Persistence**

Building Store Loyalty with Private Brands

Getting On Base

The Vi-Jon Team and the American Dream

· · · · · ·

One Hundred Years and More with the Brunner Family

Copyright © 2010 by Vi-Jon, Inc.
8515 Page Avenue
St. Louis, MO 63114

All rights reserved, including the right to reproduce this work in any way whatsoever without permission in writing from the publisher, except for brief passages in connection with a review. For information, please write:

The Donning Company Publishers
184 Business Park Drive, Suite 206
Virginia Beach, VA 23462

Steve Mull, General Manager
Barbara B. Buchanan, Office Manager
Richard A. Horwege, Senior Editor
Nathan Stufflebean, Graphic Designer
Derek Eley, Imaging Artist
Cindy Smith, Project Research Coordinator
Tonya Hannink, Marketing Specialist
Pamela Englehart, Marketing Advisor

Neil Hendricks, Project Director

Library of Congress Cataloging-in-Publication Data

Lemay, Edward A., 1952–
    Getting on base : the Vi-Jon team and the American dream one hundred years and more with the Brunner family / by Edward A. Lemay.
        p.   cm.
      ISBN 978-1-57864-585-5 (hard cover : alk. paper)
 1. Vi-Jon, Inc.—History. 2. Toilet preparations industry—United States—History. 3. Baseball—Social aspects—United States. I. Title.
    HD9970.5.T654V554 2010
    338.7'6681092—dc22
    [B]

                                                        2010001483

Printed in the USA at Walsworth Publishing Company

Dedicated to
the Vi-Jon Associates,
a "World Series" Champion Team.

Contents

Prologue *by John G. Brunner* 08

Pregame Briefing 10

Acknowledgments 11

I. JOHN BURGESS BRUNNER'S STORY

    1. **First Inning**: Leadoff—Founding a Legacy 12

    2. **Second Inning**: Securing the Right Lineup—The Roaring Twenties 30

    3. **Third Inning**: We Hit a Slump—The Great Depression 46

    4. **Fourth Inning**: The Rundown—From the Frying Pan into the Fire 68

II. JOHN WHITE BRUNNER'S STORY

    5. **Fifth Inning**: An Official Game—The Rookie Steps In 84

    6. **Sixth Inning**: Looking for a Rally—"Camelot" and Chain Stores Expansion 106

    7. **Seventh Inning**: No Time for Stretching—Gas Lines and Watergate 118

III. JOHN GAMMON BRUNNER'S STORY

    8. Eighth Inning: High and Tight Inside—An Actor Takes Center Stage **126**

    9. Ninth Inning: Victory within Our Grasp—A Millennium Milestone **152**

    10. Extra Innings: A New Century—Nothing Can Stop Us Now **184**

    11. Postgame Wrap-Up from the Heart: A One-Hundred-Year-Old Love Affair **202**

About The Author **214**

Postscript: Next Season **216**

Addenda: **218**

    Vi-Jon Laboratories, Inc., Boards of Directors, 1966 to 2009 218

    Awards Presented to Vi-Jon 226

    Chairman's Award Winners over the Years 228

    The Eighty-One Charter Associates of Vi-Jon's New Beginning in 1995 231

    Veterans Working at Vi-Jon 233

    Vendor of the Year Recipients 236

Epilogue: The "Perfect Game" *by Mel Turner* **238**

Patriotic Prayer *by Reverend Peter Marshall, Chaplain, Senate of the United States* **240**

Prologue

It was a warm August day and I was spending a rare, lonely afternoon in my former office at the old Etzel Avenue Plant. Rays from the glowing sun penetrated through a small window into the dimly lit room. Sitting at my desk, I looked around the office and noticed like never before the familiar wall ornaments and family picture. I heard the same old creaking sound from my chair as I eased back. A hollow, scratchy echo from a radio down the hall floated into my office, filling the room with play-by-play stats of a recently broadcast Cardinals game. My son, John, or J. B., lounged quietly on the worn couch in the corner, waiting for me, much as I had waited on numerous occasions for my dad in this very same office.

John G. Brunner's office in the Etzel Avenue Plant.

View from reverse side of the old Etzel Avenue office showing the side table, flags, and family portrait.

As I sat there, I reflected on memories of a friend whose funeral service I had recently attended. I realized he was actually more than a friend—he was a fellow Vi-Jon associate and a wonderful person—always a "half-full glass" versus a "half-empty glass" kind of a man. I try to consider a person's character, and their positive impact on the other folks around them, before I take note of their pecking order on the production floor. Today the glass looked decidedly empty and his absence made me think about how many Vi-Jon associates I had paid my last respects to over the years, people who had worked for the company and had passed through the sands of time. Each name and face streamed into my memory like a collage of images, a huge mass of good people, hard workers, and loyal friends.

At the same time, I realized that the Vi-Jon centennial anniversary was fast approaching, and it was my profound desire to put together a story that would express the total experience that this business institution had created over the past one hundred years. I also wanted a way to give all of the Vi-Jon associates over the years a heartfelt thanks by dedicating a very special story to this company and to its legacy before these memories are lost to the ages.

But how would I go about beginning this project? And where in the story should I start? My head swirled. I had so many questions. Who could I turn to? Where were all the wonderful people whose passionate support I had always counted on? If only I could talk to my dad and my grandfather now. They were the real storytellers, the keepers of the company's treasure troves. They held the many personal stories and fond remembrances that were truly Vi-Jon. If they were to tell the story, what would they do?

Then I realized that although I had never met my grandfather—he had passed away many years before I was born—his legacy lives on in me and in Vi-Jon. In a way, he had always been a part of me deep down inside. The story of how he had started his company on $400 in 1908 has been a part of the history of not only the company, but of our family, and of myself.

As I thought about what I knew of him, I realized that his story was also part of mine now. And the telling of this story of our family and associates, the Vi-Jon family, was in some ways so natural and entertaining that I just needed to honor the facts, be faithful to all the interesting and compassionate details, and allow the story to emerge on its own.

Yet at the same time, I wanted everyone to be able to embrace the story, be familiar with it like an old friend. I wanted folks to turn the first page and then need to turn to each succeeding page, moving through each chapter with a burning desire to read on. I wanted them to consume the entire story with the same dedication and intrigue as they might with a John Grisham or Stephen King novel. Was I hoping for too much? Yet those who do know our story have often expressed that they feel enriched and rewarded by the many moving moments that capture the warm human spirit that Vi-Jon has always stood for and that I now hope to honor within these written pages.

The portrait in the old Etzel Avenue office showing four generations of Brunners.

And so, I have decided to let my grandfather and father speak for themselves, in a way, in this book. The early years of the company's history are portrayed from their points of view. Largely based on company records and the memories of Vi-Jon associates, the following chapters recount the history of our corporate family from the perspective of its founder, my grandfather, John Burgess Brunner, and his successors, my father, John White Brunner, and myself.

So without further ado, I turn the beginning of our story over to the man who started it all—my grandfather, John Burgess Brunner.

—John G. Brunner

Pregame Briefing

This book was truly a collaboration of love, respect, and honest testimony. It was authored by the thousands of Vi-Jon associates who have worked for this wonderful company over these many years. I put together this story as we all would choose to hear it, and as it should be told—"directly" from the men who originated and guided us through one hundred years of splendid history and accomplishments. This is simply a monument to the American Dream and a family and just a few of their friends that made a difference.

John Burgess Brunner

John White Brunner

Close your eyes right now and you can hear the regal tenor voice of John B. Brunner, the founder, with his contagious laugh eliciting similar response from his closest subordinates. There are the lively sounds of an animated John W. "Jack" Brunner, courteously but effectively making a salient point about a favorite sales pitch to some of the many cohorts he trained in that prestigious art. And John G. Brunner passing through the offices and production areas of the company's many locations, with a quick smile and a warm friendly "how are you doing" that is enough to brighten any room he enters. And J. B. ("young John") as he talks about the international opportunities.

Acknowledgments

- To John G. Brunner for his commitment to this project in the face of overwhelming schedule demands that made his time and focus a particular challenge but a most rewarding result.

- To Ed Lemay, who since November of 2007 invested countless hours in the early morning and late evenings on top of long weekends to answer John's wish to scribe a "page turner," a book that all Vi-Jon associates past, present, and future could identify with, enjoy, and carry forward into the new and ever-expanding Vi-Jon Corporation of the future.

- To the Brunner family who provided support throughout the process of accumulating information, reviewing content, and providing direction on various parts of the process.

- To Pat Swinger who came in early in the process, gathered and documented the main sources of information, and provided a base document with these facts that was used repeatedly in the creation of the final manuscript for the book.

- To Mel Turner who provided a "sanity check" all along the process for both content and overall presentation of the final book.

- To Virginia Becker (John G. Brunner's daughter) and Julie Wan for their extremely valuable contributions in performing key reviews and edits on the manuscript prior to printing.

- To Margie Wilson who despite a challenging illness provided editing support and some degree of discipline in the development of the final manuscript.

- To J. B. Brunner who worked with Ed during various parts of the editing process. He served as one of Ed's sounding boards giving a good deal of direction at critical parts in the process.

- To Sharon Giacomo whose timely support during the key editing stage energized and sustained our efforts going all the way through to the final phases prior to printing.

- To Larry Sims, Brian Capstick, Jon Null, Faye Smith and the entire Vi-Jon Art Department for their support in both the photo inclusions and the development work associated with the design of the book and its cover, dust cover, and interior art design presentations.

- To Patty Lorenz who accumulated and monitored a good deal of the support materials that were critical to what became part of the final book presentation.

- Finally, to each and every Vi-Jon team member from the past and present who provided the motivation, basis, and most of the real content of this book. Remembering especially those past Vi-Jon employees who have departed their plant responsibilities on this earth. We are quite confident that they are in good hands and on John B. and John W. "Jack" Brunner's production staffs in the heavens above.

I. John Burgess Brunner's Story
1. First Inning: Leadoff—Founding a Legacy

For many of us, baseball—that quintessential American pastime—has served as a central clearinghouse and bridge between our dreams and the reality of daily life. I, John Burgess Brunner, like to think of Vi-Jon history as a nine-inning game, with the first one hundred years finishing in extra innings. I think it's safe to say we won that first game going away, and that we and our associates all did pretty well in the clutch. I see the second hundred years as the second game of a doubleheader. As a company we compete, we sometimes get the clutch hit, we sometimes go down swinging, but we always walk off the field as teammates and friends, having done our best and looking forward to tomorrow's competition out on that baseball field called life.

Now you have to understand, this was America in 1908 and, although it was considered the Progressive Era, it was still a time when lots of people did not exactly know where their next dime was coming from. I was always a believer in industrial pathways and opportunities, but it did not mean the same thing to the average Joe on the street. Everything was maybe as much of a gamble getting started years ago as it is now. Of course, I did not have an elite Board of Directors or the knowledge derived from an advanced MBA degree. But I had an awareness and gut feeling that there was something out there for me—I just needed to open my eyes and find my opportunity. For me it was time to start getting ahead or just continue to fall behind. I can truly say that I was a confident sort of fellow and above all would rather depend on myself than on anyone else. With two men out and the tying run on third, I always wanted to be at the plate, and I believe that was the way my teammates felt as well. I wanted the people around me, and those who depended on me, to feel that same way about my leadership.

Like I said, in 1908 America was in the midst of the years that would later be referred to as the Progressive Era. Industry was flourishing, small businesses prospered, and the rural population, along with the many new immigrants, were moving to the cities in record numbers to search for their share of the "American Dream." It was a time of peace and a time of social reshuffling. With the incomes these new jobs provided, people had a bit of disposable income for the first time in American history, and a brand-new middle class began to emerge. The appearance of this new middle class was part of my core business plan. I was betting on this social enclave who did most of the living, most of the growing, and yes, most of the dying in this great nation. They were my new customers. Cities went about the business of creating the department stores and recreational facilities to meet the needs of the rising middle class, and organizations sprang up to address the needs of the new urban poor.

It was against this backdrop that I resigned my position as a salesman for the Royal Glue Company and decided to start the Peroxide Specialty Company for less than half the price of Ford Motor Company's newly introduced Model T. I thought I had made the deal of the century! Who knew a century later, my grandson, John G. Brunner, would continue to sit at the helm of a company that survived and prospered through the Great Depression, two World Wars, and the challenges of an increasingly competitive and constantly changing marketplace. I couldn't be more proud of our "magnificent obsession."

In the Beginning

I guess for me to properly tell this story I need to go back in history—way back to 1804 when some of our relatives, the Burgess family, first came to the United States and settled in Baltimore, Maryland. This is a long time before the St. Louis Browns moved there to become the Baltimore Orioles. It was just three years after the close of the Civil War that I was born on March 4, 1868, the ninth of ten children born to my mom and dad, James George Washington Brunner and Catherine Jane Robinson Brunner. I was born in Washington, D.C., but shortly after my birth my dad, a carpenter by profession, built the family's homestead—"The Maples"—in Falls Church, Virginia. Dad worked as a contractor, and many of the homes in Falls Church still stand as a testament to his craftsmanship. I took great pride in knowing this. There is no finer legacy than that of having descended from a family of craftsmen. For a time, he also built frame houses for shipment to California by way of Cape Horn, a business he continued until his death at age eighty-one. He was a clutch hitter in all aspects of life as well and probably could have been quite a pitcher in baseball if he had been interested in pursuing that career. Dad purchased a seven-acre farm in Virginia, for the express purpose of making farmers out of his eight living children. Well, that never happened, as you'll soon see.

James G. W. Brunner, John B. Brunner's father.   Catherine Jane Brunner, John B. Brunner's mother.

Mom was a devout member of the Southern Methodist Episcopal Church and a devoted mother. With that many kids she needed a firm grasp on religion and faith, as you can well imagine! A history of Dulin Chapel in Falls Church lists mom (Mrs. James Brunner) among a group of women who were, "leaders in a successful crusade to drive out a saloon from the town of Falls Church in the 1870s." When the temperance movement gained momentum in the early 1900s, she became an active worker in the Independent Order of Good Templars. You know, my mom was very similar to my Viola. I guess that's why I fell in love with Vi so completely years later. I guess all the women in our lives had to have special qualities in order to support our demanding obligation in taking care of our customers.

"The Maples," Falls Church, Virginia—built in 1868 and occupied until 1905.

First Inning

My school learning extended only to the eighth grade level. In those days there was a sense of duty to get on with your life even at an early age. Then, of all things, I had this idea that I was quite the athlete, and an opportunity showed itself about this time.

The city of Washington fancied itself as a baseball-worthy town. Before the turn of the century I took a shot and played for the Washington National League franchise. I was a gamer and tried it long enough to know this was not my cup of tea, so you won't find me pictured on one of those baseball cards. Come to think of it, though, there really is nothing like being on a baseball field on a hot summer day, kicking up the dust, and enjoying the simple smell of well-worn leather mitts. Anyway, in 1899 the team shut down because of financial problems. A new Washington team, the Senators, made its appearance in 1901. My decision to quit the sport was strongly validated by the team's disastrous 1904 season when they had their worst season with a record of 38 wins and 113 losses. You never know, maybe I should have stuck with it, because a fellow by the name of Walter "Big Train" Johnson would show up in 1907 and turn the prospects of the team completely around. Funny, I always have ended up in towns with strong baseball traditions. You'll notice that this sport is always somewhere in the back of my mind. Like I said earlier, I see a lot of similarities between America's pastime, business, and plain, simple everyday life.

A young John B. Brunner, 1888.

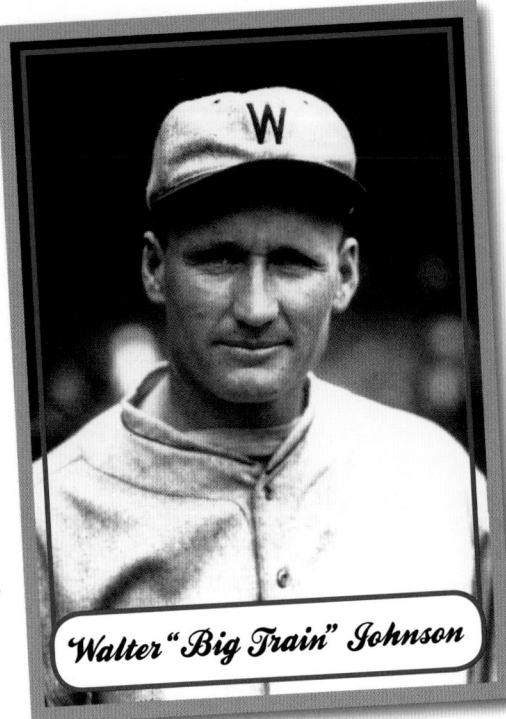

Walter Johnson, pitcher for the Washington Senators.

16

The Peroxide Specialty Company

After my "illustrious" career in baseball ended, I also decided that farming was not my chosen profession. Back then it didn't make sense to me to walk behind a mule for the greater part of the day and stare at his intelligent end. Dad was disappointed but still supportive. He wasn't interested in baseball and I wasn't interested in farming, so we were in perfect agreement. I did, however, feel compelled to do something better with my life. I took a flyer on a job with the Royal Glue Company in New York and joined their team as a traveling salesman. It turned out that this was just the kind of experience I needed. I learned a good deal about the ins and outs and the dos and the don'ts of sales. In addition, back in the eighties I started the program that I firmly believe ultimately brought about the success of the Peroxide Chemical Company. Invaluable friendships came to me through the courtesies bestowed by the buyers of jobbing houses when I was detailing the retail trade for many years prior to 1908. In essence they provided the nucleus around which this business was created. These houses were a type of wholesale merchant business that bought goods and bulk products from importers, other wholesalers, or manufacturers, and then sold them to retailers located in the principal cities of the United States. So you see, my move into business was not done on a whim but was carefully crafted and well thought out years before I made my move. There were 122 of these contacts who gave me their assistance in 1908, and many continued to give me their loyal support over the years to follow. I would like to acknowledge here and now my thanks for their sterling cooperation during the years that I was actively involved in the business.

Based on these friendships and the fact that I thought I had learned so much in my young sales career, in February of 1908 at age forty, I resigned my position with the Royal Glue Company, and with $400 of my own money started the Peroxide Specialty Company in St. Louis. That was a lot of money back then, and it still brings a twinge in my stomach to this day when I think of it. Some families back then might only see $400 in an entire year! In essence, I was betting on my ability to make a mark on this world. You might say that this was the first inning in my business ownership venture.

Roll Up Your Shirtsleeves

I called my old buddy from back east, Fred T. Barrett, to come join me in my new and growing venture. Fred Barrett was a good friend and business associate and stayed with the company until his passing in 1926.

John and Viola Brunner in 1912 with Fred T. Barrett, who remained a partner of J. B. Brunner from 1908 until his death in 1926.

First Inning

Left: At the start, our goods were put up for us by the Roosa and Ratliff Chemical Company of Cincinnati, Ohio, in the third-floor space outlined by the lines on this photo.

Right: In 1910 this Cincinnati building was leased, and occupied until 1912, when the company moved to St. Louis.

I moved the business to Cincinnati, Ohio, and Fred joined me there. Did I mention that Cincinnati had a pretty fair baseball team as well? Fred and I worked out a deal that would allow us to hit the road and sell while the Roosa and Ratliff Chemical Company of Cincinnati did the manufacturing and shipping. That was a sweet deal and could have lasted for a good long time if we hadn't been so successful and sold so much that Roosa and Ratliff couldn't handle our work on top of their production. As a result, we literally had to get our hands dirty by leasing a building and starting our own manufacturing plant to package hydrogen peroxide.

Fred was a very close friend of mine. In some ways, we knew each other's thoughts and moves before we said a word. Now, Fred and I lived pretty skinny back then. And during one period, we had only one nice overcoat between us at the office that we shared as each of us needed to make sales calls. I don't think I'll appreciate another coat quite as much as I appreciated that one. You know, I have to say that the average person has a whole different perspective and appreciation of money and property when they are at the low water mark on personal wealth and property! I also think that everyone has their own version of a "shared overcoat story" that has a special meaning to them and represents some of what will always be considered their version of the "good old days."

We were both new to this entrepreneurial life, and it's fair to say that we literally saw our lives pass before our eyes on a weekly basis. But times were exciting, and it was good to be doing something on our own. We traveled most of the Midwest, East Coast, and West Coast, and welcomed every one of the new territories becoming states in the good old USA as well.

We experienced the normal amount of growing pains for a young business. I sought the assistance of Samuel Lehman, president of the Pearl Street Market Bank in Cincinnati. He was a sound businessman—someone we could tap into and whose counsel and opinion I respected. You know, when I first went into this business I thought it was a one hundred yard dash and you simply tried to finish first. I quickly found out there was also some benefit in pacing oneself and trying to survive by finishing second, third, or fourth in some instances. By 1910 the company proved profitable enough to incorporate the Peroxide Specialty Company under the laws of the State of Ohio.

The first rail-car shipment of hydrogen peroxide shipped by the Peroxide Specialty Company from Cincinnati to Sacramento, California.

First Inning

The gripping April 15, 1912 *Post-Dispatch* headlines detailing a sinking *Titanic*. Notice the paper reports that even St. Louis reportedly had some victims included in the tragedy.

Not long after, we landed a big order from Kirk, Geary and Company of Sacramento, California. This was the first ever carload order of hydrogen peroxide in the United States to be filled, and shipped from Cincinnati to Sacramento in 1912. What a red-letter day for the company! It appeared that being energetic, inspired, and having some amount of success was all that was needed to feel fulfilled as a complete person! News of the day included the horrible tragedy of the *Titanic* in April of that year. I never felt too comfortable, even when I was on a big boat, and this accident validated that line of thinking.

For me, business and business relationships were all good and continued to move in very positive directions. However, business partnerships weren't the only type of relationship that I was interested in initiating.

Partners for Life

In every person's life there comes a time when passion for living takes hold of a person's focus. The company was having some degree of success and I was feeling professionally fulfilled. But, personally, something was missing. I was interested in finding a partner for life. I have purposely kept this part of my life very private. Most men do. But I must say that Miss Viola White captured my interest sincerely and completely the first time I laid eyes on her. She romanced my intellect as well as my attraction to her beauty and charm. I believe it's fair to say that our tender feelings occurred about the same time for both of us. I was the typical traveling salesman with an overload of vim and vigor, and here was this attractive and intelligent secretary who literally took my breath away. I can't ever remember looking forward to a sales call as much as I did when I was able to see Miss Viola. I don't rightly recollect whether or not I ever sold anything on those calls, but it didn't matter because she was so special. We hit it off from square one and soon decided to "incorporate" our lives. We were married in St. Louis on May 4, 1912, and honeymooned in Salt Lake City, Utah.

You might say that she joined the team and pinch-hit for me on numerous occasions, with every amount of command of the situation as I prided myself on being capable of delivering. Over the years she shared my triumphs, shortcomings, and accomplishments, and made my life totally worth living. I could not have asked for a more complete or wonderful partner for life.

John B. Brunner and Viola White, circa 1912.

On to St. Louis

The St. Louis Cardinals had not yet won their first World Series, but our business was now stretching across a continent. I made the decision to move the business to St. Louis, a city that was rapidly gaining in stature as a transportation and distribution hub. Its baseball renown would soon follow Vi-Jon's success and I felt honored and was glad to lead the way for both of us. The city's central location made it both an efficient and economical shipping point, a fact that contributed greatly to the company's growth. Viola and I proudly made St. Louis our new hometown. We purchased property that was adjacent to the Wabash Railroad tracks and a brand-new factory was built at 6300 Etzel Avenue in St. Louis, right down from where the former picnic grounds for the 1904 World's Fair were located on Skinker Boulevard. The adjacent city of Wellston also appeared to have a very bright future, as a mercantile center. In addition, I could shoot down Page Avenue, then over to Grand, make a left turn, and faster than you can say "peroxide" I was at Sportsman's Park, home of the Cards and the Brownies. It took less than twenty minutes if too many horse drawn wagons didn't get in the way.

Vi-Jon staff in 1913.

Outside storage St. Louis warehouse, 1913.

Getting On Base

The Etzel Avenue laboratory in 1913—rustic but effective in its time.

Peroxide vats, 1912.

St. Louis warehouse, 1913.

St. Louis office, 1913.

Peroxide packaging line, 1913.

Hydrogen peroxide processing, 1913.

23

First Inning

While still in Cincinnati, I had made a decision that one way for our business to improve quality and service levels at a competitive cost was to take on the printing of the product packaging and labels in-house. I hired a twenty-one-year-old "Turk" from Cincinnati named Charles Hall Krebs. He had some print shop experience, but more than that, he had a fire within him to handle the job and put his mark on the effort. Consequently, when we announced plans to move to St. Louis in 1912, young Mr. Krebs convinced his dear pregnant wife that this was "the opportunity of a lifetime for them." To soothe her animosity towards leaving her family and friends, Charles promised that if after three months she was unable to adjust to this new city, they would simply move back to Cincinnati and he would pursue another career, maybe baseball. Just how well did he like it? Well, he didn't play any baseball, and I understand he stayed with the company the rest of his life. It was a pretty fair decision for all of us.

I must admit to you that while I mentioned earlier that St. Louis had a pretty good baseball team, that wasn't exactly true as of 1912 when we moved there. In fact, from 1908 to 1912 the Cardinals had a mediocre 304 (wins) and 457 (losses) record for a .398 winning percentage. I was starting to lose faith in them. They had never won a World Series, but surely things were going to be different now that we were going to be part of the St. Louis scene. Unfortunately, the rest of our first decade in business saw the ball team continue to fall short of winning a pennant. However, in 1915 the Cardinals added Rogers Hornsby to the team. In 1916 they hired Branch Rickey to the front office, and Miller Huggins, a spunky little second baseman, took over as manager. He sort of reminded me of our sales manager, Howard Short, who would join our company a few years later. In 1920 the team acquired Jesse Haines and moved to Sportsman's Park. Boy, did I see a lot of good baseball in that stadium! The only negatives were the shortened season in 1918 because of World War I and the Black Sox scandal in 1919. I still don't understand that calamity.

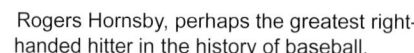

Rogers Hornsby, perhaps the greatest right-handed hitter in the history of baseball.

The June 29, 1914 *Post-Dispatch* front-page reports on the assassination of the Archduke Ferdinand and his wife, an event that seemed so small, insignificant, and remote at first would mushroom into World War I, "The War to End All Wars."

War Clouds on the Horizon

The dark clouds of war appeared on the horizon in 1914 just as my young company was starting to grow. This conflict sort of sneaked up on all of us. Most of those European countries were run by royal families, and it was pretty common knowledge that they were all related in some form or another. It seemed like one day we talked about this problem between some of the monarchies in central Europe—not a page-one story—and then soon after, the countries of Germany, Turkey, and the Austro-Hungarian alliance lined up on one side against Britain, France, Italy, and Russia. It could not have seemed farther away, until shipping difficulties and raw material embargoes started to creep into our everyday business reality. For me, personally, this could have been the end of my world. We ultimately did not enter the war until 1917; however, shipments of the raw materials used in the manufacture of hydrogen peroxide were halted. Germany and England were the only sources of these raw materials and neither would allow the other to ship to the United States. Eventually, as the result of many hand-wringing conversations and much planning, the leading English producer of hydrogen peroxide came to the United States, and along with the Peroxide Specialty Company, established a manufacturing facility in South Charleston, West Virginia.

Daily reports detailed in the *Post-Dispatch* like this October 2, 1914 front page covered the war "over there." So far away, but yet closer than anyone ever imagined.

Wave That Grand Old Flag

St. Louis was abuzz with all the spirited patriotism that went along with the new position of the United States on the world stage. There were plenty of young men spoiling for a fight. I saw this in some of the young fellows that worked for me and witnessed this type of patriotic eruption three times in my lifetime. The first time this spirit was displayed was when we as a country entered the Spanish-American conflict. The second time occurred as we were entering World War I in 1917. The third time was when we entered World War II. I think we all took a personal interest in that war. There was little time for confusion back then for anybody.

Everybody pretty well knew who they were for and who they were against. There was great honor to the process and all felt patriotic, even though the war resulted in a good deal of sadness and loss of life. The 1904 World's Fair, and the resultant industrial expansion in the years to follow along with World War I, helped to make St. Louis a leading business force in the United States like it would never probably see again. We as a company were touched by the war as well. You can't own a company and remain on the sidelines for very long when such worldwide events occur.

November 11, 1918 *Post-Dispatch* headlines announced the end of World War I. As planned, the war ended on the eleventh month, of the eleventh day, on the eleventh hour.

    Back then business existed in all shapes and sizes, from sweatshops to highly organized and mentored specialty craft shops. I guess we fell somewhere on the higher end, and we stood for something special to our people. I have always had the utmost respect and admiration for our associates. I knew them and they knew me and my door was always open. They did not feel the need nor were they compelled to seek intervention from a third party to change the relationship that I had with those people who were doing all the work on the factory floor. It was a two-way street all the way, as it always should be with the guy in charge. We operated in an honorable and fair manner for everyone to grow and prosper and have a career in which they could show great pride.

    I have always been proud of my country, the places where I lived, and the cities that I have called home. However, the feeling that comes over me when I hear the national anthem ranks right up there with getting married to my wife, Viola; the birth of my son, Jack; and the success of my business. Being an American was always considered a privilege and an identity that I wore proudly and with sincere conviction.

First Inning

As you're going through life, you don't always recognize all the events and happenings that have historical significance. History is a phenomenon that never sleeps, never takes a day off, and can never be put on hold. When you're in the flow of historical events you don't really understand what you have been a part of until you see it in, well, something permanent like a history book. During this point in time, the "war to end all wars" ended on the eleventh hour of the eleventh day of the eleventh month, and life as we knew it in America before 1918 would cease to be as simple and uncomplicated as it once had been. I've wondered a number of times if a mother who had lost a son on the tenth hour of the eleventh day of the eleventh month of 1918 would appreciate the irony and numerical significance of this preconceived marker in time.

In a few short years, the United States had grown up and isolationism was no longer the order of the day. The country would forever be intertwined with foreign interests. From a political and business perspective the United States was committed to global presence and there would be no place where they did not feel the impact in some way, shape, or form.

There was also a change for the boys who would take their first trips away from their birthplaces to go to Europe to fight. I had a few of these pure hearts from the "boot heel" of Missouri come to work for me and then join the Army just in time to be in the first expeditionary "All American" Division. They joined the likes of well-known Alvin C. York from the Valley of the Three Forks in Tennessee, along with little known Albert "Ab" Agnew of Harrisonville, Illinois. They left their sweethearts Gracie Williams in Tennessee and Lucille Schaeper in Harrisonville, Illinois, not fully comprehending their role in the war that was an ocean away. For all they knew, these country boys coming to St. Louis for induction thought that the Mississippi River was the ocean and were ready to cross the Eads Bridge to do battle with the Hun. Those were proud but sad days because we did not know which of these boys we might not see again. One thing for sure, the boys we sent to war would return as men. And we did our best to take care of the families of those who were called.

St. Louis was a very patriotic Midwestern city and St. Louis boys were welcomed back in style. In April 1919, St. Louis troops returned and were celebrated with six days of parades on Twelfth Street. Like thousands of other proud St. Louisans, we waved our flags and cheered the returning doughboys. As I watched the men march to a lively "Over There" overture and beat, I could not help thinking about the thousands of still, white crosses in the fields at the Argonne in France, those young boys who would stay "Over There" so that millions of Americans could resume their lives in peace and tranquility "over here."

I was quite ready to say goodbye to this decade as January 1, 1920, approached. All in all it had been a good decade for our company, but the world had taken a severe hit from the war. Everyone really wanted to believe that it truly was the "war to end all wars" but, as we all too soon would find out, this was not to be. In business, new government regulations, new middle-class buying patterns, and women's rights would make the next decade a real decade for change.

Getting On Base

ST. LOUIS POST-DISPATCH

The Only Evening Paper in St. Louis With the Associated Press News Service

NIGHT EDITION

VOL. 71. NO. 80.

ST. LOUIS, TUESDAY EVENING, NOVEMBER 12, 1918—18 PAGES.

PRICE TWO CENTS

Two to One! The POST-DISPATCH sells, in St. Louis and suburbs every day, in round figures, TWICE as many newspapers as the Globe-Democrat.

SOLF'S ALARM BASELESS; ALLIES WON'T LET GERMANY STARVE
HOLLAND WORRIED OVER WHAT TO DO WITH HOHENZOLLERN

Influenza Ban on All Forms of Business to Be Lifted Tomorrow

STORES, FACTORIES, CHURCHES, SHOWS ARE TO REOPEN

Certain Restrictions Will Be Announced Later by the Board of Health to Prevent Spread of Disease.

FOUR-DAY ORDER OFF AT MIDNIGHT

Regulation Regarding Street Cars Unchanged, Starkloff Says—350 New Cases of Disease Reported.

ONLY A LINE OF CAMP FIRES MARKED FRONT LAST NIGHT

Americans Rushed Into Stenay, Their Last Capture, Fifteen Minutes Before Hour That Armistice Went Into Effect.

FORMER EMPEROR MADE INGLORIOUS ENTRY TO HOLLAND

Erstwhile Martial Figure, Sat in Automobile, Huddled and Bent Over a Walking Stick, With Eyes Staring Ahead.

"ASSASSIN!" CRIED REFUGEES AT STATION

Reported Shots Were Fired at Windows of Imperial Train at Point Where He Entered It.

ARMISTICE TERMS WILDLY CHEERED IN FRENCH CHAMBER

Prolonged Demonstration Follows the Announcement That Alsace-Lorraine Is to Be Occupied.

LONDON CELEBRATES PEACE IN THE RAIN

"God Save the King" Sung Repeatedly When Royal Family Greets Crowds at Buckingham Palace.

The Socialist Head of the German Government Today

WILSON TO GIVE PROMPT ASSURANCE

German Foreign Secretary, According to Wireless Received in London, Calls Upon President to Help Mitigate "Fearful Conditions."

TELLS OF CRITICAL FOOD SITUATION

Message Expresses Fear That Blockade and Surrender of German Transports Will Result in Starvation of Millions of People.

This November 12, 1918 *Post-Dispatch* front page details more Armistice information but more interesting yet might be the second headline, which describes the lifting of influenza bans. The influenza of 1918 killed over 50 million people worldwide. A Germ-X product back then would have been greatly welcomed.

I. John Burgess Brunner's Story

2. Second Inning: Securing the Right Lineup —The Roaring Twenties

Well, enough of the world stage. The end of the war signaled a new era in St. Louis I have heard called the "Flamboyant Years." As a company we survived the restrictions that war imposed on commerce and we had continued to grow. I learned a lot from 1908 to 1920 and grew as a business owner and as a man. Like I said earlier, 1919 brought baseball the "Black Sox Scandal," and this noble profession had its first major black eye. I must admit that if Shoeless Joe Jackson had come looking for a job about then, I would have hired him in a heartbeat. Of course I would take Rogers Hornsby first, but Joe comes in a close second. It is my educated opinion that in business many financial "Black Sox Scandals" happen day in and day out, and each dishonest person cuts a little out of the heart and soul of America. But don't mess with the national pastime—that can never be forgiven.

I believe quite strongly in a conservative type of government, but there were some significant things that happened in the last half of the nineteenth century that helped industrial progressives like me spread our business wings and jump into a wonderful free enterprise economy. Congress passed laws regulating railroads in 1887 (the Interstate Commerce Act), and a law preventing large firms from controlling a single industry in 1890 (the Sherman Antitrust Act). When these laws started being enforced by Teddy Roosevelt (1901–1909) and President Woodrow Wilson (1913–1921), and other leaders sympathetic to progressive business practices, it enabled entrepreneurs to initiate their business dreams. I might add that there was another significant development that took place that I opposed, in regard to the ratification of the Sixteenth Amendment in 1913—the all too infamous Income Tax Law.

Public spending started to rise during Mr. Wilson's presidency and the country never looked back—it has risen and expanded ever since. The Federal Reserve was created. This has turned out to be a very complex business-government partnership that created a central bank with the intention of controlling the economy during extreme changes in economic environments, both good and bad.

There were many muckrakers in business when I started in sales years earlier. It really was up to the business community as a whole, of which I was a proud member, to police all of the bad-intentioned members of this fraternity. Therefore, I understood the message that was delivered by activists like Upton Sinclair when he published *The Jungle* in 1906 showing what conditions were like in the Chicago Union Stock Yards and meat processing plants of the day and their poor standards. I took great pride in being part of any improved production processes at our establishments for the sake of employees and customers alike, and for not ever simply looking the other way. It was because of these types of travesties that the new regulatory Food and Drug Administration was created. I guess although I had both good and bad feelings about this control, in the scheme of things for some people it seemed necessary. In addition, during this time many of today's other U.S. regulatory agencies were created, including the Interstate Commerce Commission and the Federal Trade Commission. I was never much for government regulation, but even I had to give the devil his due on these agencies.

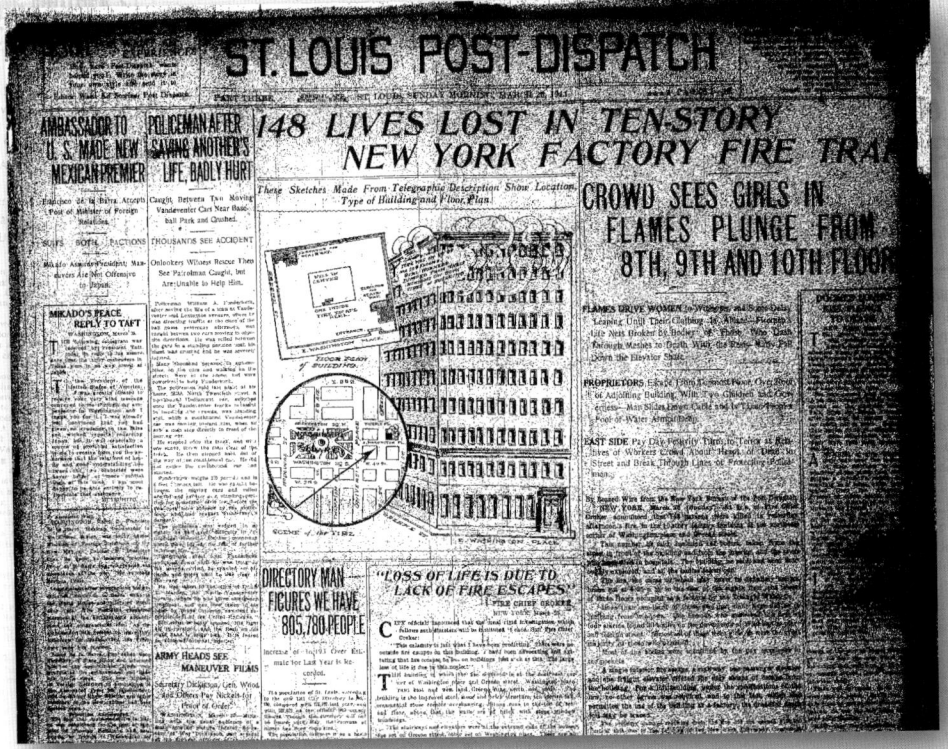

This March 26, 1911 *Post-Dispatch* front page tells about the horrible loss of life in the Triangle Shirtwaist Factory Fire. Safe working conditions and fire safety received a much-needed boost in public awareness.

Safety for the Team

You know, having some level of success and being able to realize one's dream is not only a reward but also a sacred trust—a trust that one will do the right thing for those who depend on them and the responsibility to measure one set of priorities against another. Profit versus the well-being of one's employees is the most high-profile example of this concept. On this subject, one point I would like to make has to do with the plant operations and how much the safety and well-being of our people always meant to me. You have to understand that these folks were my friends, and we depended on one another to survive as well as to grow. The plant was attached to the office; in fact, they were inseparable. A fire hazard in one area was a fire hazard for all. I think about the Triangle Shirtwaist Factory fire in lower Manhattan back in 1911 that killed 145 workers, a loss that cannot be measured in dollars and cents, but only in all the lost memories and young lives that were snuffed out on that horrible day. It makes me cry when I think about the common sense precautions that could have and should have been taken to avoid that tragedy. No government oversight can stop things like this. It really was up to the individual operator of each plant to do the right thing. Well, we always did the right thing even when it hit us in the pocketbook. Back then, and probably to a good extent even today, the boiler plant was the heart of the operation. This central utility needed to be kept up to standard at all times. Even when we would lose valuable production time because we had to shut down the boiler routinely in order to safely work on it—we did it and without complaints.

"Tank Stretchers"

Back then, hiring was done on more of a gut feel or based on the credibility of who might have referred someone for a particular position. I always walked through the plant area with a smile and a genuine feeling towards those folks who showed up every day and did what a few would consider some of the most monotonous, repetitive, and uninspiring tasks that one could imagine. But I felt that even the most routine duty measured up against any check I ever signed or any major policy decision I ever made. The way I figure, they did their share and I did mine. I enjoyed sharing with them the latest "tank stretcher" or "wheelbarrow seed" story. It was customary for new associates to go through kind of a rite of passage or initiation into the fold. One gag that was pulled frequently was sending a new hire to the next department to get the "tank stretcher" that was apparently needed back from the crew who had used it last. Once the new guy went to ask for the "tank stretcher," he was quite unceremoniously led from department to department until he ended up back in the original department where the original supervisor said he no longer needed the tool since it had already taken so long. Funny, in all my years that "tank stretcher" was never located! In addition, many a green recruit went to Jewsen's Market down the street to pick up a sack of "wheelbarrow seeds." The fellows at the market played along and dutifully promised to send them over the following week. Funny, they never seemed to get delivered either!

Incorporation in Missouri

In 1920, I formally incorporated the company in the State of Missouri. This had nothing to do with baseball but had everything to do with business growth. The business had expanded to include regular shipments of hydrogen peroxide to Mexico, Australia, China, and India, among other countries. We were now in a whole different ballgame. This expansion came at a price, and additional capital was needed to meet the needs of increased production. I reorganized the company as the Peroxide Chemical Company with Fred Barrett and me retaining control.

We went through a number of changes over the years. We were even called the Western Peroxide Company for a short time, with offices in St. Louis, Chicago, and Philadelphia. Back then the good news was that a business could operate and change on the fly for whatever reason necessary and convenient for survival and growth. The bad news was also that a business could operate and change on the fly for whatever reason necessary or convenient. Unfortunately, there are more than a few "bad apples" in the business world. In other words, the business rules that governed the average small business were quite unstructured and widely interpreted back then for both business dealings and also personnel matters. A firm handshake and a sincere business discussion were the backbones of any business deal. Ethics in business back then for most companies amounted to whether or not a person had what I'd like to call solid character. My gut instinct was my best measure of a business transaction at this point in time, and I put my trust in people of character. When most people are people of character and you have a great republic like America, well—it is the American dream that brings so many hardworking new citizens to our shores.

Common stock for "The Peroxide Specialty Company" issued December 23, 1912, in St. Louis County, Missouri.

Cards Improve—Vi-Jon Continues to Grow

Baseball in St. Louis during the 1920s started off ominously with the deaths of two fine young Cardinals ballplayers—William "Pickles" Dilhoefer at age twenty-seven and Austin McHenry, also at the age of twenty-seven. But the Cardinals had great success through the rest of the decade. They won their first World Series in 1926 against the hated New York Yankees. In a way, I see Vi-Jon as the underdog Cardinals and the "name-brand" competitors as the New York Yankees in our business league. Frankie Frisch then made another valiant attempt against Babe Ruth and the Yankees in 1928, but a three-homer performance by "the bambino" in game four cinched the four-game sweep and another World Series victory that year for the "Bronx Bombers." Vi-Jon and the Cardinals have continued to meet the challenge over the years.

You may notice I have not mentioned the other major league franchise, the St. Louis Browns, only because they really had not done much to this point in time. I watched many an enjoyable game with the Brownies and other notable teams and players. One game in particular against the Yankees I recall with fond memories occurred and resulted in "the Babe" hitting a home run over the Grand Avenue wall and breaking the display window at the Chevrolet dealer across the street. I couldn't help but think he ruined a wonderful display with that mighty clout. Guess I'm revealing the consummate salesperson inside of me.

Getting On Base

A young ball player for the St. Louis Cardinals complained of headaches at the start of the 1922 season and died of a brain tumor two months after his twenty-seventh birthday.

Frankie Frisch exhibited the gritty underdog style that made the Gas House Gang famous during the 1920s.

Second Inning

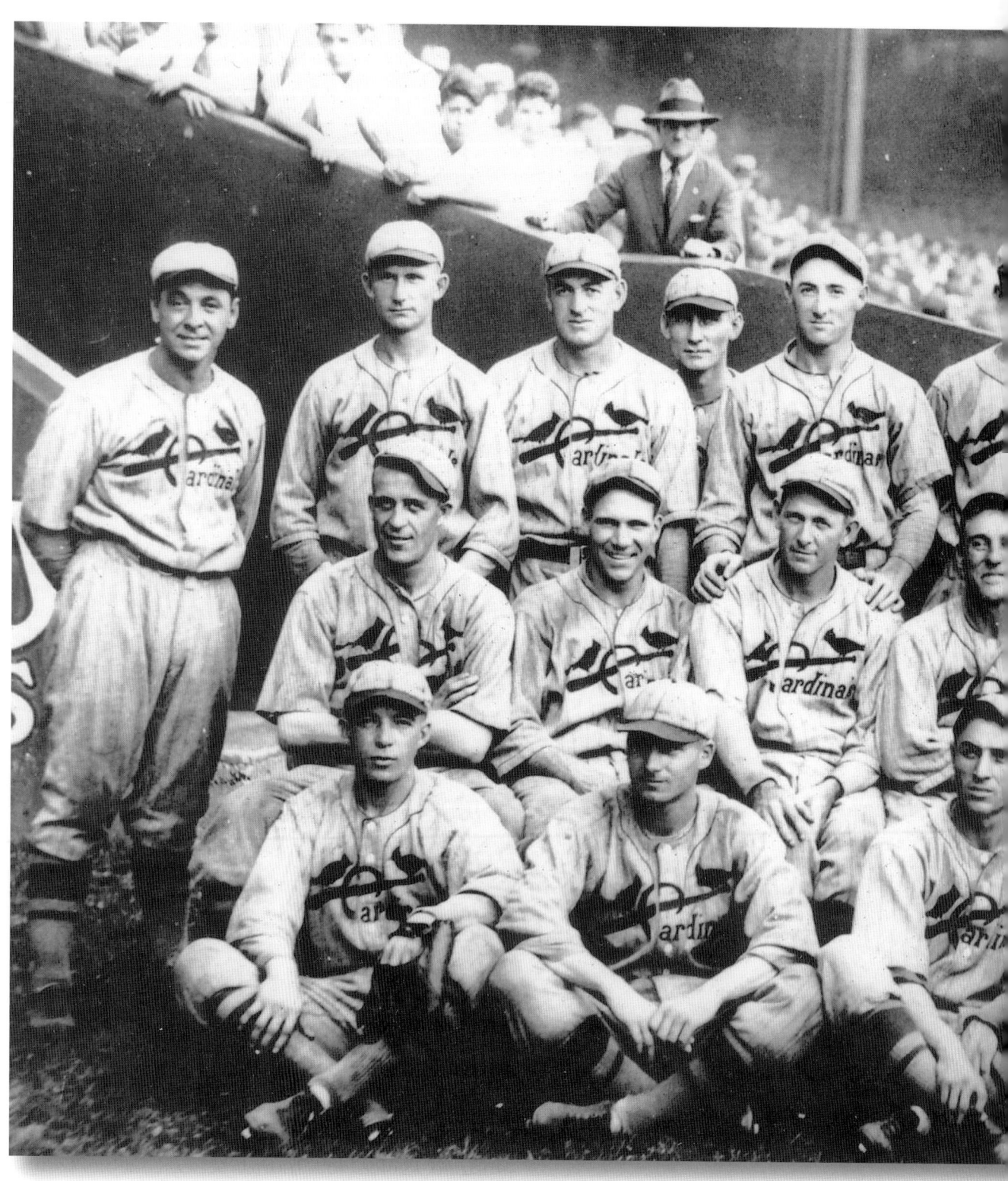

The 1926 St. Louis Cardinals beat the New York Yankees who included the likes of Babe Ruth and Lou Gehrig.

Politics, Pride, and Prohibition

Politically, during the 1920s, without any large-scale social programs, Presidents Harding and Coolidge presided over one of the more economically prosperous times in American history. The United States did quite well during this decade. American business set production records. I know as a company we increased our productivity significantly. The wage level increased and the number of hours worked decreased as well—all this when labor union membership was undergoing a rapid decline. The standard take on this period of time was that there was a dramatically reduced level of government activity domestically and internationally. Another interesting thing to point out to you was that, during World War I, the top income tax rate had been increased from 7 percent to an incredible 73 percent! Andrew Mellon, secretary of the treasury under both Harding and Coolidge, a man I grew to respect greatly, supported the theory that such rates stagnated the economy. He influenced a rational decision to reduce rates across the board. The top rate was lowered from 73 percent to 40 percent and later to 25 percent. There is no doubt in my mind that these tax reductions played a role in promoting greater economic growth in this decade.

For my part I could see the benefit for my employees. Most of my people lived from paycheck to paycheck. I promoted bonuses based on productivity, to provide a little something extra because it was the only way these folks could save for a rainy day. We even gave our work force personal loans to help tide them over. We tried to be partners both on the production floor and to some relative degree in their lives away from the plant.

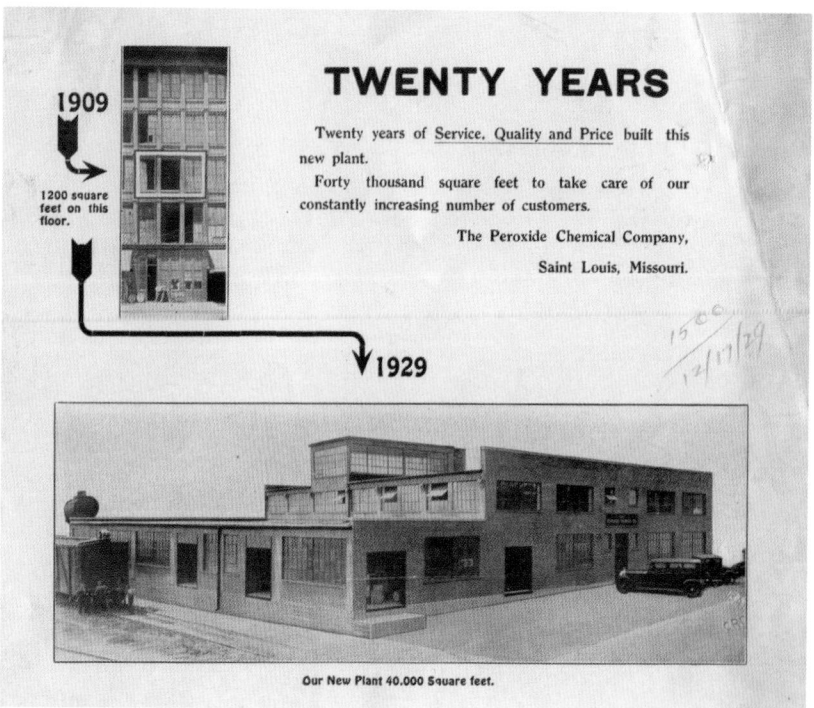

This flyer boasts of the great progress shown in twenty years from the second-floor Cincinnati location to the current Etzel Avenue plant location in St. Louis.

Back then we took great pride in receiving testimonials from our customers for the type of service we provided and how satisfied customers were with our products. I always said that the greatest compliment a customer can give you is a repeat order. I have always told the people in the plant to determine if they would buy the products that they were making in order to properly put the best interests of our customers first. As a unit, I was especially proud of showing off our production lines for any visitors to our plant. We would get the crew together and plan a passage or pathway that would bypass less desirable aesthetics, thus giving us the best opportunity to make a good impression. It was a common practice for me to glance back to the crews in each area we passed through and give a wink that gave everybody the "thumbs up" that we pulled off another good walk-through. I did a lot of winking over the years.

When I took inventory in 1920, I realized that in eight short years the company had outgrown the one-story frame and stucco building built in 1912. Like I mentioned earlier, we had to "add on a 'doghouse'" every now and then, until half our lot was covered with improvised warehouses. It was not until 1929 that we made major changes when we tore down the old building, section by section, and built the first phase of a two-story plant on Etzel Avenue.

Prohibition Dries Out St. Louis

Now a new business and social restriction appeared on the horizon called "Prohibition." It had a minor impact on our business since some of the products had alcohol-based raw materials in the formulations. But, obeying the law and good recordkeeping was the extent of our impact. We purchased the neutral grain spirits we needed for blending from a local supplier, the John Bardenheier Wine and Spirits Company. They were located nearby on Cass Avenue and provided barreled spirits as our batching requirements dictated. I knew the owners, Joe Bardenheier Sr. and his sons, John E. Bardenheier and Joseph A. Bardenheier Jr. They were good friends and business associates. They converted to making elixirs and providing spirits for medicinal purposes for the duration of the eleven-year Prohibition period.

Other St. Louis based businesses had a bit more of a business interruption. Take Falstaff breweries—they converted to making root beer. Anheuser-Busch started making pancake syrup. I will tell you that more than a few of our friends knew of some local speakeasies where one could get a bottle of "medication" to soothe what ailed them. Some of the plant people had relatives down in southern Missouri that had a booming business in making illegal moonshine. This illegal spirit business was all around us in the city and was even more prevalent in the "sticks" outside of most major towns in Missouri and Illinois. Why in Clayton, a small town about ten miles from downtown St. Louis, there was a 100,000-gallon stash found in a warehouse, while raids that found substantial amounts of spirits were frequently covered by the *St. Louis Post-Dispatch*. It is safe to say that it was popularly felt they were only scratching the surface of what was available. If they found one gallon out of every ten gallons I would have been surprised.

> **NOTICE TO OUR CUSTOMERS**
>
> If I were a dealer in Peroxide and had been buying it from time to time ever since the present War began, and I knew the price of Glassware, Acid, other matherials togather with Labor and Taxes had advanced anywhere from 10 to 50% and the manufacturer would correspondingly increase his selling price to me; You know what I would do.? I would say that manufacturer has good judgment and courage by refusing to accept orders with a loss. I would also raise my prices accordingly and congratulate myself on being able to buy my Peroxide from a firm who refused to lower the standard of their goods in order to claim they "Still Sold at the Old Price".
>
> We advance our prices only when it is necessary, but NEVER Lower our Standard.
>
> John B. Brunner, Pres. - Treas.
>
> THE PEROXIDE SPECIALTY COMPANY,
>
> ST. LOUIS   CHICAGO   PHILADELPHIA

A communication sent to customers by John B. Brunner explaining the Peroxide Specialty Company's philosophy of maintaining pricing versus providing quality and maintaining high standards all in our joint best interest.

Practical Business Sense

I have always considered myself a very straightforward, hard-driving fellow who lived ethically and morally according to my parents' upbringing. I liked to think the secret to my success was based on my uncompromising approach to doing business. Business is a two-way street and both parties need to benefit and not feel compromised in doing the next transaction. Also, I liked people and wanted each interaction to be as good for them as I preferred it to be for me. I would not set up a sales or production system just to support friends or legacies from past business dealings. We would simply roll up our sleeves and fight high cost by doing most of the practical functions ourselves. Not the easiest or most motivational way of doing things, but if you remove the middleman, along with various multilayered outsourcing activities that add cost, you can make a pretty fair living. That's simply what we did. We did not take the romantic approach to doing business, but our practical approach was the right balance for the customers and it kept us flying straight. I tried to explain my approach to my customers through company brochures. I think that one should congratulate a customer for having the wisdom to buy their product from a company that is so dedicated to quality that it refuses to lower its prices. Integrity times a fair price equals a satisfied, lifelong customer for Vi-Jon.

I went further by stating in a 1933 intercompany memo to department heads what my expectations were on how each department should be run. I asked each to "follow instructions in a gracious manner" or to "be man enough to come to me with your decision" if they felt they could not comply. I don't think that you can be fairer than that. I feel strongly that you should set your expectations clearly and without collateral comments. Then you pay your supervisors the ultimate compliment by giving them the respect and a functional level of complete trust in the decisions they make day in and day out in your name.

Women Change Old Standards

The women's suffrage movement was quite an extreme change for the country and especially for dyed-in-the-wool old standards like me. But it can readily be stated that women's liberation would have clearly been a step back for my Viola. Personally I was blessed, because my wife and I had a great relationship. But I have to tell you she was her own person. I could wield little influence over her if she did not buy into the point being discussed. Ours would probably be called an unconventional relationship during that time period. When the business was young she would accompany Fred Barrett and me on day coach train trips between St. Louis, Cincinnati, Columbus, and Pittsburgh and back again. In the scheme of things she was a feather in the cap of the effort by women to attain equal status in American society.

In 1920, with the ratification of the Nineteenth Amendment, women were granted the universal right to vote. Over time, all the old salts like myself soon accepted the inevitable, and it sort of made sense when you consider that we were promoting a greater independence to our number one customers for our products—women.

Another major change to the American industrial scene, including our plant, was the entrance of women into the general workforce during World War I. These women entered the workforce to provide for families whose fathers, brothers, and sons had gone off to war. Well, even after the war, many women kept their wartime jobs or moved into other careers, enjoying the independence and advantages of earning their own wages. It made sense and it was a change long overdue. Viola was a trendsetter in this regard. She had a career when women's careers were not considered commonplace. She continued to provide valuable support for the business and my aspirations through to the end of my days.

Viola was especially sensitive to the female workers in the plant. She once visited the plant and insisted that I allow the women to wear pants when it was particularly cold. I was happy to get her good suggestions on subjects like women's clothing. Before the start of World War I, women's styles maintained a Victorian influence. Clothing was quite traditional and not very practical. Women's hairstyles were equally drawn out, combed, and pulled into a bun to create the illusion of luxuriously thick hair. There was little in the way of makeup and what was available was reserved for ladies of the theatre and other disreputable pursuits.

However, mass communication in the form of the introduction of motion pictures seemed to create its own brand of makeover hysteria. Popular movie stars, Greta Garbo, Janet Gaynor, and Claudette Colbert gave the masses a peek at cosmetic extravagance through the use of intensely colored lipsticks, extreme shades of eye shadow, and hair styles that sent many movie patrons directly from theatres to the closest hairdresser. For women, some level of enhancing the gifts God gave women seemed to be the trend—a trend that from what I have been able to see has only increased tenfold over the years. The age of cosmetics was upon us and Vi-Jon was going to get on board that train.

All these factors came together to radically change the lifestyle and appearance of American women during the 1920s. Unlike the longer locks women had previously worn, short hair couldn't just be pulled back into a bun or braids; it required styling. Curling irons were heated on the stove and, with enough practice, ladies learned to curl their hair before it burned—sometimes. Waves were crimped with fingers and clamps or "pin curled" and then held in place. Some ladies boiled flaxseeds in water until the solution thickened, and then added rosemary oil for scent and used the resulting concoction as a styling gel. One of our best selling products was called "STA-BAC." It was the first mass-produced styling gel and the ladies just loved it—even the guys started using it to hold back their hair!

In the 1920s, peroxide, peroxide creams, and other face and hand creams were our biggest sellers, and peroxide was still an important ingredient as an antiseptic and bleaching agent. At the same time, the consumption of toiletries and other household preparations in the United States reached $765 million, nearly twenty times the amount spent on the same products in the late 1880s, far outweighing the increase in the nation's population. I could not ignore the obvious and our new company, the Peroxide Chemical Company, was poised to manufacture and distribute across the country and grew with this phenomenal change in style.

This world was fast becoming a trendsetting contest that allowed companies like our Peroxide Chemical Company to grow and present this new middle class of women the things that they so desperately wanted to buy. Viola and I loved every aspect of this brave new business world. We built our lives to address the business side as well as our personal goals. You can picture Viola, Fred, and me jumping off on our sales calls, taking the train to our various appointments, and see we were having the time of our lives. I always felt most comfortable making sales calls. Like playing first base, it was the most natural thing for me to do and I think I was pretty good. These calls that the three of us went on were by far some of the happiest days of my life. Viola was a true partner, with the type of intelligence and business savvy that made her opinion so very valuable. We were described by friends and business associates as being "inseparable" and "a perfect match." I could never imagine life any different than how it turned out.

The Legacy Continues

On March 22, 1924, when I was already in my late fifties, Viola gave birth to John White Brunner. His middle name is a tribute to the first Brunner ancestor born in America, Peregrine White, born to Susannah and William White in Plymouth Colony in 1620. Another ancestor was a soldier in the War for Independence, John White, of Mansfield, Massachusetts.

John White enlisted in the army of General George Washington in January of 1776 and was in the Battle of Long Island and the Battle at Harlem Heights. Some of the old records tell us that John was part of a nucleus of brave good men who were much more efficient than they looked. In addition, John was part of a regiment that uncovered a plot to assassinate General Washington in June of 1776. At the time, Washington's army was encamped near the North River and Washington had his headquarters in a house at Richmond Hill which stood very near the bank, so that the conspirators had dug a trench, from a concealed place among the bushes under the bank, directly under the house, working by night and carrying their gravel into the stream and covering the mouth of the trench with brush during the day. The regiment to which John White belonged was stationed about one hundred yards from the house. They saw Washington coming down alone, and the men were called to arms. The whole gang of conspirators was captured and tried by court martial, and the ringleader Thomas Hickey was sentenced to be hanged. When Hickey was hanged, White was one of the guard of fifty-two men chosen from as many different companies to perform that duty.

Jack was born before the start of the 1924 season, a season that would see Rogers Hornsby bat a whopping .424. This company and all that it stood for took on new meaning in our lives after Jack was born. This company would be developed from that point onward for him, if he chose to take that endeavor on. There is no greater accomplishment for a man than to leave a standing legacy for his son. And Vi-Jon was such a legacy.

Proud papa John B. Brunner holds his one-year-old son John W. "Jack" Brunner.

Second Inning

Life in St. Louis

I was pleased to see St. Louis continue to prosper through this period of time. It made my decision to locate here a good one. Mayor Henry W. Kiel of St. Louis seemed to motivate the town with his spirit and enthusiasm. At this time also, we continued to appeal to a female customer base with a wide range of our products.

I must tell you now that, as I have reported on the good, I must also report on some of the bad. During this decade we had gone far in reclaiming our lives from a war-influenced state of existence. One unforgettable day that I must relate to you now, occurred on September 29, 1927. The morning started off pretty normal, although it was a bit sticky and there was a very fine drizzle, complicating my hopes for a good Indian summer day in hopes that the afternoon game between the Cardinals and Cincinnati would be played. I planned on going to the game to see one of my old favorite teams play my new favorite team. It's funny but there was a strange feeling on the plant floor that morning. I walked out by the screened doorway by the railroad tracks and one of the mechanics pointed to the sky to the south. It was pitch black and the clouds around us appeared to have an almost greenish hue. The wind was kicking up and a thunderhead merged toward the central west end just to the south of us, and I knew something bad was about to happen in the central part of the city. We were hit with torrential showers and deafening thunder, but in twenty minutes or so the worst had past. My thoughts then went out to what was happening just directly to the east of our plant. I jumped in the car, drove due east down Page Avenue until I got just shy of Delmar Avenue, and I saw devastation like I had never witnessed before.

A tornado had touched down around Kingshighway and Maryland Avenue and proceeded east all the way to Grand Boulevard and St. Louis Avenue. I walked through the area and we stepped through one-inch thick broken glass on the street. I sent back to the plant to get peroxide, rubbing alcohol, and other necessary emergency supplies to the makeshift aid stations being set up. Vi-Jon always responds to the needs of their neighbors, especially when natural disasters occur. The damage was extreme, and when Friday morning arrived we were able to assess what we knew was a dreadful hit for our town. There were eighty-two people killed and over thirteen hundred injured in that gruesome ten minutes of horror. The cost was over $10 million ($100 million in today's dollars). The damage occurred in an area of around six square miles and, by the grace of God, just missed us. The old car barn a block and a half south lost part of its roof. If the tornado had struck just fifteen blocks to the west it could possibly have wiped out our Etzel Avenue plant. A number of our employees sustained losses during the storm, and we cried together that day and joined hands on the next day to start to rebuild the more that five hundred thousand buildings that were ultimately involved in the storm damage. I will never forget that day—as will most of St. Louis. But Vi-Jon and the Vi-Jon family moved on, as we always do.

The horrible reality of nature's random might is captured with this gripping September 30, 1927 *Post-Dispatch* front page, which lays out the details of the shocking carnage. The storm came within blocks of the Vi-Jon Etzel Avenue plant.

I. John Burgess Brunner's Story

3. Third Inning: We Hit a Slump —The Great Depression

Well, if the Roaring Twenties didn't get us, it appeared the next great challenge on America's horizon might. The Great Depression was a very real space in time for all the folks that were close to me as family and in the business. Those who didn't go to bed with a stomach clenched in hunger every night went to bed with stomachs consumed by fear and uncertainty. Some of our customers had to close their doors or make severe cutbacks to their operations.

I took a different approach to the situation and expanded our company's product line. I too had fear, but you know, fear can be useful and can be turned into strength and motivation if you channel it properly. It acts as the great equalizer and a mighty motivator. So I used it for both purposes during my entire life. I also turned it into focus and chose to step forward, not back.

Down on Bartmer Avenue, close to the Etzel Avenue plant, I would drive by the local soup kitchen and see poor, former breadwinners lined up along Olive Street selling apples. I never bought so many apples in my life! It was literally the fruit of the earth becoming the fruit of life. I always scanned the lines for people I knew, hoping in the back of my mind that the faces I saw would remain nameless and quite distant. All I could do was to maintain what we did for my family at home and my business family at work. We didn't even keep track of the small change that was given to the people on the production floor, because those folks didn't have it, and maybe it was our way of thanking God for sparing us from what had affected so many.

The Cardinals—The Only Team Not Hitting a Slump

Well, on the lighter side, the Depression had more impact on my St. Louis Cardinals. They started off the third decade by losing the World Series to the Philadelphia Athletics in six games—a sign of things to come for the business prospects as well? It didn't appear so in the near term. One big plus, however, was the start of the great career of Dizzy Dean. He touched the hearts of most Americans, from the countryside to the corners of South St. Louis. Plain-spoken and, yes, he even butchered the king's English at the same time, giving vocabulary teachers headaches through this period of time, I might add, as children liked to imitate his slang. The Cards did rebound for World Series wins in 1931 and 1934, which helped to soften the impact of the realities of the Depression on thousands of St. Louisans for at least some period of time. I especially enjoyed watching such players as Dizzy Dean and his brother, Paul, along with Jim Bottomly, Leo Durocher, Joe "Ducky" Medwick, Johnny Mize, and a skinny kid from Pennsylvania the Cards signed up in 1937 by the name of Stan Musial. Wonder if he ever amounted to much?

Third Inning

The 1931 World Champion Cardinals helped St. Louis get through the malaise of the first years of the Depression.

St. Louis Cardinals

The 1936 version of the St. Louis Cardinals finished second.

Dizzy Dean joined the Cardinals during the 1930 season, and the English language would never be the same.

Struggling to Survive

The decade of the 1930s found most people without work, with their hands out for help or their hands in their pockets. We were able to maintain a pretty constant work force and the people really appreciated the stability that our company provided. More than half of all Americans in 1929 were living well below the poverty level. The annual per capita income was $750; in rural areas, it was only $273. Like I said, some of my saddest times were the days I drove by the bread and soup lines that many Americans were forced to depend on for their daily existence. There was not a day that these makeshift kitchens did not run out of food, forcing hungry people to wait for the next ration the following day. Like most businesses, we provided food and support for our folks. We wanted to—after all—they were family. On the other hand, a few upper-class Americans managed to maintain the legacy lifestyle of their pre-Depression existence with only a few minor adjustments. Isn't it amazing that apples were being sold on Kingshighway and a few blocks away was Kensington Place where there was no sign of hard times!

During this tough period it was common practice at most factories to have what was endearingly referred to as "mystery back alley hobo stew." Its content from day-to-day was the mystery. It consisted of taking a good-sized stew pot that was set over a gas burner and everybody would contribute some type of ingredient before the shift started, to create the "stew recipe of the day." The company contributed bowls and spoons and some balance of ingredients to make this "daily bread" more balanced and enough for all. The various cultures brought their unique contributions to each batch. From Italian sausage and pasta to German potato salad additions to southern greens—you never quite knew what each day would bring. You could not believe how good a warm bowl of soup tasted, especially when, for some of these folks, it was probably their only solid meal for the day! Nothing went to waste and what was left always went home to the kids. I bet even today when you have company provided meals the good folks don't waste anything and take what's left back home.

Bailing Wire and Elbow Grease

During this time, I developed even more of an admiration for the resilience of my plant production people. Times were rough and everyone, including businesses, had to make do with less than they would prefer. I consider myself a fair judge of another person's raw capabilities. My mechanics and line workers would take bailing wire and keep our machines running, against all odds. I was so proud of their creativity and ability to adapt. It was this type of daily "in plant" performance that complemented our own creative efforts to accomplish sales during this especially difficult time. Buying a part that was actually a factory replacement part was rarely seen in our establishment. Back then we did our own electrical wiring and plumbing, machined our replacement parts, and upgraded equipment on our own to meet the new growth that continued to occur even during these tough times. I sort of think that you fellas have probably had similar people working for you in the years since then. Over the years, I've found that our own people are more creative and cost-conscious than most of the outside experts.

St. Louis Survives

The Depression had pretty much the same effect in St. Louis as it had in other cities across the United States. Economic conditions were in a downward spiral and large-scale unemployment was rampant. Most major building construction had ceased to take place. The construction trade was most significantly affected. Fortunately, in the city of St. Louis there were many projects from a 1923 bond issue that were still not complete during the height of the Depression. In addition, a supplemental bond issue in 1934 helped carry even more workers through this period. I was most pleased to see that the Memorial Plaza construction helped move some of the building further west and closer to our neck of the woods.

Unfortunately, land value had also taken a hit throughout the area. This compounded the efforts of businesses trying to recoup value from their properties and capital equipment. The city fathers all determined that a major civic attraction was necessary in order to give the people of the area a major shot in the arm. In 1935 the Jefferson National Expansion Memorial on the riverfront was their vehicle to accomplish this boost. Desperate to right their "sinking ship," St. Louisans voted for a bond issue to pay for the city's share of the project cost. The U.S. National Park Service was a partner in this interesting venture. I used to take a Sunday drive with Viola to see the demolition proceed on the riverfront. A good portion of the project was done before the war. However, the rail systems would take many years to fully relocate. Many designs were submitted through an architectural competition in the mid-1940s. The result was something that occurred after my time, but let's just say that its start during the Depression and its impact on the spirits and pocketbooks of the people might have been its most important accomplishment.

A Struggling Marketplace

I would have to say that the toiletries market was pretty well developed by 1930. Middle-class America was marching and sometimes hobbling towards better days that meant the need for more services and more products. Our folks were determined to do a good job to make sure we had our share of the "American Dream." I used to discuss all the current thinking with Viola and she was a tremendous asset in setting and maintaining a profitable course. She really knew her stuff when it came to outlining the grooming and household needs of American women. The Depression actually created a greater demand for inexpensive lines of quality cosmetics at prices that working folks could afford. Viola and I spotted this "cry in the wilderness" for products that made people feel special and like they deserved better, and I was resolved to provide it. I was determined to merge this concept into the Peroxide Chemical Company and add yet another dimension.

"The Vi-Jon Girl," 1933, was seen in window displays across the entire country.

About this time, along with some of our moves in product lines, we decided to take a dramatic step and rename the company. Now Viola and I had really talked about this for a good amount of time in previous years, and for the life of me we could not come up with anything that really fit the image that we felt the company represented. I wanted it to be identifiable, respectful, but most of all to have a name that said "this is who we are." We must have gone through a dozen Indian-brand writing tablets before it hit us—it had been forecast by our friends for years! I can't count the times I heard, "Hi Vi. Hi John. Good to see you." We came up almost in the same breath—Vi . . . Jo(h)n. Anyway, who ever heard of the Brunner Company?

The name *Vi-Jon* was not stuffy, not chemical sounding, but had a classy sound that made items that the ladies of America would like to buy. Our packaging for the Vi-Jon beauty products was adorned with purple *vi*olets and yellow *jon*quils, making an attractive, eye-catching display on drugstore shelves. That was Viola's touch—I would have never put that idea together. Yes, we were ready to make some kind of history with the products we were going to field!

I was set on a retail strategy that would meet the demands of the Depression-era market. We would put emphasis on price, quality, and service, and develop a complete line of drugs and cosmetics that would sell for five cents to twenty-five cents. It was also very important to provide the retailer an excellent markup. The acceptance was outstanding from coast to coast!

Politics and Economic Stagnation

In June of 1930, President Herbert Hoover signed the Smoot-Hawley Tariff Act into law, much to my disappointment. It raised tariffs an average of 59 percent on more than twenty-five thousand items. Exports were knocked down 90 percent. Some of the more than twenty-five thousand items impacted by this tariff included corporate taxes, estate taxes, cars, tires, gasoline, energy, and—yes you guessed it—"toiletries." The corporate and estate taxes meant that in the middle of this Depression, as private investment was needed, it was very unattractive. I ignored the obvious impact of these taxes and kept right on investing in the company. How could I do any less for my dream and my people who depended on Vi-Jon for their daily bread!

I would like to touch on one very important guideline that I felt very strongly about and that was my commitment to my fellow Vi-Jon associates. The position that I was in to help make a difference in their lives, especially during the Depression, was a very real responsibility—sometimes scary, sometimes motivating, but always very much a part of my everyday reality. As I said earlier, when I walked through the plant, I looked everybody in the eye as I said good morning. I wanted them to know my interest, support, and belief in our team. My expectations have always been so high, and just a simple smile and glance would do most of these people for days. What a clean, pure spirit to dwell within. I always felt that I got most of my people directly from the Lord, made to order!

Dime Store Revolution

A new pipeline came into being during this particular period of time—the five-and-dime store chains. It was a concept born in the late 1800s, fathered by Frank Winfield Woolworth. He was working

Getting On Base

as a clerk in a store in his hometown of Rodman, New York, when he proposed cutting the price of goods that weren't selling. It defied the most obvious logic that bean counters of that era would buy into. Woolworth's epiphany was a huge success. In 1912, F. W. Woolworth Company was incorporated when he bought out several five-and-dime store chains. He then proceeded to make the "five-and-ten-cent store" an integral part of the American retail landscape. Through the Depression and the years that followed, a homemaker fortunate enough to have a moderate income could stash enough "pin money" to take an occasional trip to the local "five-and-ten." There she could scan the aisles and, for mere pennies, treat herself to a new barrette or a new apron or try the latest face cream.

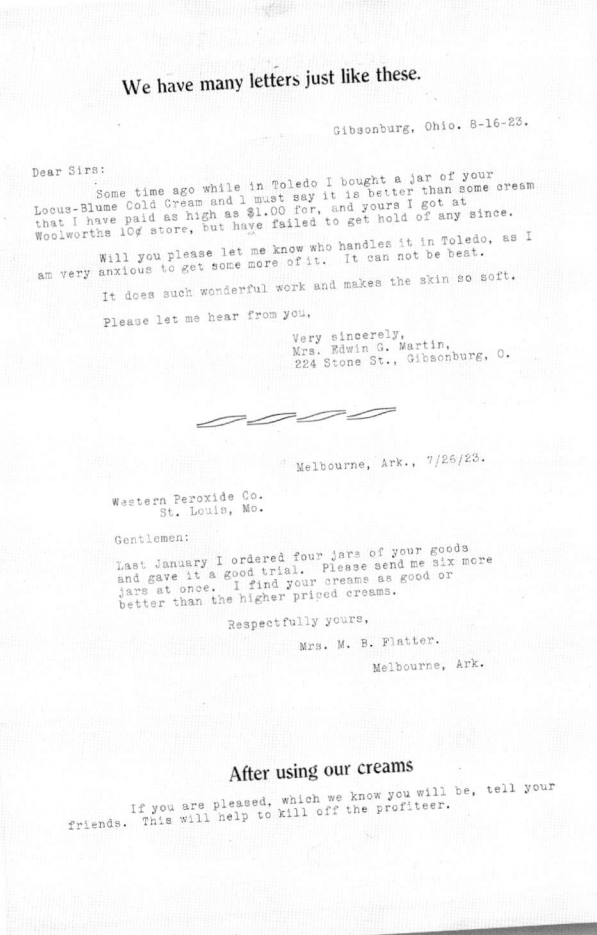

Right: "F. W. Woolworth 5 & 10 Cent Store" display poster for Vi-Jon products during the 1930s.

Above: Letters from customers sent to F. W. Woolworth's touting their pleasure with Vi-Jon products.

F. W. Woolworth cream and lotion display, 1942.

Yes, the "five-and-ten" developed into having a major role in American life during this particular period of time. The shopping experience was taking on a whole new concept for the average Mr. and Mrs. America. The general store where people got necessities now was coming of age and had expanded to a new activity that people simply called "shopping" that encompassed a whole new experience. People would plan their shopping trips, which included stops at the lunch counters with chrome swivel stools, and clerks called "soda jerks" served up grilled cheese sandwiches and dispensed fountain sodas, shakes, and ice cream sundaes.

"Quality Products" poster of the Peroxide Chemical Company from the early 1930s.

The neighborhood dime stores were to be a critical part of our success during the 1920s, 1930s, and 1940s. The design of the stores availed a great deal of window space for product sets and specials that were now a keen part of our marketing schemes. We actually had to get very creative and were able to do things that were not considered in previous years. The true entrepreneurial nature in salesmen like me was allowed to grow and thrive. We could now entice shoppers into the stores with displays of the latest hair products and the latest nail polish remover, or lotion, almost always accompanied by pictures of movie stars and big screen heroes.

Third Inning

"The Vi-Jon Girl" graces the Christmastime window display of a Woolworth five-and-ten-cent store. Fittingly, the vanishing cream, cold cream, and cleansing cream all sold for ten cents.

Vi-Jon's Sales Team

Our new, bona fide entries into the retail market dictated the need for a sales force to get our products out on the shelves. Now it's pretty clear to me that a Brunner is a natural salesperson, and we are pretty hard to convince that we have found the right sales associate to represent us. However, the first person I chose for the job was a young man from St. Louis named Carl Mueller, hired in the mid-1930s. Carl and his young wife had only been married three days when they were sent to Chicago to run the sales and distribution center. I apologized sincerely for the timing of this move. Carl was a Lutheran minister and I guess that their line of work suffered, like most everyone else, during the Great Depression. One would have thought anyone in God's work would have been in greater demand at church during this Depression. But, like I said, I trusted in people of character.

In these days Chicago was the second largest transportation hub. We were pretty industrious back then as well. Take for instance the fact that mail was delivered three times a day. So we would get the morning mail, package the orders and prepare them for the next mail delivery and pickup. So the concept of quick response and customer service was illustrated back then early in the company's history. Carl turned out to be quite the ambitious young salesman and caught on fast and rose rapidly through the organization. By 1946, I am pleased to say, he was vice-president and general manager of Vi-Jon's St. Louis plant.

Sales Manager Howard Short, left, with Jack Brunner in 1958.

One of the next ambitious young men I hired was Howard Short. It just so happened that I was visiting one of Vi-Jon's customers, the S. S. Kresge store in St. Louis, a competitor of the F. W. Woolworth chain, when I noticed the store's assistant manager. I saw an energetic young man, Howard Short, who just happened to be decorating a window filled with Vi-Jon merchandise. I struck up a conversation with him and discovered that we shared a passion for merchandising and sales. Before long, I offered Howard a position in Chicago to replace Carl Mueller, who had been promoted to plant manager and relocated to St. Louis. Howard accepted the position immediately. The years during which I had Howard manage the Chicago territory I would describe as being the biggest and best years we had in our Chicago branch. In 1944 I brought Howard back to St. Louis to take the sales manager position, a job he held for many years, along with his office of secretary of the company.

We Continue to Grow

Through the 1930s I expanded the company significantly. In my creative, industrious pattern I directed that temporary "sheds" once again were to be built to accommodate the growing business. Vi-Jon's gross sales in 1933 were just over $800,000. By the early 1940s Vi-Jon employed about seventy people and sales exceeded $1.1 million—an impressive increase when you consider that most items retailed between five and twenty-five cents. I bet our "dog houses" will last a hundred years.

To everyone's great relief, the Great Depression was drawing to a close. Our business had expanded during the Depression and it stood to reason that our business would expand even more effectively during the post-Depression period.

Throughout the entire history of the company our focus was everyday products at great values. One of those values was friendship, along with the importance of family. Loyalty was also a value that I placed very high on the list. There are so many examples of loyalty throughout Vi-Jon's history. There is no finer reflection for me to consider than stories about the loyalty that has existed between our company and its employees.

One such story of loyalty that I can tell you about involved a close friend of mine, Frederick W. "Billy" Herb. Billy announced in 1937 that he was leaving the company to make his mark in the fast-growing state of California. Billy had served the company as a sales and general manager and was sixty-eight years old at the time. I convinced Billy to open an office to accommodate the growing West Coast business, instead of completely leaving the company. I chose San Francisco as the site for the new manufacturing facility because of its central location to other West Coast cities. It also had the shipping facilities that would be needed to provide overnight service anywhere in the seven western states the company served.

We jointly decided that Billy's son, Armand, would join him at Vi-Jon's new San Francisco plant, and the two of them would work together establishing the manufacturing facility, building up the customer lists. According to the business plan we agreed upon, the two of them visited every city on the West Coast with a population of twenty thousand or more. Before too long, to my great pleasure, the San Francisco plant was one of the most productive and profitable branches of the company. In 1943, we were all stunned when Armand Herb was killed in a tragic airplane accident, a tremendous loss to his family and to our company. Billy continued to work for the company and in 1948 we moved the San Francisco plant to Oakland, California. I worked for many years with Billy and I can truly say that he had the energy and optimism of a man "thirty years his junior."

Two other fellows I would like to mention from our West Coast family were Ernst Bolte and George Summerfield. Both men had extensive experience in the drug business and were considered two of the company's key inside men. There were so many valuable associates that made Vi-Jon what it has become through the years!

Front view of the Vi-Jon office and factory in Oakland, California.

Third Inning

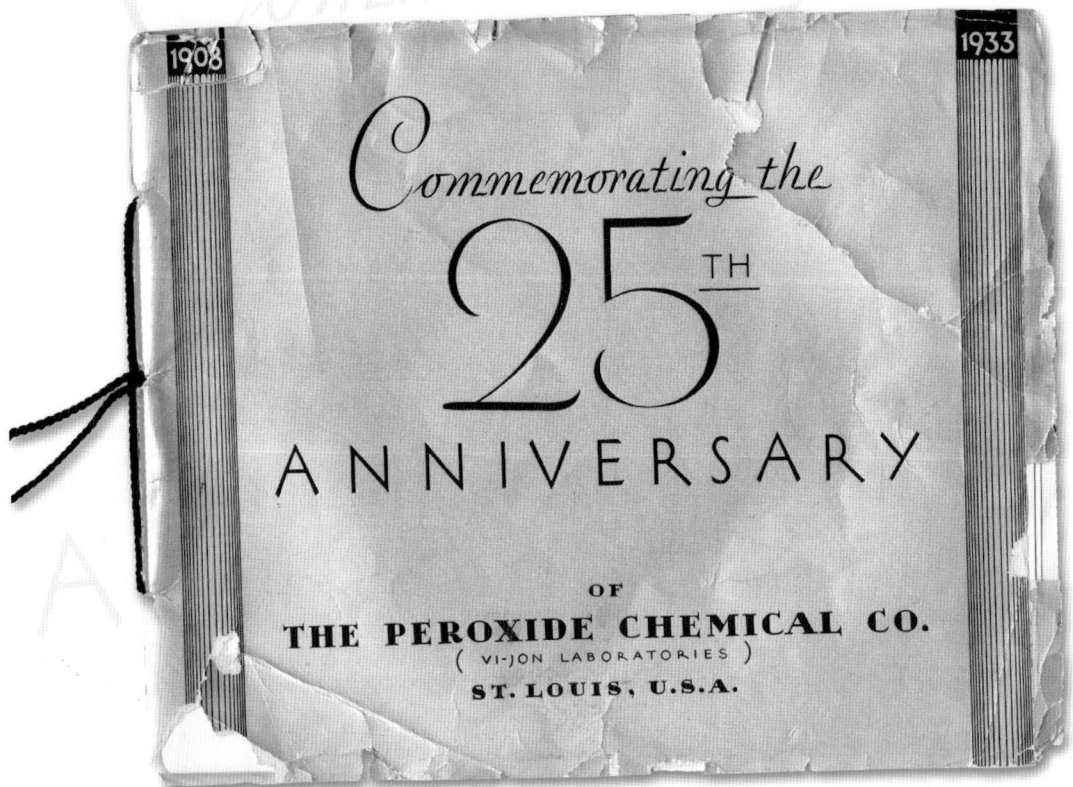

Cover of the 1933 brochure, "Commemorating the 25th Anniversary of the Peroxide Chemical Co."

A Grand Old Plant

Since the very beginning of Vi-Jon I can recall many pleasant business experiences. I humbly thank the Lord for my life and the time he allowed me to share with my fellow associates. I noted in our twenty-fifth anniversary brochure that I felt the programs that ultimately brought about the success of the Peroxide Chemical Company were really started back in the 1880s. I had initiated invaluable friendships that came to me through the courtesies bestowed by the buyers of jobbing houses (a type of wholesale merchant business which buys goods and bulk products from importers, other wholesalers, or manufacturers, and then sells to retailers) located in the principal cities of the United States when I was detailing the retail trade for those many years prior to 1908. The nucleus around which this business was created was the 122 firms that gave me their assistance in 1908, 44 of whom were still in business at the time of our silver anniversary. They, along with many new friends who joined us over the years continued to give us their loyal support.

Manufacturing in 1933

I will admit to you here and now, that I owe much to the talented people who were able to provide their expertise to develop a sales, marketing, and manufacturing system for providing all the products that served as our core business. I want to especially comment on the manufacturing capabilities that we developed during that first twenty-five-year period. By 1933 we had expanded into an efficient, modern plant with a floor space of over forty thousand square feet, with most of it used exclusively for the manufacture of high quality drugs and cosmetics. The Etzel Avenue location afforded us a home base, serviced by the Wabash Railroad tracks that allowed us to load and unload carload lots. We also had shipping and receiving capabilities that could routinely handle as much as one hundred thousand pounds daily—pretty big in those days!

Wave set production line, 1933.

Third Inning

Note John B. Brunner in the far left back of the St. Louis office in 1933.

We had gone from a one-sink, ballpark, experimental approach for basic batching to a modern analytical laboratory with expanded capabilities to achieve greater control of our daily product quality. Our labs were ultimately expanded to the point of providing control for all manufactured goods by analyzing all raw materials used in batching and packaging, and consistent high quality was maintained. I had the opportunity to tour many of the country's leading manufacturers, and I must tell you that in most of these locations quality was measured more on the basis of what you could get by with, than on the basis of what was right for the customer and overall company integrity. Our sustainability, I felt, would survive on the basis of this type of long-term common sense value, versus some of the shortsighted actions that were found at most of our competitors. It's important to note here that we felt cleanliness was the main element in the laboratory, and you could see this anytime you walked into the lab area.

Our compounding area, on the second floor, had over twenty stainless steel supply tanks that were connected to the filling department on the first floor below. An important point to keep in mind, fellas, is to keep your product supply close to the production lines. I felt our design was cutting-edge because we had product made almost directly overhead, and it was ultimately transferred to the fillers through a gravity-flow process. The hydrogen peroxide plant—our bread and butter—was able to make twelve thousand pounds every twelve hours. The Etzel Avenue plant allowed us to have a compact layout that could be operated economically. We also tapped into the good Lord's natural sunlight by having over forty-five hundred square feet of window glass.

Hydrogen peroxide filter press operation, 1933.

Third Inning

Our plant had equipment capable of handling preparations that needed to be filled while hot, such as cold creams, petroleum jelly, hairdressings, and more. We actually had heated pipe runs from the batching areas on the second floor overhead. We had a new carrier setup with five belts that took thirty minutes to deliver the filled jars to the packer. This design allowed a period of time sufficient enough to cool the jars and contents so that they could be sealed. We were able to make one hundred gross (we talked in gross or 144 units) per day. We had other smaller two-person operations that allowed for the production of smaller items, giving us an additional forty-gross daily capacity. We had railroad cars deliver loads of around two thousand cases that would be set onto a conveyor belt for transport to storage on the second floor to maximize our storage capabilities. A railroad car could be unloaded in just under two and one-half hours.

I was particularly proud of the STA-BAC Curl Set Department. As some of you may recall, STA-BAC was quite the hair preparation that would dry the hair in place. It was a tacky glue-like substance that within minutes would put your hair where you wanted it, and if you wanted it to stay in place, well a little STA-BAC would do it! But getting it into a jar fast enough was the key. I am proud to say that I was part of the design and special construction of the systems that allowed this department to accurately and speedily prepare these products. The preparations that went into these products were specially blended in the laboratory and then sent through one hundred feet of specially constructed piping to the filling machines. The fillers operated through a vacuum process, which allowed for very accurate measurement into the jars. The maximum capacity of this department was calculated at around two hundred gross per day.

In our cold cream and lotion laboratory, no expense was spared in carefully planning and equipping this department with necessary, up-to-date stainless equipment, so as to produce nothing but perfect Vi-Jon products. We took a section in the Etzel Avenue plant and specially constructed the area to eliminate posts, allowing for an uninterrupted span of thirty-two feet from one side to the other. We had the capacity to produce twenty-five hundred pounds of cold cream a day. In addition, we produced four hundred gallons of lotion every eight hours.

The brilliantine and talcum powder production department offered a combination of bottle washing, labeling, filling, capping, and packing devices in one operation. We maintained here a capacity of over one hundred gross per day. The talcum powder filling operation started with the powder being manufactured on the second floor just above, and then moved through gravity to the filling machines, through hoppers direct from the sifters. A machine for weighing and filling the cans, that was invented and exclusively used by Vi-Jon, has almost unlimited capacity. Standard production rates of up to five hundred gross were regularly accomplished.

All of our batches had formula cards in order to guarantee product with perfect uniformity. If you had told me the level to which our in-house productivity and quality concentration had risen by 1933, I don't know if I would have believed you. There is a spirit within the people that make up this company that, I felt deep inside, could be passed forward for many generations to come. It was this spirit in the plant that I just described to you that allowed us to supply our eleven warehouses, located across the country in New York, Pittsburgh, Cleveland, Atlanta, Chicago, New Orleans, St. Louis, Minneapolis, Dallas, Denver, and San Francisco.

The Great Turtle Shell Mystery

I can remember this very interesting story like it was yesterday. As I recall, one day the telephone rang and I answered only to hear the voice of my floor superintendent in an apprehensively concerned tone relating a problem I never saw coming down the line. It concerned turtle shells that had just arrived on the dock. Apparently about a hundred more had arrived today and this was fast becoming something of a major predicament for my little group. It all started when I contracted with a California company for the purchase of turtle oil. I thought I was pretty smart when I asked that they throw in the shells along with the refined product. My merchandising idea was that we would provide our customers a free turtle shell with every gross of product.

Turtle oil newspaper article in the *St. Louis Globe-Democrat Sunday Magazine* on December 24, 1933.

Third Inning

Turtle shells on the roof at 6300 Etzel Avenue.

The first shipment included about fifty shells that measured about three feet by two feet. As luck would have it, they also had a less-than-desirable fragrance. More specifically, the truck they arrived in reminded me of a pungent fish market. One of our warehouse staff stated the smell was so bad it "would make a billy goat puke" and I was inclined to agree. The day after the first shipment, we received fifty more, and then a hundred more, and more were on the way! I immediately sent a desperate message to the supplier: "SEND NO MORE SHELLS BUT RUSH OIL." This note appeared to take the immediate pressure off of the crew. Somebody had the bright idea of taking all the shells to our flat warehouse roof. There they sanitized in the natural hot summer sun. They started looking mighty good and resembled the turtle shells that everybody could recognize and appreciate. We even were able to separate the top shell from the bottom shell and stack them so they took even less room.

I often had daydreamed about taking a trip down to the Gulf of Lower California where these turtles thrived. They were hunted by Indian and Mexican crews, who were experts at harvesting these sea creatures with spears. I have never been on anything that was even remotely related to a turtle hunt. It sounded quite interesting. At Vi-Jon we specialized in blending the turtle oil into our cosmetics. But these animals actually represented a great deal more than oil and attractive shells. We greatly valued having the turtle oil as a skin beautifier and never gave much thought to the overall exotic adventure that was related to this most recent endeavor. This interesting cavalcade all started when I spoke to a man in San Francisco who told us about a crew that was going to Mexican waters where he expected to find enough turtles to supply potentially all the turtle oil that would be needed to treat the skins of all the women of the world. Based on this information, we asked him to take his team to the Gulf of Lower California just off of the coastal town of Guaymas in the state of Sonora. According to this man, he talked of the warm waters of the Gulf as having been able to support the population of thousands of these large turtles.

The average weight of these sea creatures ranged from one hundred pounds to over five hundred pounds. They swim to the beach to burrow in the sand and lay their eggs in this natural incubator. Apparently, the mother turtle never actually sees the newly hatched turtles. Just days after hatching, the baby turtles join the massive population that circulates in these warm and nurturing waters. Down in this part of the world turtles have been the center of a major industry, but the oil was not used for anything in particular. Their meat was considered quite delicious and was valued in Mexico and in other parts of the world as a delicacy. Fleets would go out into the Gulf waters and tap into the turtle population on a seasonal basis. They are then sent ashore to plants where the meat is prepared by slight curing, then wrapped in paper, and canned or boxed for export. I understand that the average-sized turtle will provide about 175 pounds of meat that can be used as steaks or as the prime ingredient in various soups. The oil itself is extracted from fat deposits around the stomach that are cooked in vats with slow, steady heat, refining the oil that is then strained and filtered until it is determined to be pure. The material is then put into containers and shipped from Mexico under special permit.

Well, I'll tell you this, I have done my share of fishing in my life. However, what these natives do in this form of fishing for turtles is utterly amazing. Their process depends on techniques used in deep-sea fishing, with a refined, almost factory-like approach to yielding their product. Yaqui Indians and other native Mexicans are recruited and operate canoes, which can be used in some fairly rough waters. These "turtle technicians" are experts with spears and also need to be capable of using high-powered rifles from time to time. These crews go out after the turtles and remain at sea for days at a time. Once the schools of turtles are located, the hunt starts with all the immediacy and cruel reality of any type of hunt for a warm-blooded animal. Spears have ropes attached and after an accurate throw is made the turtle is then pulled to the boat. After several turtles have been collected, a larger boat offloads this catch and sends the load to shore. Ultimately, the boats make their way to the shore where wagons transport the turtles to packinghouses and the refinery where the oil is harvested. It is interesting to note that Mexican law determines how old and what size the turtles must be to be harvested. We must protect and maintain all of God's creatures, even to the point when one pulls back when it is not always financially prudent.

Once we got into this raw material I did a little research and found out some very interesting information. Turtle oil has been available and sold in Mexico for a long period of time. This is one reason why the government has strict inspection detailed for turtle by-products. The folks down there do not recognize the oil's value for skin care. Rather, they take it internally and regard it as a primary cure for tuberculosis. All through the Southwest it is taken much like cod liver oil for its high vitamin content. Everything we have seen and use this material for, takes advantage of its use in cosmetics, not in any medicinal capacity. There is a prevalent value when used in conjunction with dry scalps and on wrinkles. It's amazing that this awkward-looking, archaic holdover from prehistoric times would be a harbinger for use in beauty treatments.

This story got some level of press coverage as well. Articles, which were as good as gold, started popping up in national and local publications. Other companies were using this raw material in their stable of ingredients. There was nothing unique in that. We just were able to get a little timely focus, which never hurts business or the bottom line.

Like this turtle story, the 1930s with the Depression and collapse of world governments around the globe turned out to literally be a shell game, with the real payoff coming in the 1940s. No one knew it then, but things were building up for a major showdown on the world stage that would have impact on the lives of everybody—even in quiet, serene St. Louis. We would soon find out that the days of sitting in the backyard and listening to a Cardinals ball game and wondering how warm it would get at the Veiled Prophet Parade downtown (that St. Louis tradition I'll talk a bit more about later) were going to be long gone. Once again we would need to look within ourselves to see how we might survive another tough period for the business and another tough conflict that would test the mettle of our nation as a whole.

I. John Burgess Brunner's Story

4. Fourth Inning: The Rundown
—From the Frying Pan into the Fire

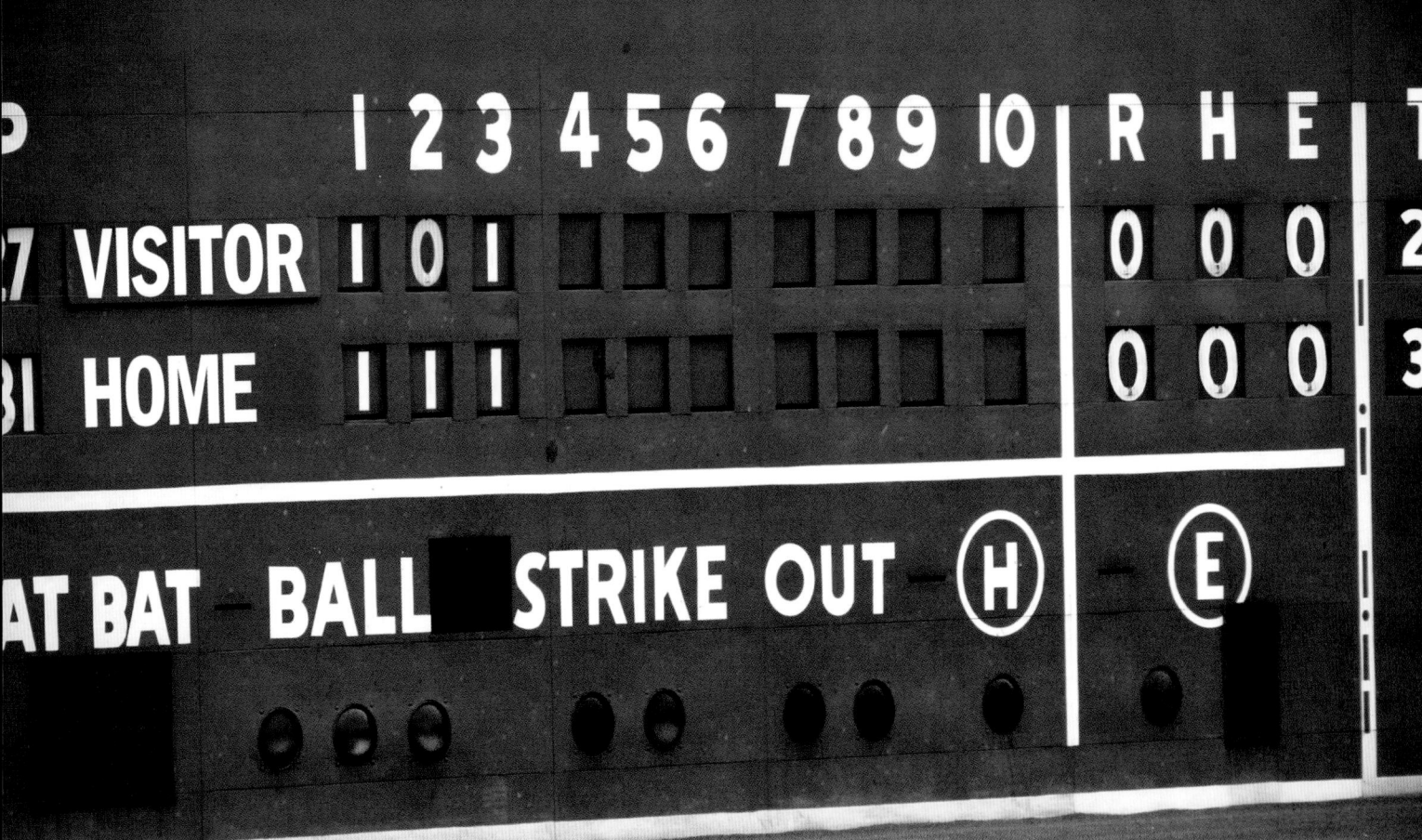

We went into our fourth decade with great relief, optimism, and confidence. This would soon turn into despair, pessimism, and confusion. We had survived World War I, Prohibition, and the Great Depression, so many of us said, "bring on the forties." Little did we know that this next challenge would be even greater, more ominous, and devastating than anyone could ever have imagined! As an American citizen deep in the heartland, I was totally oblivious as to how we fit into the scheme of world events. As a businessman with a growing industrial concern, I had dealt with some international influences and had "dodged some bullets" leading up to the World War I. My conservative overview served to filter out certain obvious social challenges to our times leading into the 1940s. This would turn out to be like the precipitous challenge of World War I—but with every corner of the earth threatened with weapons of mass destruction and political changes that would forever change social barometers, technology, and world order.

I hope the company never again has to deal with the challenge of volatile pricing, availability of raw materials and packaging, and quality and transportation uncertainties to the same degree we had to during the Depression and periods of war. Our sourcing people and inventory control folks had their hands full, but all the action from World War I and the Depression would prepare them for the biggest challenge to come in the not too distant future.

President Franklin Roosevelt once said that during the 1930s: "One third of the nation was ill-fed, ill-housed, and ill-clothed." The great experiment he brought to the table in 1932 worked to some extent, but more importantly he actually brought to the masses some degree of hope and belief in the future. Politically we were on different pages, but as patriots who believed in this great country, we ultimately all pulled in the same direction.

Going into the 1940s the economy was not skyrocketing, but it was growing at a decent pace. The GNP from 1933 to 1940 had doubled, so there was some reason to be enthusiastic. One number that escaped most everyone's attention, other than mine and the average wage earner's, was the fact that in 1940 the unemployment level was about 10 percent. That just seems way too high for a nation that places so much importance on employment levels and support for the family. Keeping people working has always been my concern and guiding principle. It's quite interesting to note that despite some of the negatives from 1932 to 1940 the economy grew nearly 60 percent. From 1940 to 1945 the economy would grow almost another 60 percent, all due to a wartime economy. In the coming war, the economy would operate under quite different conditions than during peacetime. During the war you would have massive spending, price controls, war bond campaigns, rationing of raw materials, prohibitions on new housing and new automobiles, rationing of consumer goods, guaranteed cost-plus profits, subsidized wages, and to top it all, the drafting of 12 million soldiers.

Fourth Inning

In the Good Old Summertime

As you may have already noticed, I slid into the next decade with guarded optimism and moderate expectations. The slow, sleepy pace of the early 1940s in St. Louis fit my senior standing and pastoral mood perfectly. The summers of 1940 and 1941 were typical hot St. Louis summers. The boys of summer, my Cardinals, finished third, with a record of 84 and 69 in 1940. Highlights during this period include the first night game in St. Louis—a game the Cardinals lost to the Brooklyn Dodgers 10 to 1—despite a 5-for-5 performance from Joe "Ducky" Medwick. I am not so sure about this new idea of night baseball. As a former ballplayer I think that you can see the ball better during the day. I would have lost pop-ups in the lights for sure. Don't know if the night thing will ever catch on—doubt it. And in 1941 the Cardinals finished two and a half games behind Brooklyn.

Soon baseball would feel the impact of future events. Nothing, not even the sacred institution of baseball would be left out of this period of infamous world events. It would be said in St. Louis that in the 1940s two major events took place: World War II occurred and the Browns made it to the World Series against the Cardinals. Had the Brownies won, I suspect all life would have changed in St. Louis.

Getting On Base

First night game held at Sportsman's Park, May 24, 1940.

The Days of Wine and Roses and Veiled Mysteries

Even during the darkest days of the Depression, Vi-Jon as an institution had progressed and became a highly respected corporation within the St. Louis community. Both Vi and I were deeply involved in civic organizations and our church. We enjoyed an active social life. We had been blessed with success, and it was only natural to share our prosperity with our friends and our extended family who worked at the company. Our good intentions were meant to reach all of our acquaintances, no matter what socio-economic level they occupied. We especially were fond of giving dinner parties and, to keep them from getting stuffy, we enjoyed handing out silly gag gifts to our guests. Sometimes our guest list extended well beyond the capacity of our expansive dining room table, whereupon additional tables were placed at its end so that everyone would be seated as one group together at the main table—everything for everyone at one big table—pretty novel idea.

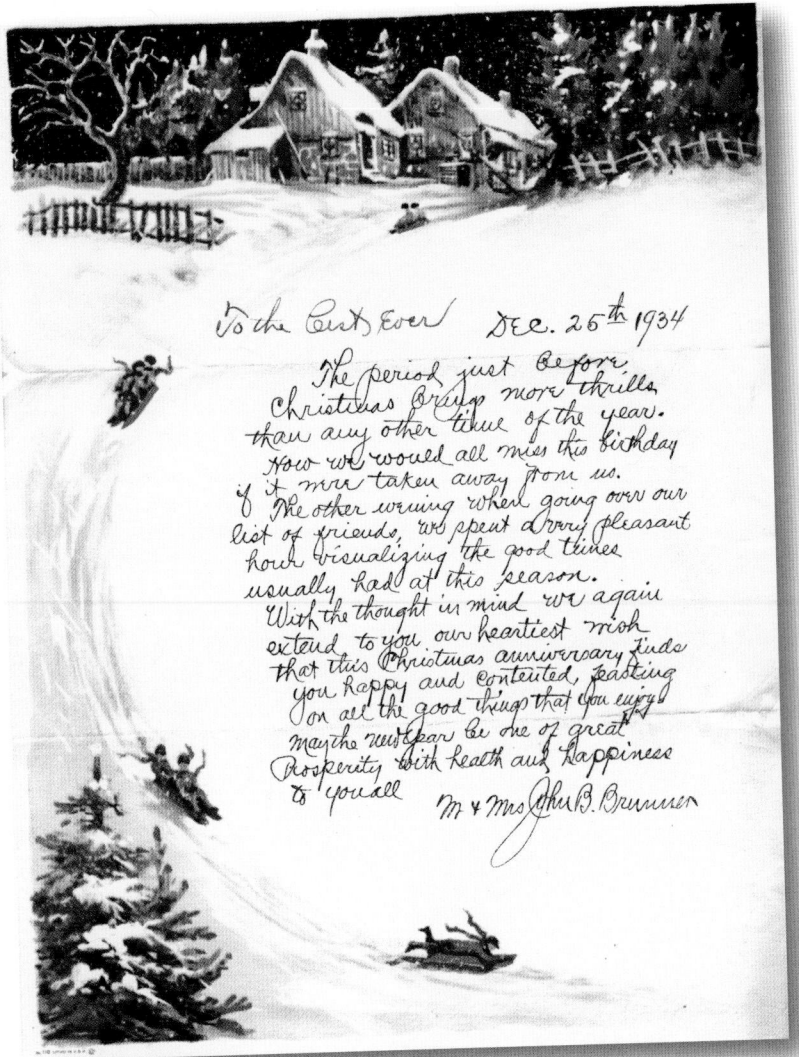

A Christmas letter sent December 26, 1934, signed "Mr. And Mrs. John B. Brunner."

Getting On Base

SEASON'S GREETINGS

1886

1935

Season's greetings from John B. Brunner noting his "50th Year" in business.

At this time, the Fiftieth Anniversary of my business life, on behalf of the Company I extend to those of you who knew me back in the Gay Nineties, and other friends of more recent years, my personal thanks for the part you have played in our success. May we greet each other many more years.

I wish you the most Joyful Christmas and Prosperous New Year you have ever had.

Sincerely,
John B. Brunner, President
The Peroxide Chemical Co.
Saint Louis, Missouri.

A young John W. "Jack" Brunner poses for a picture at about age ten.

73

Fourth Inning

We did the same at the plant for celebrations, sometimes just simply bringing out sawhorses and laying pine sheets of wood over them, then finally covering our improvised, makeshift dining table with a clean tablecloth—all the comforts of home—because our plant *was* home to our Vi-Jon family. Nothing like a potluck to bring the true neighbor out in everyone!

Leading up to Christmas every December, I could count on hearing some of our printing technicians circulating that my Vi was on her way down to the print shop with her arms loaded with boxes of stationery on which our family's Christmas cards were to be printed. Some years I would get ambitious and provide some handwritten letters. However most years Vi would make sure that there were photos of Jack or myself extending season's greetings on our family's behalf.

As Jack grew older, he, Viola, and I would travel together to various business and social events, as we had done before his birth. When he was younger, the Knox family (Vi's sister's family) stayed with him; in fact they literally moved their entire family into our household to care for him while we were away. For a time, our home was on Clemens Street, not too far from the Etzel Avenue plant, but for most of Jack's life we enjoyed living in the new, suburban Webster Groves. I must confess, having a son born when I was fifty-seven was quite a change for Vi and me. Being more mature parents, we had to balance our established lifestyle with that of raising a youngster. But we adapted and I think I was a pretty fair father. I believe that I was able to instill in him a drive to succeed, and he also became a pretty fair ballplayer. I like to think he was a chip off the old block.

Let me add that some family members went so far as to gossip that both Vi and I "doted" on Jack. I will say here and now that I stand guilty as charged. I confess to being an expert "doter" as will Vi, with great pride. The challenge of operating the business and maintaining a healthy home existence was difficult at times. But Vi always operated as "the balance wheel" for the three of us at home, and she kept us pointed in the right direction.

Thinking of those calm days of the early 1940s brings back many memories to me. Anybody who lived in the St. Louis area during the thirties or forties is quite familiar with many St. Louis legacies—Art Hill at Forest Park, the Cardinals and Brownies, Fairgrounds Park, the Highlands (amusement park), and the Veiled Prophet festivities.

As de facto members of St. Louis society we made our mandatory appearance at the Veiled Prophet Ball where the young daughters of the chief benefactors in St. Louis, most of whom were friends, made their social debuts. I have to be honest with you, while most local businessmen would probably have considered this an honor, I really didn't get too turned on by all the pomp and circumstance. You might say I had an almost irreverent but realistic "common man" view of this event. I had several friends who were very much a part of the Veiled Prophet organization. Out of respect for my close friends I won't name names, but one admitted to being the Prophet himself during several of the yearly events. For the record he was a nice guy, but not mystical by any stretch of the imagination!

Getting On Base

This picture shows all the pomp and circumstance of the regal "Veiled Prophet Ball" in 1948.

75

Fourth Inning

The Veiled Prophet organization was founded in 1878 by a collection of well-known St. Louis businessmen. The group patterned itself after the New Orleans Carnival society, the Mystick Krewe of Comus. I don't know what that means or even if they still exist, but I do know that the Veiled Prophet organization has continued to thrive in St. Louis. The start of this group was originally targeted at countering the growth of Chicago and to reestablish St. Louis's position as a preeminent manufacturing center and agricultural shipping point—great idea for a great city! Anything that promotes manufacturing and agriculture, especially in the St. Louis area, has to be well received.

St. Louis was the center for agricultural fairs before the turn of the century. The 1904 World's Fair was at its core an agricultural celebration. But after 1904, St. Louis seems to have drifted behind other great metropolitan efforts to lead the Midwest into the agricultural spotlight. I did get a chance to stop by the World's Fair, and it sort of helped sway me towards my ultimate decision to come to St. Louis. So I supported the Veiled Prophet concept at its core.

Also, I am here and now going on the record to set straight the rumor that my friends and I did in fact attend the Veiled Prophet Ball in a unique style one year. The story that got back to me was that I had the gall to borrow a dirty old dump truck to transport my party and me to the ball. Nothing could be farther from the truth. As usual, this legend, as popularly reported, was slightly off center and in fact was what I like to refer to as the real garbage within this story. The truth of the matter was that the vehicle in question was a brand new, shiny, white dump truck that was used to transport our party to the Chase Park Plaza Hotel for the evening's festivities. Any red-blooded American truck driver would have been proud to drive this impressive piece of equipment. I might add that we tipped the valet appropriately. After all, Vi and the rest of the ladies had expensive gowns on and the gentlemen were wearing fine formal tuxes! My sense of humor has no bounds and was clearly understood by only my Vi. She sort of kept my overt expression of what I found humorous somewhat in check.

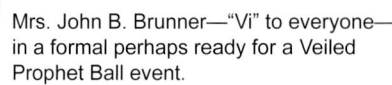

Mrs. John B. Brunner—"Vi" to everyone—in a formal perhaps ready for a Veiled Prophet Ball event.

How Naive Were We?

I must confess that most Americans like me had this shortsighted, romantic notion that this big mixed-up world would continue to roll along and somehow get wished into better times. Well I placed my trust in the Lord, and—how does that saying go?—"The Lord protects fools and little children." I guess I will admit to having the blind faith of a child and the informed, projected foresight of a fool in regard to seeing what was coming down right smack dab in the middle of the main world highway to our front doors. Circumstances over the next several years would bear me out. We all were living in a dream world that depended more on the power of hope than the reality of circumstances as they actually existed throughout the world.

For myself, I can honestly remember over the next several years, replaying in my mind a poignant scene from the popular 1938 movie *Drums Along the Mohawk*, which concerns survival on the frontier in the upper Mohawk Valley, located in what was then New York. In this particular scene there is a rare celebration of peace sandwiched between skirmishes with the British-sponsored Indian tribes during the American Revolutionary War in this quiet little valley. The pioneer wife, Lana, reflects on that moment and the state of her happiness then with her husband, newborn child, and their community. She tenderly prays and beseeches God, softly saying, "Oh dear God, please can things stay this way forever?" I quietly said somewhat the same prayer on many occasions during the early 1940s. I guess I had this feeling that my immediate family—Mom and Jack, along with my Vi-Jon family—were in for some very challenging and changing times in the not too distant future.

The peace and tranquility of baseball sure did not calm the fears that were brewing in the country, with all the negative news coming back to us from overseas. First, there was trouble in Germany with Hitler taking advantage of a leadership and economic depression vacuum. The depression that hit Germany was worse than our earlier economic downturn in the United States. So it's no surprise that the starving masses would support the guy with the loudest message and the biggest mouth. That loud mouth happened to be Hitler. But like I said, things were pretty bad over there and he sort of had everybody over a barrel. I guess the closest we came to that reality was the short-lived popularity that Huey Long—the "King Fish"—had down in Louisiana. Friends overseas in Europe were quite nervous and felt that the economic and political events during the thirties would ultimately lead to a world conflict. I was hoping and praying that they were wrong, but as it turns out we would soon be drawn into the conflicts in Europe and the Pacific.

In the meantime, the business continued to grow, and our escape from the thirties and the Depression was a great relief for all. With the ominous clouds of war in the distance in Europe and Asia, I once again started to have concern for a new generation that, like the generation before, would apparently need to go through a baptism of fire by means of great destruction and human sacrifice. Except now, I had a unique additional interest in how things influenced this generation since Jack would be of age for military service over the next number of years. All those wonderful years raising Jack, and it never occurred to me that he would someday enter the mainstream population out from under my protective umbrella and face such things as a worldwide conflict. I felt similarly about all the young people who worked in our plant. They were just kids, and it bothered me a lot. These thoughts perplexed my mind and caused me endless hours of distress right in my office. That very room had served as a chapel for prayer many times.

Fourth Inning

The reality of what happened on that peaceful Sunday morning is vividly captured in this December 8, 1941 *Post-Dispatch* front page. One story on the front page communicates President Roosevelt's emotional retort that "We Will Gain the Inevitable Triumph."

Day of Infamy—Nothing Would Ever Be the Same

You know how they say that everybody remembers where they were, what they were doing, when monumental events in world history took place? Well it's absolutely true. I can remember everything that took place that late fall morning, the morning of the first Sunday in December of 1941. It's as if those few hours were frozen in time. I remember what I ate for breakfast, what suit I wore to Sunday services, along with every detail of my son Jack's description of the previous night's Christmas Ball that year,

I remember that it was unseasonably warm that morning. I wore my brown suit and Vi wore her light blue winter long-sleeved dress. I sat in the living room, pleasantly recovering from a second helping of Viola's chicken and dumplings. The radio beamed clear channel KMOX in the dining room as we listened to CBS radio's broadcast of a seasonal December concert at New York's Radio City Music Hall.

Suddenly, CBS news broadcaster John Daly broke into our peaceful existence with news that Pearl Harbor in the Hawaiian Islands had just been attacked by military forces of the Empire of Japan. Jack came running in with a stunned look on his face. Vi dropped her favorite soup tureen to the floor with a gut-wrenching crash and it hit and shattered into a thousand pieces. Shock and dismay gripped us all at that same moment in time. The broken tureen seemed symbolic and ironic, for our lives were shattered and "peace in our time" as Prime Minister Neville Chamberlain claimed, was gone in a split second. Vi and Jack rattled off a nervous list of questions in staccato precision to me as if they could not understand or deal with this bitter dose of reality that had been force-fed to everyone in one mass countrywide feeding. My mind went into a repetitive rewind of events as I considered this horrible event. We knew very little except that things appeared to be very bad. We sat by the radio, hoping for more news, good or bad—anything that would give us more details to grab onto. You know, you stare at these old Atwater Kent Radios long enough and the faceplate appears to take on any number of emotions, especially when the set is delivering bad news.

I instinctively called Carl Mueller, our plant manager, and told him that we would meet early Monday at the factory to discuss a number of key issues related to the day's events and those that were certain to follow. The only edge that I figured could work in our favor was to be prepared for any changes that were going to take shape over the coming months and years. First, as was the case going into World War I, the demand for peroxide would become a tremendous priority almost immediately because of its medicinal properties. Second, many of our employees would probably answer the expected patriotic call for duty. I supported their noble patriotism, but I also operated a company that would need to support all of our families and provide important materials for the war effort.

Almost immediately rationing was initiated. It was common knowledge that there had been a national planned response program for such a crisis in the top drawer of most prominent public officials. I had heard some of the details but now these plans would be brought out, dusted off, and initiated. We now had to learn how to operate in a wartime state of affairs. We also had to learn how to conserve on things that we formerly took for granted just last week, oil, gasoline, and public services. On Monday, December 8, President Roosevelt challenged all of us to join the war effort as he addressed the full session of Congress. He said, "No matter how long it may take us to overcome this premeditated invasion, the American people, in their righteous might, will win through to absolute victory."

To a large degree, everyone was drafted to participate in this nationwide effort. Folks in our part of the country were scrounging scrap metal to help the war effort and ladies were sharing ration coupons for flour, sugar, and shoes. At Vi-Jon Laboratories we had to work hard to maintain production, juggling the rationing of our own supplies, and holding onto basic personnel in order to meet the wartime production schedules. It could be said of the folks at Vi-Jon, as well as for most people in the United States, that everyone's efforts were important and everyone had a stake in this conflict.

Everybody put such overwhelming efforts in at work, and on the home front you would have thought that the Germans and the Japanese were just down the block on Olive Street. Vi-Jon felt the impact of the war every day over the next four years. Our New York plant manager, John Ashmead, was called into the Navy and his wife, Margaret, stepped in and ran the Eastern operations from 1943 until V-J Day. In St. Louis, Carl Mueller, C. C. Lewellen, J. Louis Lenz, and many loyal department heads held the plant and work force together, operating at times on a shoestring in order to keep production up for the war effort.

Fourth Inning

A Long Four Years

We all did our duty and we all carried the load. Few families were left untouched, and pennants in the front window symbolizing family members in the service were plentiful and proudly displayed. One of the little known details during the war includes the fact that the workweek in manufacturing increased by seven hours between 1940 and 1944. The massive increase in production numbers was clearly related to the construction of armaments and military equipment. It should be noted that this increased production was not geared toward things that civilians needed. However, our productivity at Vi-Jon did increase and our ability to become more efficient was effectively displayed by how many people we were able to replace with simple machine adaptations. It should be remembered that most of our talented young men were away serving around the world in the armed forces. As I mentioned before, the 12 million men and women who served in the United States armed forces during the period between 1941 and 1945 were surely our finest generation.

During the war, unemployment for all intents and purpose disappeared. With 22 percent of the prewar workforce pulled into the war, it's no wonder the unemployment rate was so low. This fact led to the next big revolution in the manufacturing industry, namely, the introduction on a large scale of the use of women for all jobs in the production plant. Six million women occupied jobs in manufacturing and production during this time frame. Many were new jobs, making armaments, but many were not. The popular fictional character of "Rosie the Riveter" was the image that was seen by most. While most replaced men in the military, a lot of these women trail-blazed new inroads for good capable workers, who just happened to be women. I supported this move because it was the right thing to do and it was long overdue anyway. The real impact that this new workforce would have on our economy and family structure would not be clearly seen until after the war. Before the war Vi-Jon had a good number of female employees, so the increase was a natural direction to complement our plant employees. Our early moves towards merging women into the work force turned out to be somewhat of a salvation. Now, with fewer men available, the roles of lead people, supervisors, and plant management would open up to women over the next number of years, a new concept that these deserving women earned many times over.

It should be noted that however unified we were behind the war effort there was ongoing "butter or bullets" discussion. For the most part, Vi-Jon produced products that consumers wanted and used. The peroxide, rubbing alcohol, and other clearly medicinal materials went chiefly to the war effort. However, all other materials such as perfume-based products and other beauty aids were basically limited by the amount of raw materials that were available for these types of products. We were in position to launch back into our basic health and beauty aids after the war because of the type of management we practiced during the war. And we continued to stick to our guns, offering a good value at low prices.

The headline everyone had been waiting for—the end of World War II. The Japanese surrender announced in this August 14, 1945 *Post-Dispatch* tries to capture all the emotion released with the end of this crippling world event.

The End in Sight

I firmly believe the one major event that overshadowed the Great Depression was World War II. Gearing up for the war had started many years before Pearl Harbor. Nobody knew this until it was reported after the war. The war effort gave a sense of productivity to the average citizen. I think people were getting ahead because they were saving larger amounts of income. The fact of the matter is that this income was not spendable because there were few goods to purchase. We all bought bonds and most socked away hard currency, which was a remnant of Depression-style thinking. No one during the war was able to buy a new car, house, or major appliance because production of these items had been put on hold by the government—for good reason. With the end of the war just over the horizon, my staff and I started to come up with aggressive postwar business plans. We would be ready to sell "Rosie the Riveter" her beauty aids after the war and also welcome her as a permanent part of our production teams!

Fourth Inning

VE Day and VJ Day months later made everyone cry! I cried—no, no, that's not correct. More accurately, I would say I bawled like a baby, and I am not ashamed to admit it. I was drained. I saw my whole life, and my family's, pass before me in a second, and then time stood still. Both Vi and I felt a special tug to our hearts because of Jack. With him right in the middle, knee-deep in the war in India and China, the end could not have come soon enough for us. The war effort had been such an all-out countrywide endeavor that when it ended it seemed like such a coarse, empty feeling—as if we had been on a roller coaster and now instead of another twist and turn we sat motionless not knowing what to do. We had been going one hundred miles an hour for so long we forgot what standing still was like.

Everybody reacted in different ways. We had all lost someone we knew. Things were changed and life would never be the same again for thousands of families. We had gotten so good at this new Spartan way of survival that we didn't know how to act when we got the word that we won—that it was finally over. We had all worked hard and had developed a real respect and dependency on one another. We were truly a nationwide team. I hate to say this, but I hope as a country we don't go drifting back to the nonchalant, sort of selfish people we all may have been before the war.

A Tragic Turn

Well, the war had ended and things were looking quite positive for the future of Vi-Jon Laboratories, Inc. Then something happened that I am not able to explain or fathom to this day. Our sales had topped the million-dollar mark since the beginning of World War II, and with the end of the war came the promise of much better times to come for all of us personally and for the business as well. Jack was serving in the United States Navy in Shanghai. I remember that his wife Virginia (or "Ginny" as she was known by her close friends) was visiting us in St. Louis over the Easter weekend. She was like our own daughter, and we treasured each moment she was able to share with us. Her strength and presence really took some of the sting out of Jack's absence during the Easter holiday. I had promised Ginny that I would find some silk stockings for her, which were really scarce because of the war. From here on things are a little blurry. I remember helping Ginny to board the train. She waved and smiled and I think I caught a tear or two. She was so fragile and yet so brave. I was particularly distressed that we had to go through the busiest areas of Union Station. People were rushing, carts being pushed recklessly in and out of pedestrian lanes—a collage of general confusion. We had to go all the way to the far west end of Union Station to Track 24 where the train to Indianapolis was located. Like I said, I am a little confused on this, but I don't recall hearing or seeing anything until. . . . Well, I'm sure my son, Jack, can provide fuller details on this event. So let me turn the story over to him.

MARCH FOURTH
NINETEEN-FORTY-THREE

Today is another milestone for me. I am grateful for this long period of life, health, and happiness. My life has been an active one. Full of adventure with many mistakes, but lots of experience from which I have profited much. I feel my good guesses have exceeded my errors or I would not be here today. I believe my present day condition is wholly due to optimism of which I am, and always have been, packed full.

It is said: "Work hard, take chances and you will come smiling through"—eventually. I have done this and am happy, grateful to God, the supreme jugde, for his guidance and help. Let's go forward through faith, truth and hope.

John B. Brunner,
101 south rock hill road,
Webster Groves, Mo.

"Should Old Acquaintance Be Forgot".

"Should Old Acquaintance Be Forgot" was John B. Brunner's sentiment when he celebrated his seventy-fifth birthday on March 4, 1943.

John W. "Jack" Brunner on duty with some Navy buddies during World War II.

II. John White Brunner's Story

5. Fifth Inning: An Official Game
—The Rookie Steps In

If only I could have been there. It was an accident plain and simple. Dad was struck by a motorized baggage cart while moving through the loading and passenger walkway areas at St. Louis Union Station. Witnesses said it appeared that he simply didn't hear the cart approaching. They rushed him to McMillan Hospital on Kingshighway and he went into a coma. He fought hard to stay with us, but he lay in the hospital unresponsive and passed away three days later as a result of the head injuries he received in the accident.

An April 28, 1946 U.S. Naval Communication Service telegram notifying "LT JG" Jack Brunner that his father had been injured April 21, that he was in guarded but satisfactory condition, and that the doctor had recommended his presence to help his mother, who was deeply upset.

Fifth Inning

Above: An April 29, 1946, U.S. Naval Communication Service telegram from Senator Forrest C. Donnell directing immediate action on the request to have "Lt. John White Brunner" be given immediate leave to proceed home to his dying father. Senator Donnell asked for notification of the resulting actions.

Right: An April 29, 1946 U.S. Naval Communication Service telegram from John W. "Jack" Brunner to his mom, trying to console her by telling her he had talked with God and all would be okay, and to tell his dad he would be home soon and then he could teach him about Vi-Jon.

Bottom: A "29 Apr 46" U.S. Naval Communication Service telegram from the Navy to Senator Donnell, advising that "LT JG John Brunner" was headed home and due to arrive at Pearl Harbor on "ten May."

86

I wasn't informed of the accident until almost a week after he passed. There I was ten thousand miles away, with him laying in the hospital in critical condition. He needed me, Mom needed me, Ginny needed me, and there I was en route from Shanghai, not able to be reached, on that proverbial "slow boat from China." I sent a series of telegrams trying to help prop both my parents up. Even with all of the fine political friends our family had, there was no way to get me home any sooner. We had lots of people trying to pull strings, including Governor Donnell and several senators, all from Missouri. Their collective political clout wasn't enough to get me home in time for the funeral. I had not thought about this for many years, but I actually left Shanghai to be discharged from my ship on the day Dad was injured—talk about timing! I didn't know about the process then, but it took about a week to get me discharged. Again—and here is the crusher for me—it wasn't until after the discharge mess that I actually learned of his death. The Navy dropped me off at Pearl Harbor to catch the next boat to San Francisco. I always dreamed that I'd wave to my parents as my ship passed under the Golden Gate Bridge, but it wasn't meant to be. I came back to St. Louis as soon as I could to help pick up the pieces with Mom. Almost immediately I started my tenure at Vi-Jon in May 1946. I was only twenty-three years old. It was a very troubling and traumatic time for all of us.

Dad was laid to rest at Bellefontaine Cemetery. Mom insisted on having her pet name for him entered on the tombstone. There he was, interred with many prominent world figures in that beautiful setting, with names on tombstones like explorer William Clark, General William Tecumseh Sherman, World's Fair President David R. Francis, bridge noteworthy James Eads, and on his the name "Bunny." Rumor has it that David Francis' wife's nickname for him was "Cupcake." I don't believe it made the tombstone. Anyway, we all liked "Bunny" much, much better! Mom's nickname was widely accepted and used with great affection by the entire family.

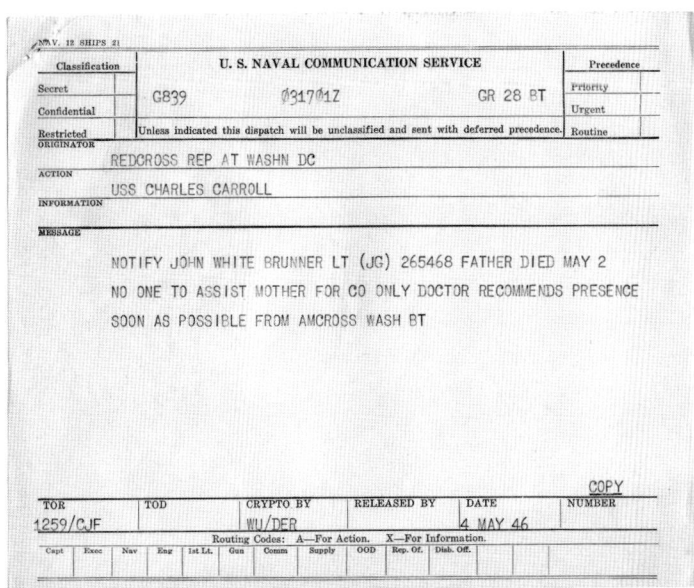

U.S. Naval Communication Service telegram notifying "LT (JG) John White Brunner" that his father died May 2, that there was no one to assist his mother, and that the doctor, once again, recommended his presence as soon as possible.

Fifth Inning

John and Vi Brunner just prior to John's untimely death in 1946.

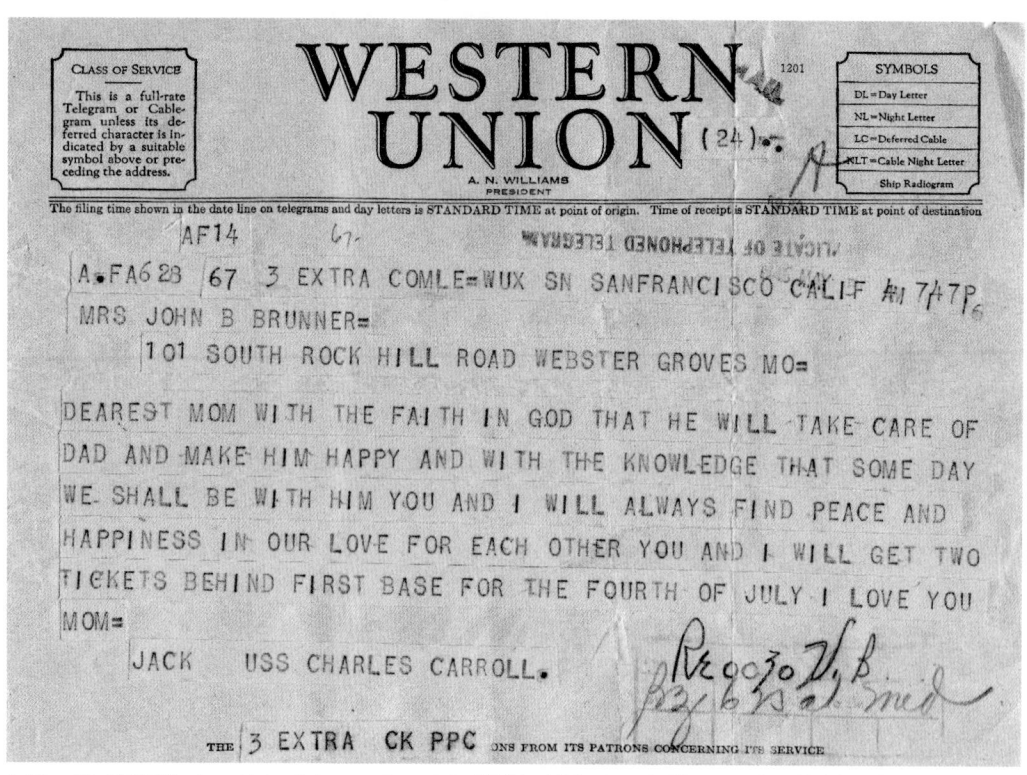

A May 15, 1946 Western Union telegram from John W. "Jack" Brunner to his mom, in which he tries to console her and prop her spirits by promising to take her to that baseball game he promised his dad, and they would sit in those seats behind first base as earlier committed.

We all kept close vigil on Mom after Dad's passing. I guess I never fully realized how inseparable the two of them were until that exact moment in time. She was lost, and for some time she was beyond consoling. Her sister, Aunt Orissa, made it a point to call Mom every day after Dad was gone. Mom tried to keep somewhat active in the business in the years to come, but she never again participated at the same level that she did during the years she traveled with Dad. I also saw her sit for hours in this same dimly lit office, staring into the distance, trying to connect with one lost, distant memory of him. She was quite insistent that, on my return from overseas, I should take over the company so that the Brunner name would remain a fixture in the Vi-Jon business. In part, her commitment to Dad's memory was the continuation of the Brunner family involvement in Vi-Jon.

The Buck Stops Here

Well, the nation switched gears from a wartime economy to a peacetime economy and did it under the direction of a crusty old bird named Harry S. Truman. After President Roosevelt's death, Harry was thrown from the frying pan into the fire. Even his fellow Democrats didn't appear to be totally on his side. The story goes that during the 1948 presidential campaign he used to have to go through his train coach and pass the hat in order to have enough money to make it from one whistle stop to the next. Now that's scraping the bottom of the barrel for funds!

Harry S. Truman's election is proclaimed on this November 3, 1948 *Post-Dispatch* front page. For most of the pre-election period, Truman was considered a significant underdog to then-Republican candidate Thomas Dewey.

I think Truman was a good man, but he had an abrasive side as well. He was tarnished slightly by his association with and start from the Tom Pendergast political machine in Kansas City. He also relaxed by having a scotch with a card game, which was not publicized too much. I recall a funny story that I heard back then about Harry's use of the king's English, especially some of the more colorful words. While in the White House, Harry's daughter, Margaret, was quite cautious about bringing beaus over to meet her dad. She brought over one lad who seemed to hit if off with her dad while walking through the Rose Garden. When the young man asked how the roses thrived so successfully and were so attractive, Harry responded that "manure" was the key and went on to describe the "manure" application process. Horrified, Margaret went running to her mother, Bess, tearfully describing the current subject of discussion between Harry and her beau. Bess just slowly shook her head and responded to Margaret, "It could be worse. You know how long it took me to get your father to use the word manure"?

Just What Did We Gain from This War?

This terrible war and the events of the 1940s had a major impact on everyone's sense of fair play and concept of world order. I was no different. My apprehensions confronted me every day. I was fighting to understand what real influence this conflict had on my view of the world going into the late 1940s and 1950s. I really could have used Dad's counsel to understand this new world order after the war. Hearing him describe things with his calm, consistent logic always made me feel better no matter what the issue was. I just could not figure out how this all made sense.

I'll try to explain my quandary. The big picture amounted to the fact that the war was won by the Allies with the loss of 50 million lives, along with catastrophic destruction. Here is the kicker and what I had a hard time coming to terms with. I understood Pearl Harbor, Nazism, and Fascism and fighting and defeating the countries that propagated these events and philosophies. I got confused when comparing the world order balance sheet before and after the war. It was like mankind went to bat, stood at the plate, and watched three strikes without even getting the bat off their shoulder. Let me explain. Britain and France went to war to save Poland from Hitler, only to hand Poland back over to the communists (Soviet Union) after the war—strike one! The takeover of Czechoslovakia by Germany was hotly contested and contributed to starting the war, and then Czechoslovakia was handed over to the Soviet block—strike two! Finally, Japan's invasion of China was the major straw that broke the camel's back in Asia, but by 1949 the Chinese were living under the Communist tyranny of Mao Tse-tung—strike three! We were out and what had we gained for all the pain that the world had suffered through?

Postwar Prosperity on through the 1950s

After getting back to St. Louis, things were coming at me so fast that I sort of responded instinctively for a while. The good news was that Dad had the foresight to set up a company with deep management resources. The bad news was that I was going through what amounted to a "baptism of fire." I was fortunate to have come into an operation that had been put together with strong family values and a fair amount of patriotism added on top for good measure. Dad was always a flag waver, and it made me proud to have been brought up with such strong national feelings. This patriotism was further validated by his and Mom's involvement in local politics. My wife Ginny's parents were also very active in politics in their home state of Indiana. They were very influential and inspirational, which also motivated my strong feelings for the United States and what it stood for. Along with their support of more serious and very worthwhile values, there were some light times as well. Like the time I made the mistake of using the term *Hoosier* in their presence in a less than positive light, which I definitely should not have done. They gently reminded me which state—Indiana not Missouri—was settled first and was therefore more civilized. (I never understood that brand of logic.) In any event, I never made that mistake again.

I graduated from Webster Groves High School in what could only have been described as idyllic settings. Dad went out of his way to keep business at the plant separated from life at home. I sort of wished that he had taken me to the plant more often. Maybe my crash dive into the business might not have been so steep. That's why I included my own son, John, in the business a bit more than I had been as a young man. Back then I had so many friends that I never paid too much attention to the fact that I was an only child. Who could argue with having all of Mom and Dad's attention whenever I wanted it? I attended Westminster College in Fulton, Missouri, and graduated in 1944. Everyone who has ever heard of Westminster College equates it with the "Iron Curtain" speech that Winston Churchill made there not too long after the war. They have a great museum dedicated to that memorable event that you should go see when you have the time.

Chip off the Old Block

Dad was able to puff out his chest about his ball-playing prowess. Well, I believe I was a chip off the old block, because I too think I was also a pretty fair ballplayer. I played first base at Webster Groves High School, and was on the Westminster College baseball team, and anchored a pretty fair ball team I don't mind saying so myself. Now, in St. Louis everybody knows that baseball is king, and every boy's dream is to play for the St. Louis Cardinals. I was no different. In fact, I was fortunate enough to get a tryout with the St. Louis Cardinals! My idol was Dick Sisler, who made playing first base a science. Back then the big leagues really depended on the informal traveling tryout to fill their need for prospects in the minor leagues. A man by the name of Branch Rickey developed an outstanding minor league system for the Cardinals during the 1930s. Mr. Rickey went on to do other groundbreaking work with the Brooklyn Dodgers when he brought Jackie Robinson into the National League in the late 1940s—the first black player in the major leagues, a move I think we all feel was way long overdue.

Well, back to my tryout. Like I said, walk-on tryouts were still pretty commonly used by the Cardinals. I must tell you that I was a crackerjack fielder with particularly "soft hands" which is an important characteristic to have as a first baseman. But I was a sucker for a changeup (pitch) that could make me look

St. Louis Cardinal first baseman Dick Sisler during the 1940s.

Fifth Inning

awfully bad at times. Swinging early and missing a changeup is enough to put a swat hitter like me literally on the seat of my pants. After all is said and done, you've only managed to stir the dust a bit. My tryout occurred before the great movement of players who left organized baseball for the service. I always said timing is everything. Heck a year later and who knows I might have been a baseball trivia answer. It still was a great honor to have had the chance to get a glimpse at the baseball brass ring—and I'll never forget it.

Sure would have been great to be a part of the Cardinal teams that made it to four of five World Series from 1942 to 1946! In an August series in 1946 against the Cubbies, Stan Musial went 12 for 13 over a three-game series. Top that off with winning the best two-out-of-three game playoff with the Dodgers after they finished in a tie with the Cardinals at the end of the regular season. That was great because I never cared for those bums from Brooklyn either. Incidentally, the Dodgers didn't much like Brooklyn either because they moved to Los Angeles about fourteen years later. The best part of the 1946 baseball experience was winning game seven against Boston with Enos Slaughter's famous "mad dash" from first base to score on Harry Walker's double in the eighth inning. That 4 to 3 victory in game seven was mighty sweet!

Webster Groves High School star first baseman "Jack" Brunner, circa 1940.

Meet Me in St. Louis

I guess I was pretty lucky to be in "St. Louis Cardinals Country." But back then there were so many things to be proud of in St. Louis. Why, even the movies during this period portrayed St. Louis in a very favorable light. Take for instance, *Meet Me in St. Louis* with Judy Garland. I must have whistled that theme song from the movie a thousand times. Wish I could have seen the World's Fair and Forest Park in its glory.

I met my wife, Ginny, while I was at Westminster College in Fulton, Missouri. Ginny grew up in Indianapolis, but she attended William Woods, a private college for young women. I first met Ginny when the two Fulton schools teamed up for a production of Thornton Wilder's *Our Town*. She was known as Virginia Gammon in the acting circles at school. I had second thoughts about participating in that play, but I am sure glad I stuck with it.

Back when I was young, it never occurred to me that we were "well off." Neither Mom nor Dad gave that impression, and the respect that they always showed to everyone, rich or poor, proved to me how humble and down to earth they really were. I actually preferred a more frugal lifestyle, and Ginny described us coming together as children of the Depression. Everyone who lived during my lifespan had the values of that time period permanently engraved into their being. To my way of thinking, the upside of a recession is a renewed focus on real values. Too many handouts have spoiled recent generations. Nothing is more sobering than the impact that a light billfold or empty stomach can have.

Virginia "Ginny" Gammon from Indiana, circa 1945.

The War and New Priorities

I guess within a year of my arrival at Westminster, the United States entered World War II and I immediately made plans to enter the Navy upon my graduation. I vividly recall how proud Dad was when I told him that bit of news. Back then, service for one's country was not a question of *if* but more appropriately *when*. Mom was so proud when she hung my service banner in the front window of our house as was the custom during the war. The big debate during World War II was whether you should get married *before* a soldier left for war or *after*. I sent my Ginny a white carnation every week while I was overseas, and she told me she played the song "Say a Prayer for the Boys Over There" on the piano constantly. Ginny must have driven her mother crazy, playing that song, hours on end!

Picture of young naval officer John W. Brunner, who writes to his sweetheart Ginny on their first wedding anniversary date, "One year which will be turned into 50—Your Jack."

Ginny's parents, Jesse and Juanita Gammon, were both professionals (a lawyer and schoolteacher, respectively) and they badly wanted Ginny to finish college before we married. I distinctly remember everything that happened when I proposed to Ginny. We were on a weekend visit to St. Louis from our respective colleges. It was late summer and it was warm, but it could have been snowing for all I cared. I was impervious to any outside influences, especially weather. Everything was beautiful to me because I was very much in love with Ginny. I saw mankind during this period of time through rose-colored glasses. One stipulation that Ginny's parents insisted on was that I promise that Ginny would finish her education while I was away at war. We were married October 28, 1944, at the Broadway Methodist Church in Indianapolis. True to our word, Ginny went on to finish her education at Butler University in Indianapolis.

Ginny Brunner with her naval officer husband "Jack" before he ships out to go "Over there" during World War II.

John W. and Ginny Brunner were married on October 28, 1944, at the Broadway Methodist Church in Indianapolis.

Fifth Inning

Around that same time I had gone to Harvard Business School, an institution that for two or three years was dedicated to the training of Navy supply officers. It is a wonderful school and continues to be one of the very highest seats of learning for business applications. Following my graduation I was commissioned an ensign in the United States Navy. That uniform meant the world to me. Those were troubled times. Everyone needed to put their efforts in, and mine were directed towards service in the Navy. The Navy determined that I was desperately needed in the Far East and thus I was sent to the China-Burma-India Theatre of Operations.

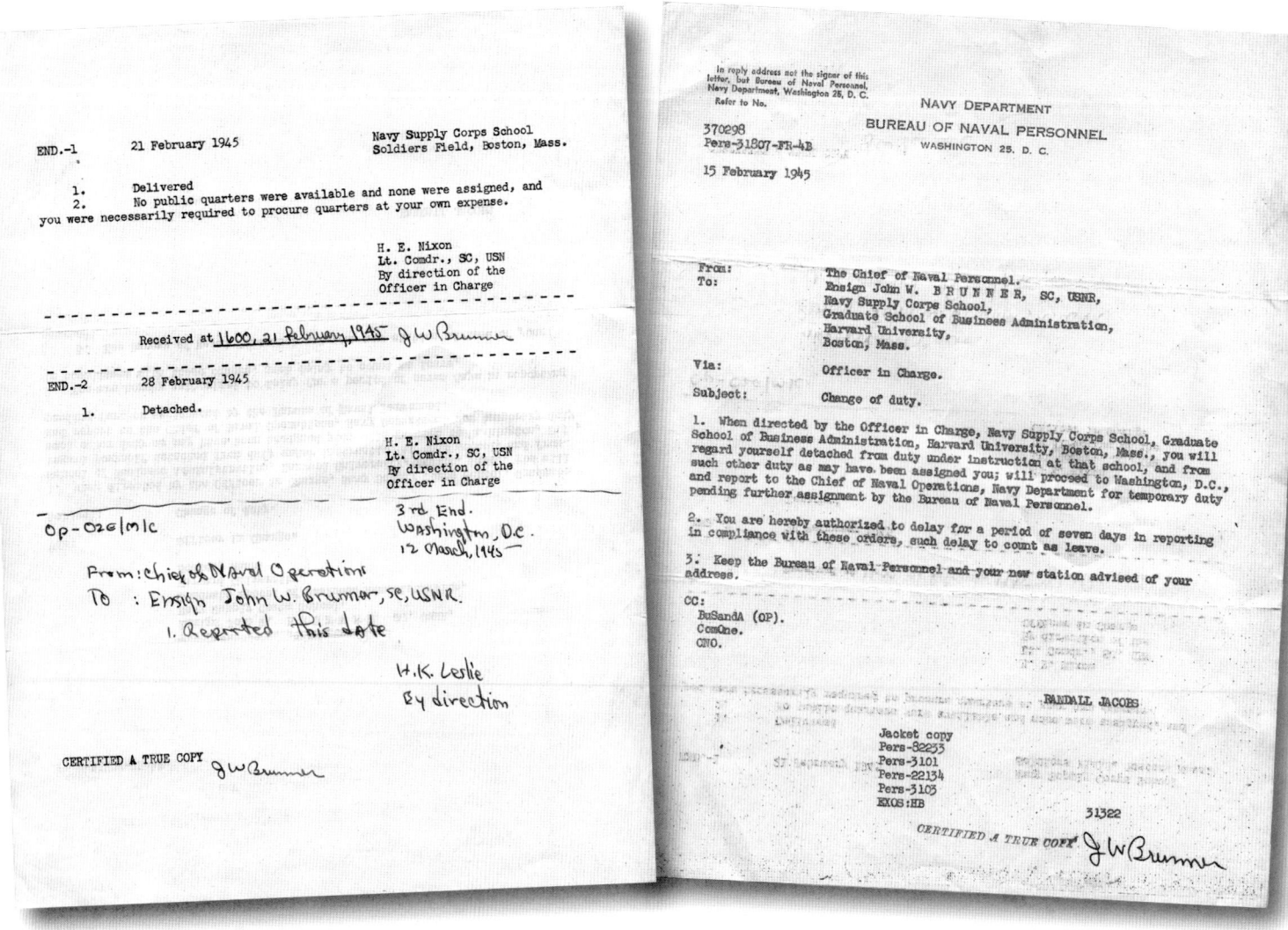

Right: A February 15, 1945 "Change of duty" directive to John W. "Jack" Brunner to report for temporary duty in Washington, D.C.

Left: Confirmation that John W. "Jack" Brunner had reported for duty and that he was to procure quarters at his own expense during his time in Washington, D.C.

Riding in style, John B. and Vi Brunner are chauffeured by Lieutenant John W. "Jack" Brunner in 1945.

One interesting point to mention here was that Navy supply officers were given the option of returning to Harvard after the war to enter the MBA program, but my priorities were family and the family business. I really hadn't known what I was going to do. I did appreciate that Dad never put pressure on me as a young man to throw in with him at the business. I actually had kind of thought about being a baseball coach or going into the ministry. After Dad's accident, my plans had to change, and I became what I would like to call a "mouthwash salesman" instead of a pastor. But my "congregation" is the Vi-Jon work force, and my "sermons" were the words of encouragement I tried to instill in them.

A Budding New Career

It was July of 1946 when I became president of Vi-Jon. The company had annual revenues of $1.3 million with approximately seventy-five employees. As I said, Dad really left a very productive and well-staffed company. Nevertheless, there was a tremendous leadership vacuum because of his absence. I found over the years that the most important mission of a company's leader is not the many checks he signs, nor the critical decisions he must make along the way, but the good form and method through which that leader injects optimism, energy, and spirit into the work force. The entire company feeds off of the daily, sometimes hourly, demeanor of the man who runs the show. The weight of this responsibility on me, at least initially, was unnerving. Being around Dad and seeing him in action, even on a limited basis, helped me to understand this concept. My being in the service helped continue this education. But being thrown into the fray when I joined the company in 1946 was the final act in this sacred training process.

I really saw this leadership capacity later in my son. His people depended on his concern and compassion on a daily basis, even more than they did on his vision. Bottom line is that you're only as effective as those key associates around you who display and apply their experience and savvy in conventional ways for unconventional results. The other point I would like to make about those years was the fact that a lot of people stayed with the company twenty, thirty, and forty years.

Into the Fire

I credit three men as being the "spinal cords of vitality at Vi-Jon" during the time I was learning the business after Dad was gone and I didn't have the benefit of his advice. Those three men were Carl Mueller (Operations), Howard Short (Sales), and Charles Krebs (Printing).

I should mention again that I came into the company at the tender age of twenty-three. I was never around the business all that much while I was growing up and believe the reason why stemmed from the fact that Dad was fifty-seven years old when I was born. In addition, there were a lot of senior employees there; people who knew the business and were very good at their jobs. I'm sure that Dad asked himself, what could this kid add to the company when so many of his people had been there twice as long as I been alive! I did, however, ultimately find my niche. I felt that the best thing I could do was to bring in orders. So I loaded up an old 1944 sedan without a back seat, where I could store product samples (you could save money at that time by not having a back seat), and called on the ten-cent stores—the mom-and-pop stores throughout Missouri and Illinois.

The same year of Dad's accident, a man named Ted Zerbe came to Vi-Jon and went to work at the Chicago warehouse and sales office. That freed up Howard Short to come to the main office in St. Louis. Ted served the Chicago-area customers for nine years until he was promoted to West Coast sales manager in 1955 and moved to California.

I inherited Dad's knack for sales but, unlike him, I wasn't particularly comfortable behind a desk. The nice people at Vi-Jon took me under their wing and taught me how to be a "mouthwash" salesman and, in time, the rest of what it took to run a company. First, they put me on the road so I couldn't do any harm and could learn the business. It was a lot of fun; I enjoyed it. I went all over Illinois, Indiana, Missouri, Arkansas, plus a little bit of Iowa, calling on every dime store in the state—and any city of a thousand people or more had a dime store. We had maybe three or four hundred customers, and I worked in advertising and promotion in towns like Decatur, Champaign, and Springfield. I would go into these stores where the owners were busy trying to make a living, and in order to get their attention I'd help sweep the floor, set up displays—whatever needed doing. In exchange, the storeowner would give me ten minutes of his time. I'd write up the order and if I had the stuff in my car, I'd fill the order right then. If I got a $25 or $40 order, that was great. After about five years I was able to contribute something. I'd phone the order in to the sales manager, Mr. Shoreham, and they would ship it. I'd come back into the office and then go out again. I don't remember that Dad traveled much. I guess he felt more comfortable running the store back in St.

Louis. It was second nature for him. But he had a very good salesman who worked for him—Howard Short—and I believe he also had a couple of brokers. I'd also go to New York to call on Woolworth and to Detroit to call on S. S. Kresge. And I remember bringing my own son along to New York and Detroit when he was ten or eleven.

I have really fond memories of the years I spent in sales with Mr. Short. Howard and I would go on sales calls and compete to see who could find the cheapest hotel or the cheapest gas or come back with the lowest food bill. We had a gag we used to pull on one another in our hotel rooms where we would pretend to call room service and order a bigger room sent up. In Vi-Jon's fiftieth anniversary book from 1958, I referred to Carl Mueller, general manager at the time as "Mr. Inside" and Howard Short, then sales manager as "Mr. Outside." The three of us, Mueller, Short, and I, came up through the Sales Department and emphasized expanding volume and upgrading service. The net result was record sales and record peacetime profits.

One of the small things that I felt most comfortable with was the fact that everyone at the home office called me "Jack." Being called "Mr. Brunner" just didn't feel right. I noticed years later that my son also liked the folks to call him by his first name. As "Jack," I had a way of turning friends into customers and customers into friends. I have always been a "people person," and I think my son is also much like me in that regard. I liked the people and the accomplishment of getting to the store at 7:30 or 8:00 in the morning and calling on them, writing an order, and getting something done. I would call on everybody about eight to ten times a year, and it was always a pleasure and a privilege to visit them and work up advertising promotions. I considered all these folks nice people and very good friends.

This picture of John W. "Jack" Brunner was taken in that famous office at 6300 Etzel Avenue in 1958.

Fifth Inning

We Like Ike

In the meantime, I was learning my sales applications during a very interesting period of history. After surviving the Truman "Fair Deal" experiment, we enjoyed two terms with the immensely popular Dwight D. "Ike" Eisenhower. He was a middle-of-the-road guy who liked small government and was a conservative who ran his office like a business-type administration. He ran a balanced ship by carrying over some of the New Deal ideas. He also bolstered Social Security, initiated huge public works programs, and the all-important Federal Highway Act of 1956. This would serve to launch our new consumer, who now would be a mobile consumer, anxious to hit all the new shopping centers and spend their new consumer wealth.

Eisenhower's period in the White House was a very productive and prosperous time for most folks. We had over just 5 percent of the world's population while producing over 50 percent of the world's goods. Technology would launch many new initiatives, with knowledge and productivity setting records in every quarter. In addition, some of the other bold new steps ushered in by Ike included the age of space exploration, the computer age, and "feeding the masses" when the first McDonald's franchise opened in 1955. The country's five largest industries—autos, oil, aircraft, chemicals, and electronics—made a quantum leap in productivity. The car industry lowered the average cost of labor required to produce a new vehicle by using high-tech equipment on the production line. We were seeing innovations in filler concepts, along with new cappers that applied new cap designs. In another raw material area that had an impact on Vi-Jon, the chemical industry provided new avenues for consumers through advanced use of synthetic fibers, chemical precursors, and especially plastics. I predicted back then that plastics would replace glass in most basic consumer applications, and I believe we are just about there.

Expanding Middle Class

This postwar boom was due to the middle class and their newfound impact on the economy. Between 1945 and 1960 the median family income, adjusted for inflation, came very close to doubling. The increasing income grew and basically doubled the size of the middle class. I would estimate that two-thirds of the population now qualified as the new middle class. This was a time of almost full employment, great new opportunities, and increased federal spending that contributed to the expanding economic landscape. It was a time during which everybody seemed to be making great strides.

This middle-class juggernaut continued as folks stretched out their arms to encompass a new suburban lifestyle. There were 13 million new homes built in the 1950s and almost 90 percent were located in suburbia. The landscape around the traditional cities was full of suburbs. The baby boomer phenomenon resulted in the birth of almost 76 million Americans.

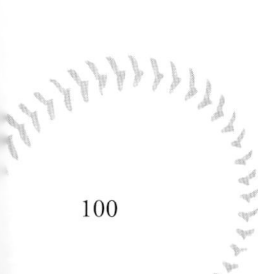

A New Progressive Type of Workforce

The way I saw it, post–World War II Americans went in search of the "American dream" at a breakneck pace. About this time also, men were returning from duty in the armed forces, and it followed that women, who had joined the wartime workforce, returned to the home front in substantial numbers. This movement back to the home happened to *some* degree; however, many women had gotten a taste of working outside the home, and said "Thanks but no thanks" to going back to their former way of life.

Now at this point in time, a huge percentage of our work force lived within walking distance of the plant; however with the popularity of the family car, many moved farther and farther away. As a result, suburbs sprang up in record numbers. It was also about this same time that American cities adopted the practice of zoning. Instead of the old neighborhoods where churches, factories, stores, and houses existed in close proximity to each other, the concept of planning and zoning dictated that buildings be grouped according to their purpose, a concept made possible by the availability of the automobile. Subdivisions replaced neighborhoods, shopping centers with big parking lots replaced neighborhood mom-and-pop stores, and industrial park complexes kept factories located next to each other and far away from residential areas.

An interesting story while I am talking about living in close proximity to work involved a couple who really took the concept of living close to work to a new level. Years ago, as I said earlier, an overwhelming number of employees lived near the plant and walked to work. However, there was one employee who eclipsed everyone else for being close to his job. Walter Stotler and his wife actually lived in the building at 6300 Etzel Avenue. A small apartment was built on the second floor across the hall from the office and was separated from the print shop by a thin wall. Print shops can generate a fair amount of noise, so I'm sure Mrs. Stotler was glad when five o'clock arrived! Walter was the resident mechanic/maintenance man/watchman and was probably the only employee who was never late for work.

The new Traffic Building, completed 1957, was constructed to allow for the 1960 expansion program of another twenty thousand square feet on the second story.

The Move to Private Label

Not long after World War II, as the company transitioned from industrial sales to retail sales, something occurred that caused Vi-Jon to undergo yet another shift in focus to keep pace with the changing market. I was calling on Kroger and other national chains, selling Vi-Jon products and trying to develop the Vi-Jon name, but stores increasingly wanted their own label. I can remember that we spent perhaps $100,000 (big money back then) for a half-page ad in *LIFE* magazine for our Vi-Jon mouthwash and I proudly took it to Woolworth's. They said, "That's fine, but I want you to know we're going to go to private label, and your competitor is now doing that business for us." It was a sobering moment in 1958 and perhaps even more of a lightning bolt full of reality. Woolworth's was sending their message, loud and clear, and I got it.

Another concept that I saw coming was the fact that the term "dime store" was being replaced with the concept of a "variety store." I guess it was pretty clear that a dime no longer had the purchasing power it once had. Given that a few giants like F. W. Woolworth and the Atlantic and Pacific Tea Company had been around since the 1920s, chain stores were just beginning to dominate the American retail landscape. Another all-American benchmark came along in 1955. Ray Kroc bought several restaurants from the McDonald brothers and put the concept of franchising on the map, along with Harland Sanders who started his Kentucky Fried Chicken franchises the same year. I can tell you that I ate at a few of those restaurants over the years! Then discount stores entered the market, offering people more purchasing power for their dollars. In 1962, my friend, Sam Walton, built his first discount store in Rogers, Arkansas, and S. S. Kresge launched the first Kmart store. The "big box" stores were on their way—and our team at Vi-Jon would be there to service them.

Another Milestone

When we at Vi-Jon celebrated our fiftieth anniversary in 1958, there were approximately eighty employees and gross sales totaled $1,931,102. Our best-selling products were hospital-grade hydrogen peroxide, antiseptic mouthwash, wave set, hair spray, aftershave balm, and the ever-present nail polish remover in its familiar non-tip bottle.

In my message to customers and friends on this fiftieth anniversary, I credited the stockholders, the loyal employees, and our faithful customers for the company's success. But above all, I acknowledged the company's debt to the very country in which it resided. I described it then as "the America that arose from a land divided by Civil War to the most productive, liberty-loving, most generous nation on earth in less than one hundred years." It is this America—with its freedom, its opportunities, its Constitution, its national pride, and its faith in God—that gave birth to this company and the millions of businesses, farms, and services that span America today.

Compounding Department at the Etzel Avenue location in 1958.

Fifth Inning

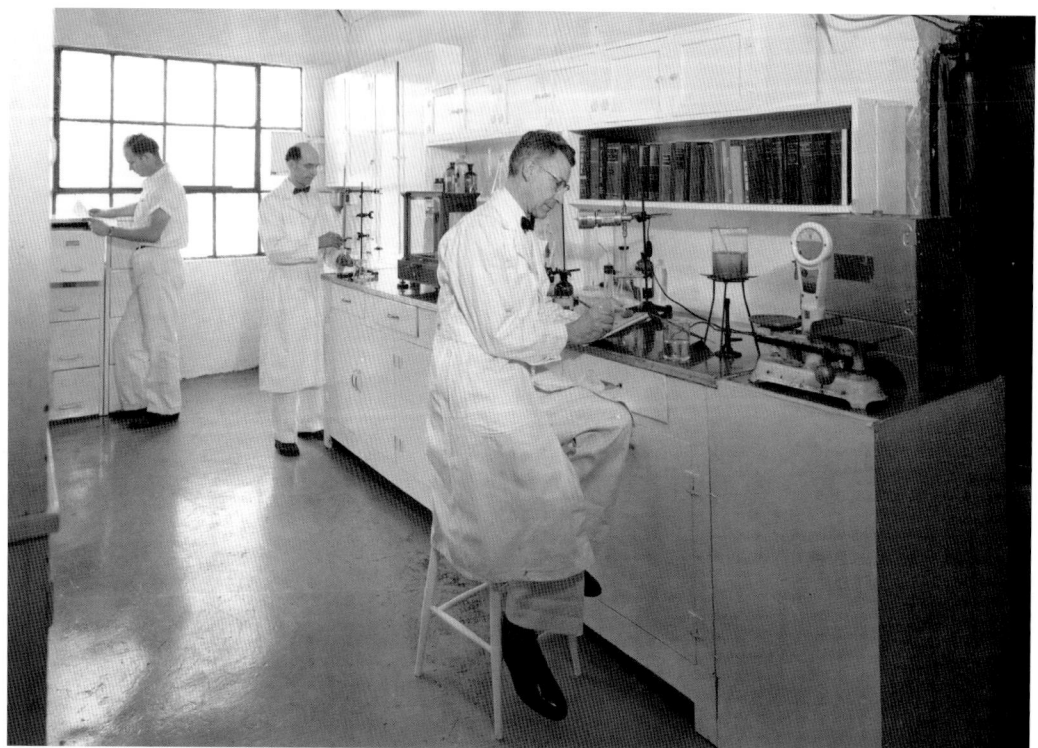
Chief chemist Raymond Moore is shown in the foreground of the laboratory in 1958 conducting an analysis for a new product.

Wave set line, 1950.

Getting On Base

Shampoo production line, 1958.

II. John White Brunner's Story

6. Sixth Inning: Looking for a Rally —"Camelot" and Chain Stores Expansion

Well, I guess the appropriate and "in" way to say this was that we "rocked and rolled" into the 1960s with an arbitrary sense of what the term *Cold War* really meant. It seemed that half the country was digging holes in the ground for bomb shelters and the other half was busy looking to the air to see the latest aeronautical breakthrough in jet design. In addition, the word *Sputnik* all of a sudden popped up on our television screens almost overnight. And what was a Sputnik anyway? Sounded like some kind of breakfast cereal with nuts. Could it be that suddenly the Russians had somehow become more capable than the United States? No way—not if our team at Vi-Jon had anything to say about it!

On the other hand, some of the more sobering events had also gripped our attention. These events included the appearance of the Berlin Wall, the Bay of Pigs fiasco, and the Cuban Missile Crisis. I can recall quite vividly having a conversation with several palletizers at the plant who suggested we might need to dig a bomb shelter by the front tank farm—you know, just in case. I guess since the palletizer is the very last guy stationed at the very end of the line stacking off cases of finished products onto pallets, they figure they should be the first ones off the line into the shelter. I told them if it made them feel any better that the "basement" at the Etzel Avenue plant could be drafted into an emergency bomb shelter for use if need be. But that gives you some idea as to the mindset of the average person in the plant. Just think of it—trying to comprehend the incomprehensible—total and complete destruction. The biggest complaint that I heard from the various "water cooler summits" was the fact that everyone felt like a herd of mindless sheep now being led by one of the fellow sheep instead of a lion, as had been the case with Eisenhower and Roosevelt. There is an Arabian proverb that states, "An army of sheep led by a lion would defeat an army of lions led by a sheep."

That Cuban missile mess really got everyone's attention. This crisis literally came out of nowhere and was splashed across our Monday morning papers with little to no forewarning. It was a very tense time for everyone, and often there was a deathly hush over the production areas and in the office, like some mysterious ghost had zapped everyone's spirits. My concern compelled me to allow our folks to leave early from work to go to their places of worship during the height of this incident. I think everybody spent many anxious days on their knees as this incident played out. The comment Dean Rusk (President John F. Kennedy's secretary of state) made about the other side blinking was about as accurate as one could be. All I can say is I'm grateful the other side blinked and cooler heads prevailed!

There was plenty of "blinking" going on in our health and beauty aid industry as well. The middle class of the United States marched on and we continued to serve their ever-changing patterns. You know, we have really seen some monumental changes through the years. Look at everything that has been mentioned in this short period, and we haven't even gotten to my son. There was some level of forecasted change during every decade. But I really believe that the 1960s were really equal to all of the previous predicted rates of change times ten.

It was sort of crazy because this new sense of world balance for most was not consistent with what had been considered normal in the 1950s. For instance, the Berlin Wall and the issues related with Cuba; our increased involvement in Viet Nam; the John F. Kennedy, Robert F. Kennedy, and Martin Luther King assassinations; antiwar protests; the six-day war in Israel; and continued trouble in Northern Ireland. Catch your breath—there's more! Add to that list the first manned space flight by Russia, the first heart transplant, the Russian invasion of Czechoslovakia, and the first man on the moon, Neil Armstrong. And, by the way, I was sure glad that my children weren't involved in that Woodstock business that happened in New York during 1969. Also, the pioneer trailblazer to that Internet you like to put so much stock in—ARPANET—was created. Don't know how far that will go, but it's certainly like another foreign language to me. I don't like a machine that can think faster than I can! I'll always remember how hard it was to convince me that we needed to convert from a card-punch system to a computer! Anyway, much was happening during this decade that would set the stage for decades to come.

JFK, Camelot, and Days of Turmoil

The person who led us into the aforementioned unpredictable and turbulent times of the 1960s was John F. Kennedy, the former senator from Massachusetts. From the somewhat stable administration of President Eisenhower we entered the youthful reign of John F. Kennedy in 1960, who was a mere forty-three when he entered the White House. I must admit that I was not a Kennedy supporter, but I liked the fact that he was a Navy guy. He certainly was quite a colorful personality and must have been considered a reporter's delight. But, he received a lot of homage that I didn't feel was rightly earned. I will admit that he occupied the highest office in the land during a time of great change and troubled times, and because of that he received my support and respect. However, I think some of the issues he may have walked into occurred because of his lack of seasoning. Now in all fairness, I'm quite sure that Kennedy made some good decisions along the way, but just the same I would have felt so much better with "Ike" calling the shots.

However, Kennedy was a charmer, and during the groundbreaking televised debates, which I watched intently, he basically left Nixon in a pool of sweat while he looked cool, calm, and collected during the event, giving him a clear edge. I guess one of my key criticisms centered on the fact that Khruschev, being the old salt that he was, probably felt that in 1961 this young politician could be pushed and this may have contributed to the Berlin Wall and Cuban Missile events. The impact from these critical events was felt across the board for the next thirty years.

The associates on the floor at the plant and in the office languished in a sea of uncertainty during this time period, and many days were spent reassuring these folks that all would be well. I put on my "game face" and rarely conceded my *real* impressions of what appeared to be happening. I expect we have all used that game face on many auspicious occasions.

The gut-wrenching reality of that horrible November day in Dallas is validated by these stunning headlines in the Saturday–Sunday November 23–24, 1963 *Globe-Democrat*.

The John F. Kennedy assassination was a terrible tragedy that left the country stunned. This was a horrible thing to happen! The news went out just past noon like a bolt of lightning. People openly wept as they stood by their machines. I must admit I had to gather myself as well. We let our people go home a bit earlier than normal after the terrible news on that fateful November 22, 1963. I can remember watching TV with my kids, John and Robin, quietly sitting on the floor, listening to the muffled drumbeat and watching the death procession as the caisson bearing President Kennedy's body rolled slowly down Pennsylvania Avenue. They said that it was the same caisson that moved President Lincoln's body nearly one hundred years earlier. I don't care if you were a Republican or a Democrat, Jewish or Christian, man or woman, it was very touching to see little "John-John" give a salute to his father's casket as it passed by. Your mother and I cried openly because it was as if some uncaring phantom had stolen the country's young and inspired spirit in one terrible swift moment. This was the less than a storybook end to the point in time called "Camelot."

The horrible events of the days following the tragedy added to the malaise. I made up my mind to re-center my outlook going forward, put my personal concerns on hold, and offer some basic guidance and support for all of our people. Life would go on as it should and must. But I knew our country that I loved so much, would be heading into some very rough water.

From Camelot to Cowboy

President Lyndon Baines Johnson came into office on a tremendously sad note. I would not wish what he had to face right out of the gate on anyone. On top of all that, back at the plant there were rumors spreading like wildfire that I'll never forget. The story goes that the mechanics got the story that Johnson was pro-nuclear and supported the use of advanced weapons and that he was looking for a reason to drop a bomb on Russia. In addition, the story had to complement the story that Russia was responsible for JFK's death. These guys had way too much time on their hands. I calmed the hysteria and told everyone that this was ridiculous and had absolutely no foundation, but you know how rumors spread. I am sure that this qualifies as folklore now. I was sure that I would find some of my folks hunkered down in our self-proclaimed basement "bomb shelter" near the rear of the plant. Isn't it crazy how rational thinking goes right out the door in times of distress?

I will have to admit that Lyndon Johnson was a real-life cowboy—stubborn, resolute, self-righteous, and a tough-as-nails, a power play specialist as opposed to Kennedy, who was a negotiator and a bridge builder. Johnson would bully his opponents and fellow democrats and passed entitlement programs right and left. You could almost hear the cash register going "ka-ching" as each new program was being shoved through Congress. The country has never really fully recovered from all these giveaway programs. None of his programs helped the real workers, like my people on the plant floor and in the office. The "Great Society" programs, along with "black hole" education initiatives and an aggressive war agenda, nearly sank this country. Health care reforms *were* needed, but everything was happening so fast it really set the economy reeling. Johnson declined to run for a second term, which to me was the noblest thing he ever accomplished during his presidency. Question was, could we recover enough to go into the seventies with some sense of optimism and momentum.

From the National Stage Back to St. Louis

These national and world events that had happened seemed so unreal to everyone living in St. Louis. But, really how could these things affect our little corner of the world on Etzel Avenue? The cultural revolution in China in 1966 seemed so far away and it appeared at that time, in the short term, that this event would have no impact on how our mouthwash or shampoo packaging lines ran. Who would dare suggest that we do business with a Communist country like Red China?! China was such a hard-line Communist country and so secretive that it appeared as if they were a million miles away and not a threat able to break into the business world. We couldn't know how far this Chinese Cultural Revolution would cast its impact on business and industry in the United States in the coming years.

From Sportsman's Park to a Concrete Bowl

Talking baseball with my son and with our associates at Vi-Jon was one of the simple pleasures of life for me that I always enjoyed immensely. It's the kind of camaraderie and bonding activity that is hard to describe to anyone who does not have a feeling for the grand old game.

Well, I took time to smell the roses—or maybe the "red hots"— just outside of Sportsman's Park. But you weren't able to smell them long because the grand old building that housed the Cardinals and Browns for so many years, Sportsman's Park, would see its last game during April 1966. It was rudely replaced by this huge concrete bowl, right in the middle of downtown St. Louis. I am not kidding you—this thing looked like a giant bowl—but I guess this was considered progress. The 1966 All-Star Game was held in the new stadium, and it was 112 degrees on the natural grass field. Keep in mind that this was before the installation of the synthetic improvement they called "Astroturf" which really promoted higher field temperatures—don't even get me started on that!

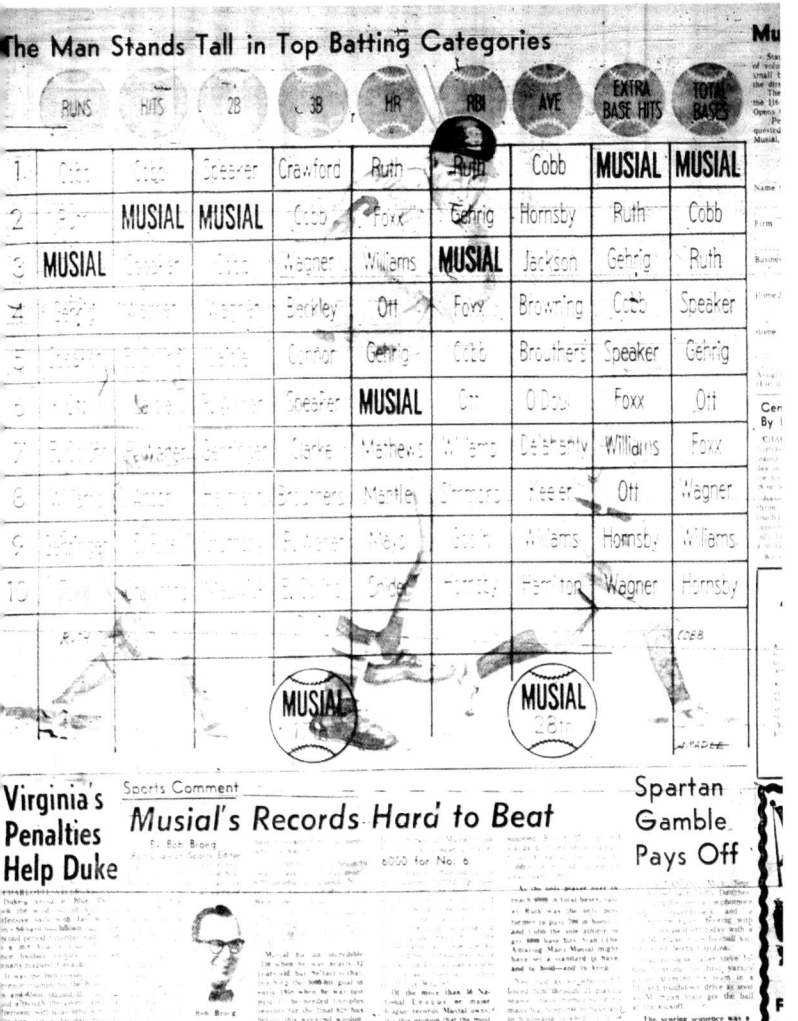

When Stan Musial retired in September 1963, this batting comparison with the game's greatest players was the *Post-Dispatch*'s way of measuring Stan's accomplishments and place in baseball history. The Cardinals then turned around, and won the World Series against Mickey Mantles Yankees in 1964.

When asked by Jay Randolph, a local TV announcer, what he thought about the new St. Louis Ballpark. Casey Stengel, then a coach in the new Met organization, said, "Well it sure holds the heat well." I never went to as many games after the move to the new Busch Stadium. But in 1964, several years before the move, we were allowed one last time to "strut our stuff" in the old ball yard with a World Series victory over the hated New York Yankees. Mickey Mantle and crew came into town—only to lose in seven games to a feisty bunch of Cardinal players who literally came out of nowhere to take the National League Pennant on the last day with a victory over the Mets. Oh, and by the way, that guy named Musial retired the year before in 1963 with some very impressive numbers during his twenty-two-year career. In years to come, a statue in front of Busch Stadium would salute Musial's wonderful accomplishments. They called him "Stan the Man"—baseball's "Perfect Knight."

111

Sixth Inning

Just like Vi-Jon, the Cardinals' longevity and reliance on excellence came through in 1967 and 1968 when they again went to the World Series both years and came away with one very big World Championship over the Boston Red Sox and Carl Yastremski in 1967. Dad would have appreciated the efforts of some of those players during this time period who displayed their talents while wearing the "birds on the bat" uniform. There was this fireballer, Bob Gibson, the fleet-footed Lou Brock, and the colorful "Cha Cha" Orlando Cepeda. We got Brock in a sweet deal from the Cubs in 1963. You have heard the "curse of the Bambino"—well I believe there is now a curse involved with the Brock trade. Chicago also had some curse involved with a goat or something back in the 1940s. Just as Boston will probably not ever win a pennant—and definitely not a World Series—so, too, will be the fate for the Cubbies on Waveland Avenue.

Lou Brock in his familiar slide going into second base. Lou stole 118 bases in 1974 to break Maury Wills' record of 104 steals a decade earlier.

We all enjoyed watching Lou Brock drive the opposing pitchers crazy when he got on base. He fidgeted and bobbed at first base, and then would steal second every time—it was a thing of beauty. Along with that, anyone who could stand up at the plate against a Gibson high and tight inside pitch had to have nerves of steel. I really enjoyed baseball during the sixties. Good thing because the Cards sort of fell off the face of the earth in the 1970s.

The Very Public Appearance of Private Label

If you looked well into the future, by the mid-1960s most of the national chain stores had shifted to private label merchandise. This was not like the random label additions Dad saw in his day. This was a real movement. The chains were reacting to what the customer wanted, as I saw it. People who bought Kroger brand mouthwash and liked it came back to Kroger. They weren't even put off by the bland nature of the most basic of label designs, all the way down to the very drab, generic white and yellow placard appearances. On the other hand, if it was Vi-Jon mouthwash, the feeling was that they could get it from anywhere. So the thought process was that Kroger wanted to keep the business at home. The dime stores may have started the trend, but the grocery chains followed maybe three or four years later. They were not into the depth of assortment that the dime stores had, because the dime stores had bigger displays. But with anything that sold well—mouthwash, nail polish remover, hand lotion, shampoo—they would get two or three cases of the product into each store. They would set up floor displays that would merchandise and capture the consumer as they walked by strategic end aisle locations. We began selling to a lot of supermarkets, which hadn't carried Vi-Jon, and our volume doubled in the next five to six years. We had to add more printing machines and factory lines at the Etzel Avenue plant, although we still worked eight to five. The growth seemed to fit; it was just something new and different we had to do in order to grow. Our next goal was to move to keeping the production lines busy on two shifts. Up to this point in time it was kind of an unheard-of proposition.

Even back then there was some degree of international flavor to this new product concept. It was apparent that Europe and Canada led the way in the expansion of the private label industry, but U.S. manufacturers weren't far behind. This trend would continue to grow into the next decade. By the mid-1970s, instead of producing one batch of Vi-Jon product, the company was producing fifty batches of product labeled for Woolworth's, S. S. Kresge, Kroger, A & P and all the other chains.

While our move into the private label market might have been inevitable, credit has to be given to two strategic departments. They were the sales department with their aggressive, creative approaches, and the ability of our R & D folks to replicate name-brand merchandise. I had always bragged that we had a very good chemist—"Dr. Bick"—and when a buyer said "I want a copy of 'Lectric Shave'—or whatever product they wanted—he would mix the oils and the alcohol and water. The standard approach was that if it smelled like the proposed target and lasted a long time, he would go with it.

The Incredible Dr. Bickley—An American Original

I had kept the original stack of formula cards maintained by Dr. Ethan Bickley, Vi-Jon's longtime chemist. Even though these handwritten cards with the various formulations of products looked archaic compared to your modern computer spreadsheets, I believe I am correct in saying that they were still being used when my son John G. joined the company in the late 1970s. Important information is never too out-of-date to hold onto.

Sixth Inning

One of the "Bicks" original "formula cards" that John W. Brunner held so dearly.

The original "Dr. Ethan Allen Bickley" in his lab at the Etzel Avenue plant during 1986.

I would like to say a few things and share a good story about my good friend, Dr. Bickley. Everyone who knew "Bick" knew about his treasure—his "baby"—that old 1949 Plymouth he drove to work every day. It had become, for better or for worse, his trademark. John G.'s famous expression "rust buckets into gold" only halfway described Bickley's vehicle. True, it was a rust bucket, but it was as far away from being a precious metal as one could get. Along with other Vi-Jon associates, I remember more than once driving down Skinker Avenue on what was normally a pretty smooth shot, only to run into a traffic jam farther down towards Washington University. I would filter through the traffic and routinely would see Bick randomly weaving his way back and forth across the width of Skinker. To someone not familiar with Bick you would have thought he was DWI (driving while intoxicated), but in Bick's case it was more of a case of DWT (driving while thinking). I questioned him about his driving technique and jovially suggested going back to using a horse and carriage. That way at least the horse was capable of helping him stay in his proper lane. He responded that his trip home was his favorite time to think about in-depth challenges that were taking place in the lab. I felt compelled to intercede for him to think less and drive with more awareness of the other traffic. I also suggested that he move a lot closer to work.

Now back to Bickley's formulas mentioned earlier. Labeling of ingredients was becoming a tightly viewed area of focus. Back then we commonly used the phrase "and other ingredients" printed on labels in order to protect a company's trade secrets. John G. described a conversation he had with a representative with the Food and Drug Administration who suggested that Vi-Jon would be the last company to use that statement intimating that there is nothing new in the health and beauty field. Maybe I was too practical, but I think that if you go back to these formulas you would see that they were much like women's fashions. They had become somewhat cyclical in their demand. These concepts would appear and reappear with ever-changing labels and snappy names and the latest new celebrity who would hawk their virtues. Looking back, those were very resilient formulas.

Private Label: A Penny for Your Thoughts or Per Unit Cost

As you might expect, private label manufacturing was still in its infancy and some companies were doing it better than others. I think you could sum up this circumstance by saying that our competitors saw what we were doing and began making cheap lines of their own, which actually weren't very good. My Dad used to say that a dishonest man can never earn enough money in his future to pay for his past. Only this was a future cost that we would all share in. People would buy their substandard version, not like it, and then not buy our product because they thought ours would also be junk, and we lost some business as a result. We were out of the aftershave business for about four years because of that. Apparently, price wasn't everything. Quality became one of my passions as time went on. Who said you couldn't teach old dogs new tricks?!

Through the years, monitoring the current trends in the private label industry has been critical. As time passed it appeared that trends were shifting toward upscale products. It's a great idea with way more profit—if only you could attract the consumer to buy the product. However, traditionally, private label has been an industry that has required constant monitoring of production costs in order to remain competitive. Our business has been commonly known as a "penny-profit business"—every bottle that goes down the line is more or less a penny profit. Dad, I woke up nights in a cold sweat after dreaming that I saw pennies rolling down our conveyors at Etzel Avenue instead of the usual bottles and jars. Nixon wasn't the only one sweating in the 1960s! This small level of profit margin required a cost-conscious mindset, one that has been part of Vi-Jon's corporate philosophy since its inception. We have always rewarded our associates for any cost savings that they have brought into our day-to-day business.

Recycle and Succeed

I tried to instill in my co-workers a cost-conscious mentality targeted at touching virtually every aspect of life at the Etzel Avenue plant during the postwar years and beyond. Our accountants used to joke with me that we were so tight that most of the time we squeaked when we wrote accounts payable checks. I used to joke with the folks that when the meat industry was packing pork they used everything but the squeal. I told everyone that we needed to find a use for "the squeal" as well. I must say that even though we were tight on money I look back on those days quite fondly.

Charlie H. Krebs with his Vi-Jon friends celebrating at the Etzel Avenue Plant in 1958.

My friend and fellow Vi-Jon associate who ran our printing department, Charlie Krebs, used to have some of the best stories about these frugal days. He told the story about a large schoolhouse-style clock that had been hanging from a pillar in the print shop long before he started working there in 1947. When Charlie suggested to his father, who still ran the print shop then, that it might be time to replace the clock with an electric one that wouldn't require winding, his dad quickly dismissed the idea. He'd bought that clock at Famous-Barr Department Store for $2.50, Charlie said. And he told me, "It's a perfectly good clock and there's no need to spend money on a new one." The subject was never brought up again—and the clock kept on ticking. Charlie said, "When the printing facility moved to Fenton, Missouri, in 1991, the clock came with us, still ticking. When I retired I brought my dad's clock home with me. I wind it every other day and it's still ticking and keeps perfect time." Charlie's dad was right—it's a perfectly good clock. And, most importantly—you can only create value products with a thrifty attitude.

A great example of recycling some years back, decades before the actual term was introduced, were the dozens of wooden squares used as paperweights in the print shop to prevent stacks of papers and labels from flying away in the breeze created by the fans prior to air conditioning. What was the original purpose of those wooden squares? At one time, Vi-Jon launched a product called "Napol" which was an individual application of nail polish in a capsule. The idea was to prevent the waste that occurred when the nail polish dried up once the bottle was opened. Each capsule was filled by hand, a task that required an enormous amount of manual dexterity, patience, and skill. To make the task easier and more efficient, rows of holes were drilled into these wooden squares in order to hold one end of the capsule. Then the line worker simply had to fill the capsule with nail polish and top it off with the other half of the capsule. The product wasn't a success, but the wooden squares provided the print shop with excellent paperweights for many years.

Slow and Steady

Well, we weren't setting any land speed records about this time, but Vi-Jon sales grew at a reliable and steady pace, from $1.3 million in 1946 to $5.5 million in 1979, when Vi-Jon employed nearly one hundred people.

Change was in the wind once again as the market for personal care products became increasingly competitive. Business practices grew exponentially in their level of sophistication. The decades following World War II were a time that most of us who remember them look back on with nostalgia. For a time it seemed as though everything was simpler. Advances in technology were about to arrive at a heart pounding pace and the world was about to be divided into two distinct categories—those who learned to embrace the technology and those who would be forever left behind. And frankly, if you didn't have a passion for "change," the world would pass you by in a cloud of dust.

II. John White Brunner's Story

7. Seventh Inning: No Time for Stretching —Gas Lines and Watergate

The 1960s left everyone reeling. It seemed as though all of our traditional values were being challenged and questioned regardless of the end result. I was to learn, especially during the 1970s that one of the tougher things to do in life is to know how something should be done and watch someone else do it wrong. But my father taught me to have an open mind and to consider all views no matter what the source might have been. However, he also taught me that you should not "throw the baby out with the bath water." What I saw happening in the 1960s was a predominant desire for change, but I don't think we clearly understood the consequences of that change. We tend to forget that "change" doesn't always mean "better." I was blessed in having a family with sound values and grounded by strong character that allowed us to think on our feet. This helped to keep us from falling into easy choices and then going in the direction of least resistance. I have always said that if you can pass only one legacy on to your offspring, make it strong character.

It seems as if we literally collapsed into the 1970s. It just appeared that the country was winded and beaten down by the war in Vietnam, the peace movement, and the country's inner strife, along with an endless list of other international challenges. I would say that some of the things that caught everyone's

Charlie H. Krebs, Howard Short, and John W. "Jack" Brunner going over strategy in 1958.

Seventh Inning

The almost anticlimactic announcement in the January 28, 1973 Sunday *Post-Dispatch* of the Vietnam cease-fire melts into history's deep crevices. The returning servicemen came back to a nation unwilling to honor their patriotic commitment to do their duty in this conflict.

attention, and were routinely discussed on the production floor every day, were right off the evening news highlights. Many of the more high profile news events we discussed are still remembered to this day: the Polish antigovernment demonstrations, Bloody Sunday in Northern Ireland, the second Arab-Israeli war, the disastrous end of the Vietnam "conflict," the exit of the Shah from Iran, and dictators calling themselves liberators. Some of the benchmark items that particularly stressed my soul included the Watergate scandal, the resignation of President Nixon, the legalization of abortion, and the world's first test tube baby. I mention these things because they were part of what shaped our conversations and frame of mind during this period. My Vi-Jon family represented a communion of spirits directly affected by outside influences both large and small. When I talked to the folks on the floor I could detect their need for some sense of structure and direction on these current events and issues. I could filter out onto that production floor or drift through the office on most any day and feel the full range of emotions that were part of their daily lives. I usually liked to keep it light and get a smile by saying to our employees that the future will always be better tomorrow. Most times I would achieve a giggle or a nervous smile. Their fears, hopes, uncertainties, and goals were all wrapped in good, trusting personalities that I would describe as sincere to a fault and honest as the day is long.

We also went through several severe recession periods. There were shortages of gasoline, plastic, sugar, and patriotism at various times during this period. My most important job these days was walking around on the production floor trying to cheer people up. People watched every penny these days. I liked to joke with the folks on Thursdays that the labels always went on straighter on payday. I even had some of these fine people exclaim to me and insist that their labels were applied straight every day. I loved our people and the important role they played in my life.

A Cardinals Recession

Well, I told you earlier that our team kind of went into the 1970s with that great Cardinals pride, but they would end up with something less than great results. One major reason was the fact that the ownership, corporate giant Anheuser-Busch (AB), gave less than stellar support. Can you imagine that AB with their brand of quality control would allow some of those fairly mediocre teams to even take the field? We used to joke back and forth that if we expanded quickly enough we could buy the Cardinals and then we could make the changes that we thought should be done. How about my son, John G. pitching, me at first base, and my dad at second? I bet the three of us together could "break a few windows"!

Early in the decade Bob Gibson, Lou Brock, and Joe Torre held their end up. But as the decade went on, they got older and there were no replacements who could match their previous thunder. But let's face it—when you are resting your chances on players with nonhousehold names like Scipio Spinks and Lance Clemons, you lower your expectations considerably. For those non-Cardinals aficionados, not in the know, in another celebrated momentous trade we sent Jerry Reuss to Houston for that name-dropping duo, Scipio Spinks and Lance Clemons.

St. Louis Cardinals third baseman/catcher Joe Torre in the early 1970s.

Seventh Inning

On top of all that, the Cardinals made their all time worst trade by sending Steve Carlton to Philadelphia for Rick Wise. The story goes that Gussie Busch was annoyed that Steve Carlton was asking in excess of $100,000 to sign in February of 1972 and in a royal fit demanded that Carlton be sent on his way. Well, I had met Mr. Busch several times before and have great respect for him and his company. However, you can't make flip decisions based on a personal whim or on the degree and tenure of your anger towards a particular person. Four Cy Young awards will attest to the questionable motivation of his decision regarding Mr. Carlton, who now has a bust in the Baseball Hall of Fame with a Phillies hat on instead of a Cardinals hat. Thank goodness we didn't trade Carlton to the Cubbies!

St. Louis Cardinals pitcher Steve Carlton, who was traded for Rick Wise in an ill-fated baseball deal in 1972.

From "Red" to "the White Rat"

The manager's office for the Cardinals was more or less a revolving door from 1976 to 1980. We went from the ageless redhead, Red Schoendienst, to Vern Rapp (now that's a trivia question begging to be asked!), Ken Boyer, and finally Dorrel Norman Elvert "Whitey" Herzog. The Cardinals finished in second place three out of the first five years of the decade, but they crashed and burned each year thereafter until Whitey (also nicknamed "the White Rat") came on the scene in 1980. They say life is an adventure in humility. It's safe to say that the Cardinals acquired some humility during the 1970s.

I had not mentioned our NFL franchise football Cardinals, because they weren't much to talk about since they had arrived in 1959 from Chicago. However, from 1972 to 1974 they played a pretty exciting brand of football with the likes of Jim Hart, Dan Dierdorff, Conrad Dobler, Roger Wehrli, and Larry Wilson. They even won a big Monday Night Football contest from the Cowboys, in Dallas, that got some national attention. I believe that was the only Monday night broadcast I ever stayed awake for an entire game—from kickoff to the final whistle. That game kind of caught Don Meredith and Howard Cossell by surprise on that telecast. It's safe to say—to Don we were number one that night.

Hitting Our Stride and Seeking Normalcy

I think I have made the point that the 1970s came in and sort of left everyone a little flat. It was pretty clear in the latter part of the 1960s that the massive economic expansion was going to slow down. A period of stagnant growth was due, and this type of economic correction activity would happen, regardless of how we approached it. Even with a Republican president—Richard Nixon—there were some (what I considered) very experimental economic wage and price controls being put into place. This had more impact on my employees than it had on the richest 1.5 percent of the population. On top of that, Nixon slammed the gold door shut at the Federal Reserve. This in effect took the United States completely off the gold standard. Like cutting the string off a helium balloon—someday our dollar will soar to worthlessness—inflation!

I was really disappointed with Mr. Nixon, as were many dedicated Americans. I am a loyal supporter of the "Grand Old Party" but he didn't appeal to me like other good Republicans and even most Democrats before and certainly after his tenure of service. A painful period that I am ashamed to even mention involved that Watergate episode. This was a time when my faith in both my traditional political and religious beliefs was clearly stressed. Most men can stand adversity, but the true test of moral turpitude is to give him status and power. In my estimation Mr. Nixon failed this test.

In spite of the political downsides, our business continued to maintain sales, with slow but steady growth. However, the country was very much the victim of an inflationary spiral that threatened to have serious impact on the country as a whole. I constantly counseled our Vi-Jon employees to save for the rainy day that was certain to come. But then, saving doesn't make much sense if the dollar is worthless.

Gerald Ford came into a real mess when he assumed the presidency from Nixon. He coined the economic acronym "Whip Inflation Now" (WIN). Good idea—if only slogans had worked. Productivity in the early part of the 1970s had dropped by 1.5 percent across-the-board in the country. A little farther into the decade, the country would vacillate between losses and gains on productivity. I had a great deal more respect for Mr. Ford than I had for Mr. Nixon. Most people are uncertain about his pardon of Nixon. I think that, as president and the leader of the free world, it was time to promote stability, reestablish order, and get the country healed. Ford literally "took a bullet" for the country because it destroyed any chance he had of being reelected as president.

Our next president was Jimmy Carter, and his policies, along with the mess he basically inherited (in all fairness), helped to maintain the turbulent times in the economy. Inflation continued to be our biggest problem during the 1970s. We saw that especially in the raw material purchases we made during this period of time. Particularly volatile were sweeteners and plastic.

Everybody Gets into the Sales Act

I must share my recollections of when my daughter, Robin, first got involved in the business. I must say that sales (as you know) is my first love. Sharing that experience with my kids was a major highlight for me. John and Robin were first set up to sell Flag and Sail men's cologne and Robin White ladies' cologne (named after Robin). After my younger daughter, Carley, was born—we had to have a "Carley" line of fragrance and powder. I know for a fact that displays with enough bravado and impact, and maybe a fragrance fountain or two thrown in, would shoot the stuff off the shelves. I am quite sure of that. It is my idea to develop and deliver creative and effective sales setups for the buying public to latch onto. I had John and Robin set up at the end of a Kmart and Woolworth store counter, close to another high impact display area that was frying peanuts and making popcorn. My two young sales associates apparently did not readily identify or appreciate this tremendous break in logistics. Not only that, you had the added incentive of having attractive fragrances softly mixed with the aroma of the fried peanuts and popcorn drift softly to your territory. (I wonder if that combination has ever been considered as a new product?)

As I recall, John had great success. His sales accomplishments ranged from selling three bottles, all the way up to being sold out. He really put me under the gun, but he was in luck—I managed to restock him in the nick of time late in the afternoon! I have to be honest, I'm not sure John fully appreciated the joy one can have as a sales associate who knows he has an almost unlimited supply of product to depend on. There were endless hours of enjoyment for him, literally working his sales corner from dawn to dusk! But I can still see the disappointed look John had when he first saw me bringing in extra supplies at that discount store. Why go home early if there was still more time to sell?

The Story Passes onto the Next Generation

Another major event in our family's life had to do with John joining the Marine Corps. I must admit that I was not all that enthusiastic about his initial efforts to join, but it didn't take long for him to win my approval and admiration. He might tell us a little about why he chose the Marines pathway instead of loading his Chevy with product and following in my sales footsteps.

I've been going pretty strong here, but maybe it's time to let my son take over this narrative. Dad and I have provided almost seven complete decades of Vi-Jon history. And now, I'll silently step to the background as I let John begin telling the rest of our story. Remember, yesterdays should not dominate today or tomorrow.

Semper Fi—New Marine John G. Brunner proudly displays his Marine dress uniform.

III. John Gammon Brunner's Story

8. Eighth Inning: High and Tight Inside —An Actor Takes Center Stage

I look back at the 1970s with fondness because of my experiences with the Marine Corps, my wife and my kids, my association with the Vi-Jon family, and my new career that was just starting to grow. Most of all, I was so fortunate to have the opportunity to work with my father.

My dad was the ultimate salesperson. He loved people, loved selling. So he thought it'd be a great idea to get me started at a young age. When I was about seven or eight years old, he brought home a bunch of Vi-Jon products, got out my little red wagon, and suggested I go door to door selling Vi-Jon products. It was a highly discouraging enterprise. Nobody wanted anything except the lady who lived next door whose son and I were best friends growing up. She bought a bottle of nail polish, but nobody else in the neighborhood bought anything.

Even at age seven, young John G. Brunner was waving the American flag and displaying his patriotic fervor.

Eighth Inning

I got some feeling even then that I wasn't really cut out to be a salesman. I guess I've always felt that selling really wasn't my calling, that I would never be the salesperson my dad was, or that I could never would understand the thrill he got from that.

I grew up with all the ups and downs of the business. I absorbed a lot about my father and grandfather's business from growing up around the dinner table. There's just never time off in a family business; no luxury of a time clock to say you're done for the day. So my dad would bring home the issues, and they inevitably came up at every dinner.

I don't recall ever having highly successful years; I recall a lot of lean years. But the company kept a lot of people in business. When I was about ten years old, I remember my dad announcing that we had lost all of the mouthwash business to Woolworth, which, during mid-1950s, was the biggest retailer in the country. And I didn't know whether the world was coming to an end. But I knew my dad had a certain resolve that we'd get through this tremendous loss of business, whatever that meant to a seven-year-old.

I went on some sales calls with my dad and remember one of the main grocery chain buyers would joke with him, "Jack, what is this? You take an order from me, you go back, put on your jeans, work on the production line, load the truck, count the inventory, and then come back and put a coat and tie on and get another order?" My dad laughed, but that was literally the truth. You just did what you had to do as a small family business.

And so I did my share too. I started working in the warehouse during a couple of summers. It was 110 degrees, and I would be loading these forty-foot long trucks by hand, one box at a time. In those days, everything came in glass bottles. There were these thirty-two-ounce glass mouthwash cases that must have weighed thirty-nine pounds a box. I'd walk into this long truck and drop one box down on the floor and go back for another. And the whole idea was to fill up this forty-foot truck. It was not easy or interesting work, but I helped out by doing what I could.

One of the Few, One of the Proud

I never felt I had the drive or thought that I'd someday be the president of the company. I always thought that at some point in time, my dad really wanted me to come back and help him full time, probably after I graduated from college. But I never really had that as a passion, dream, hope, or anything else.

In college, I decided to join the Marine Corps. Vietnam was going on, and my dad was a veteran of the Navy in World War II. It was a very contentious period, and people felt I was a bit crazy, actually volunteering. But there was always a core sense of patriotism in my family. So I wanted to do my service too, and I thought if I was going to join something, I'd join what I considered to be the best at the time, which was the Marine Corps.

I completed everything to be a young lieutenant and infantry officer, and I was in the next group heading to Vietnam. But they were just hauling people off the embassy in Saigon, so instead of Vietnam, they sent me to the Caribbean. I think my parents were very much relieved. I never really thought one way or the other. I guess I just felt they put you wherever they wanted to put you.

I fell in love with the Marine Corps in terms of the order, the structure, the talented people, the leadership training, and the people I was learning with. So much so that I extended my service for another year as an officer, and I was on my way to get a regular commission. Meanwhile, my dad was holding the business together until I was going to come home. At the time, I felt a little bit like Jimmy Stewart in *It's a Wonderful Life*, wanting to go off and be an architect, and his dad has old savings and loan waiting for him to come home and maintain. In the end, I felt that, just as it was my obligation to give some service to the country in the military, so it was my obligation to the family to come back into the family business. So I packed up my things from Camp LeJeune, North Carolina, where I did my training. I had been married for about two years, and we headed back to St. Louis to see what needed to be done.

Young marine John G. Brunner in the Atlantic, returning from six-month deployment in the Mediterranean.

Eighth Inning

John G. and Jan Brunner dash off in their getaway limousine on their wedding day.

A very familiar Brunner wedding pose as John W. and Ginny Brunner also made a quick dash away in their limousine back in October 28, 1944.

The Marines Report for Duty at 6300 Etzel Avenue

When I came home from the Marines to join my father at Vi-Jon in 1978, I returned to a company that, I'm afraid, looked like a time capsule from the 1930s. Vi-Jon was quite a change from the structure, uniforms, and organization of the military. I walked into a business that seemed to be, at that point, just barely held together.

My dad was in the Navy when his father unexpectedly passed away, and he suddenly found himself, at the age of twenty-three, having to lead the family business. He didn't know exactly how he could make a contribution to a very good running company, so he went into sales, figuring that he could bring in orders. And he just fell in love with sales and really stayed in that area the whole entire time. He left the day-to-day management of the business to the talented people already in place. But what happened over the years is that many of these people retired. And in many ways, my dad felt that he could continue to make the best contribution in terms of continuing to sell. At that point, he didn't really have the management team or the same talent available to him as when he first came in.

When I returned from the Marines, my father wanted me to go right into sales. After all, as he would say, "Nothing happens until somebody sells something." But when I inspected our plant on Etzel Avenue, I knew we had a lot of work to do. I would sometimes joke that the point of difference here was really my dad being a Navy supply officer and me being an infantry officer—a little jab in the side at the U.S. Navy there.

But I thought I could make just as strong a contribution inside the business as outside the business. It seemed to me that the overwhelming need was to get things organized. And I was fortunate to have a lot of tremendous training and experience as a young person in the Marine Corps, being in charge of 130 people, equipment, and resources, as well as being deployed on a number of operations and overseas assignments over a four-year period of time. It was a tremendous training and learning experience in how to work with people, get them motivated, and be part of a team.

So I basically tried to apply the same kind of leadership training to a small business. I started with the purchasing and inventory procedure. We had an archaic system that consisted of pegs on strings on a big pegboard. Each hole represented 144 units, so you shifted the pegs left and right based on what was shipped. But since each hole was 144 units, if there was some factor other than 144, it was always an estimate. So, using this pegboard system, it took only about two weeks before you didn't really know what you had anymore. But they had used this system for thirty or forty years. I thought keeping records of actual inventory was a lot better, so I got out paper and a pencil and started keeping track by hand. From there, computers started coming in, and then we began using spreadsheets.

Our phone system was also pretty old-fashioned. We were still using the old switchboard type of system, where you had plugs going in and out. And this was the late 1970s, early 1980s. When Southwestern Bell came in to update our system, they actually wanted to keep our model as a memento, calling it the oldest operating phone system west of the Mississippi.

At that time, we were also calling all our production lines by a confusing series of names. For example, we ran mouthwash on the "new cologne line," aftershave on the "alcohol line," and shampoo on the "aftershave line." I discovered that they had named lines based on the first products that ever ran through, and over the years, the products changed, but everyone stuck with the old names for the lines. It was confusing, so I decided just to call these lines by colors—the red line, the blue line, the purple line, the green line. And now, thirty years later, all our production lines are still called by different colors. It's been a lot simpler than naming a line after a product that at some time ran through that production line.

A Little Elbow Grease

At the same time, the Food and Drug Administration (FDA) was knocking on our door with an official Regulatory Notice saying we were out of compliance in a lot of areas.

I guess the business was getting a bit old and creaky over the years, and there just wasn't anyone there to really give it the right vitality. The plant was leaking like a sieve, with dozens of buckets hanging from the ceiling to catch the leaks. It seemed like someone had been up there punching holes from the top down. We eventually found out that when weapons were fired, the lead went up in the air, dropped back down, and punched holes in our building. Our leaks were coming from stray bullets!

There were a lot of broken windows as well. When I got an estimate from the window guy, he said we had over eleven hundred windows that needed replacement. I asked the guy if he would only replace the windows that had holes instead of just cracks and, in that way, was able to save a little by only replacing 188 windows.

And the varmints! We had rats on the factory floor that would come out at night after everyone had left. Fortunately, in the office, only the smaller mice would run around. The plant "manager" said we could solve the problem by emptying the trashcans more frequently. I ordered a forty-foot construction dumpster to get rid of all of the trash. I told the guy that it would only be one load, but six loads later I was still dumping old pallets, boxes, and an assortment of ancient history into that big cavernous container. I still remember discovering a forklift truck under a big mound of old corrugated boxes!

Once we had painted the inside of the building, we started painting the outside, I remember a police officer came by and wanted to know what we were doing. I said, "We're painting the building." He said, "Oh, well, we thought that was an abandoned warehouse." I said, "Oh no, we got people here working!"

That's the kind of state it was in. So we fixed the windows, got rid of the rats and mice, cleaned up the plant, painted it, instituted good manufacturing practices, and got ourselves in compliance with the FDA. Again, my dad was always wanting me to go out and sell, but I didn't know how much selling we could do in the future unless we got a good plant to support future sales.

As soon as I did something about the warehouse, I wanted to hire a warehouse person. I wanted to learn something about the Mixing Department in order to find a good chemist to come in and run that. I needed to find someone who understood FDA regulations.

But when we got to the Mixing Department, there were no mixers! The older guy who ran that department told me that all we needed to do is stick an air line into the batch of mouthwash and "let 'er blast" with a lot of unfiltered air from an old compressor, and when it looked "O.K." just "shut 'er off" and turn on the valve to the filling line. It didn't take me too long to order a real electric mixer with a great big propeller blade.

Since it was a small business, I had the opportunity—or maybe there was just a need for me to jump into each of these areas. And so, by rotating around to different elements of the business to try to prop each area up, I came to a really good working knowledge of what I felt was needed in terms of the job.

It wasn't a pretty sight, but I ended up encountering other people who felt like they could roll up their sleeves as well. All in all, it was a job that needed to be done, and I think anybody would have come into the situation here and clean things up, get it organized, take care of people, and start interviewing people who can bring in some expertise and knowledge to the business.

So it was a good process, and before long, we started to see that orders that my dad was bringing in could actually be shipped on time. And the quality would be more consistent, and taps were tightened and didn't leak, and the labels stayed on the bottles, and people started buying more products. So we started to finally build a little bit of momentum after a few years.

Benefits

A few years after I was back from the military, my wife Jan and I were expecting our first child. It was then we realized there was no maternity coverage at Vi-Jon—because the average age was seventy-one. So we had to get the maternity coverage started there, and Jan and I were the first beneficiaries of that.

I also recall, for one of the retirement parties of someone who had been with the company for twenty-eight years, I thought, we should do something more than just cake and cards. We needed to search our benefits and retirement program and build up the health insurance and disability.

So every year, I tried to add an extra benefit, an extra way of supporting our associates. We weren't able to do something every year, but gradually we made forward progress. And now we have a pretty outstanding 401k, retirement, disability, health coverage, and a number of other wonderful benefits for our associates.

The Lunchroom

We had no cafeteria at the time, but the boiler room is still where it was back in the old days. There were also no hot plates at that time, and microwaves weren't around yet, so employees would take their lunches and put them on top of that boiler. By lunchtime, lunches were warm, and they would eat on the steps that led up to the second floor. Some people would even sit out in front on the curb along Etzel Avenue to eat. At some point during the first year we constructed a lunchroom so people could enjoy lunch under far less challenging conditions. We created a little area, got some vending machines and some tables, and called that our lunch room. And now we have microwaves standing in for the old boiler. But I guess we could say that that same old boiler is our backup plan today in case we ever have a "hot lunch" issue!

Eighth Inning

When I came in, my job was to roll up my sleeves and do whatever needed to be done. And so whether it was to turn the front stairs into a lunchroom or put in a security system or trying to provide some benefits or trying to find good people, I just did what I needed to do.

Needless to say, not all the fixes were permanent. Some of the ideas didn't turn out very well, but, slowly but surely we started to build a team of people that were somewhat energized and passionate.

Firstborn for John G. and Jan Brunner, John B. "J. B." Brunner posing with dad in front of the Sphinx in Egypt.

Interestingly enough, some sixty-plus years earlier, John W "Jack" Brunner had posed in an almost identical setting in front of the Sphinx in Egypt.

Chain of Command

During those first years "on board" at the company I think Dad was particularly sensitive to my challenge in being the new kid on the block. I am sure he realized how difficult it was when he came on board back in 1946. As it turned out, he convinced most of the ready-to-retire management team to stay until I returned from the Marine Corps. The day I started here, I was looking around for talented people to teach me the ropes—and they were all retiring! In addition, everyone reported to my father. So one of the first things I wanted to do was to establish some enhanced system of structure and order.

So it was great when my father went on the sales calls, because that gave me more elbowroom to get the plant in ship shape. After a while, I felt that I could join him on the road. Those sales calls were some of the greatest experiences of my life. I learned a simple lesson that there is nothing like being across the desk from a buyer with a full sample case to close a sale. There was just something special about him and the customer. He had a love and passion about the sale that I never quite could catch. In just five years, the company sales doubled. I really have to give the credit for any success to our associates who were beginning to form into teams. It seems the key to solid growth and opportunity has been and will always be teamwork.

I actually started my career at Vi-Jon Laboratories as purchasing manager. Over the course of the next decade I worked in all areas of the company as a forklift driver, mechanic, truck loader, manufacturing supervisor, operations manager, sales director, vice-president of operations, and executive vice-president. I believe I stacked product from the warehouse onto the mouthwash line for a few shifts and even cleaned a latrine or two. Back then you just pitched in and did what needed to be done.

The one thing I can clearly say was that, whatever job I took in the company, I wanted to contribute, to measure up—in other words, to help the team. I'm convinced that business success in the future starts with the simple question: What should I do for a career? People do not advance by moving to a "now" industry or by taking on a particular type of management style. They succeed by keying in on the real focal point, which is the question of who and what they really are and more importantly what drives them, what motivates them. What do they really love to do? By doing this a person releases so much creativity and positive spirit that the resulting empowerment is overwhelming. At the end of the day, in life, we are held accountable for not only what we do—but just as often what we *don't* do.

I Get By with a Little Help from My Friends

Besides my father, one person in particular was there to provide some sage advice. Howard Short had helped teach him the ropes back in 1946 and was now doing the same for me. I recall that Howard was fond of saying, "We should always remember that nothing happens until someone sells something" and I would respond, "Nothing happens until someone buys something." Mr. Short's philosophy, and a pretty good one at that, was "No matter what you do, what you think, or what your direction is with Vi-Jon, stay close to the customer." I learned from Dad how important a "yes we can" is to the customer.

Eighth Inning

GOOD DESIGN
continued from page 53

this time, I would suggest that it do so. Farmer Jack is not a symbol for the 80's.

The Price Chopper supermarket chain out of Albany, New York uses an illustration of an axe chopping a coin in two. While there is strong imagery here, the general public is more sophisticated today and tend not to respond as well to literal representations. Considering too the way food prices have been going up, one wonders if this is the most appropriate imagery.

One of the problems with many new logos is they are not thoroughly tested on all the mediums on which they will work. Consequently, what may look to be a perfectly acceptable logo may be totally inappropriate when implemented over a broad spectrum of communicative elements.

Evaluating A Logo

Several important considerations to remember when evaluating a logo:

1. Does it reduce in size well? Many times logos will fall apart when reduced because of the fragile characteristics of their letter forms.
2. Does the logo blow up well? Does it look too massive or unwieldy on a large sign?
3. Can you effectively reverse the logo? This means to drop it out of a solid color. Some logos look good in a positive manner but not in a negative.
4. Is the logo effective on signs? At some point, the logo should be tested on an actual sign site.
5. Does it blend well with the private label packaging system? Many retailers simply slap their logo on their private brand packages and it looks it.
6. Is the logo easy to read? You would be surprised how many are not.
7. Does the logo have long-distance visibility? This is particularly important on signs. The actual distance that you can read the sign should be carfully measured and compared to the previous logo and other retail signs.
8. Is the logo promotional in nature? This does not mean that it has to be, but for retailers generally, a highly visible logo with good promotional elements and strong colors is desirable.

If the designer you choose is not taking all the above points into consideration, he or she is doing you a disservice. A logo that works effectively on a broad variety of media is not easy to come by. It takes creativity, experience and usually time to accomplish it. But once you have selected one, be sure you use it in a manner that makes both the logo and the medium on which it performs look good.

This is one of the problems of having a supplier design a sign or private label package for you. They usually do not understand the system that has been created and as a consequence the end product may be visually less than desirable. If suppliers are to be involved in the design of either signs or private label packages, there should be a graphics manual available that specifically spells out what can and cannot be done with the logo.

Use of Initials

The question often arises whether or not initials should be used in a logo. This of course depends upon your cor-
continued on page 57

54   PRIVATE LABEL, JUNE-JULY 1980

One of John G. Brunner's first advertising campaigns in the late 1970s.

136

Getting On Base

Above: John W. Brunner during a lighter moment in his office during the 1980s.

Right: Al Gioia, the chief operations officer, prepares for one of his numerous meetings in the Board Room at the Page Avenue plant.

Eighth Inning

In the foreground, Eduardo Alves at the Private Label Manufacturers Association (PLMA) show in Chicago. Eduardo is Vi-Jon's senior vice president of sales and is married to John W. Brunner's daughter Carley.

My father went through a period of trying to discover how he could best be of use to the company. So did I. I appreciated the work and the need for sales but I've got to admit that I did not share my father's overwhelming passion for sales. He was a "sales machine" and I guess I was a "people machine." He tried very hard to motivate me towards the sales side of the street. I can recall traveling with him during one of our joint trips down in Mexico. It was one memorable trip I know I will never forget! In his zest to accomplish sales, he was willing to drive the entire width of Mexico City so as to make one more sales call in hopes of getting one last order. I have to admit that I considered the end result barely worth the effort. After that, nothing surprised me, like when he stopped to make a sales call at the airport gift shop on the way to catching our plane, a plane that we might well have missed. To my father, a great day was starting off with a big breakfast and heading out with a sample case full of product. I remember thinking that this was not my idea of fun, so I guess we just had a different way of looking at sales. But at the end of the day, despite my personal feelings about these various sales experiences, I believe that the core strength of our company is in the unfaltering support for our sales force. Incidentally, as years have gone by, I have adjusted my overall motivation for sales. Who knows, I might even stop at the airport gift shop to try and make a sale. And sales will *always* take the lead at Vi-Jon. My father would be so proud of his son-in-law, Eduardo Alves, who is leading the current sales effort!

With sales clearly not my power zone, I had to decide which way to proceed. I considered focusing on research and development but recalled the "C's" I received in high school chemistry. What I discovered, and what many people at Vi-Jon will attest to, was my ability to find and work with people. I am very fortunate in that I find a greater thrill through finding people who are better than I am at accomplishing things. I realized early on that every time you find a good person, they multiply themselves. Our key executive team has been with me for fifteen or twenty years, and they are absolutely outstanding people! Kirk Sanders kept everyone motivated, while Bob Hess kept track of the profits. Al Gioia has a relentless passion in Operations—save every penny! And our long-term Human Resources guy, Ed Sander, has retired, but now we have a hard-charging people person in Susan Conti. And of course some of the finest Vi-Jon "originals" continue to lead us into the next century—Tom Marren, Ed Arndt, Kevin Birkner, Jon Nowotny, Jackie Hofius, Margie Wilson, Diane Mueller, Debbie Ursery, Patty Lorenz, and so many others. And the team in Tennessee—wow! Are they outstanding people, like, David Mobley, Bill Hale, Susan Brown, Terry Hailey, Cathy Crabtree, Debbie Sizemore, Alethea Murray, Bola Ogunpola, Rabbit Victory, Ronnie Breece, and so many more, too numerous to mention everyone. It's all about people—people *are* the business!

Farewell to a Challenging Decade

Time during this decade started to pass by so quickly. The reality of life's fragile nature showed its very human side when some real icons left us during the 1970s—John Wayne, Bing Crosby, and Elvis Presley, to name a few. For the first time in my life, I started to understand the concept of growing older.

Walking through the plant and having people address me as Mr. Brunner made me feel funny and uncomfortable. "Mr. Brunner" is my dad and he does not feel comfortable with that formality either. I have always tried to communicate right away that I really just wanted everyone to address me as John. The first personally meaningful accomplishment that I hoped to achieve was to get the confidence of our associates and their support for me as a fellow Vi-Jon worker. Everything was just another promotion or job title. I would take that promotion and that honor, and treat it with great respect and hope to retain everyone's confidence as I grew with the company.

During the 1970s I considered myself a rookie. I entered the 1980s with a better idea of what to expect, but I understood that second-year players always have a different set of standards to live up to as well. You know what they say about the sophomore jinx for a second-year baseball player. I was finding out that I knew a little about a lot of things. The problem was I just didn't know a lot about anything in particular. That's an important marker in time for anybody to realize. In the 1980s I was about to find out just how much I didn't know about everything in general. I still had the exuberance of a young mustang, but not quite the horse sense of a well-seasoned ice wagon horse. The reality of that concept crept up on me just like it did on my father and grandfather. This decade would serve to harden the backbone of my business sense and give me more perspective and range to develop a practical side to my business knowledge. It would be a skill set that would serve me well in the coming turbulent 1990s.

Eighth Inning

Decade of Greed—I Don't Think So

The 1980s would present a new challenge because they were eventually known as the "Decade of Greed." However, I personally felt that this term was unfairly assessed. For instance, charitable contributions grew at a 55 percent faster annual rate than they had grown over the past twenty-five years. Besides, we moved into the 1980s with renewed optimism because we had a new leader as president, Ronald Reagan, who represented a belief that government was too big, and that we should proudly display our pro-freedom way of life here in the United States. President Reagan was elected to two consecutive terms, and the confidence he displayed was inspirational. I proudly wore the colors of a Reagan spirit of freedom. He supported the business community; and he reestablished the American entrepreneurial spirit and the overwhelming public support of the free market that had suffered so badly in the 1960s and 1970s.

Some of the other highlights of the 1980s included such noteworthy events as Prince Charles marrying Lady Diana Spencer; the first report of AIDS; Argentina invaded the Falkland Islands; the Marines landed on Granada; the Chernobyl nuclear disaster; and the Russian boycott of the Los Angeles Olympics. Add to this list Gorbachev's proposal for democratic reforms in the U.S.S.R., the Tiananmen Square Massacre, the removal of the Iron Curtain, and the election of George H. W. Bush.

Pride of St. Louis Returns in the 1980s

As noted earlier, Whitey Herzog became manager of the Cardinals in 1980. Toward the end of that season, Whitey replaced John Claiborne as general manager. It was a clean sweep, with changes that left everybody's head spinning. Whitey, nicknamed the "White Rat," was rebuilding the team into an exciting, Gas House Gang type, hit-and-run machine that was suited for the Astroturf reality of playing ball at Busch Stadium. Over the next two years he acquired Darrell Porter, Bruce Sutter, Lonnie Smith, and Ozzie Smith. "Whitey ball" was born, and the stolen base, squeeze play, and hit-and-run were now seen in every game.

St. Louis Cardinal Manager Whitey "White Rat" Herzog from New Athens, Illinois, coached the Cardinals for ten seasons from 1980 to 1990.

In honor of their past performances, Bob Gibson, Johnny Mize, Red Schoendienst, and Lou Brock were elected to the Hall of Fame in Cooperstown during the 1980s. In 1982 the team won their first World Championship since 1967 with a come-from-behind victory against the Milwaukee Brewers. Star-studded moments abounded in that World Series, with Willie McGee and Bruce Sutter leading the way. Although I didn't have a ticket to the winning game, they opened the gates in the seventh inning and my wife rushed in to see the Cardinals win. I especially enjoyed the start of the games, when Ozzie Smith would go out onto the field and do a back flip and get the crowd into the game even before the first pitch.

The rest of the 1980s had some interesting ups and downs, but there was one name that would go down in St. Louis history as having a memorable impact that will never be forgotten—Don Denkinger. The setting was Game 6 of the World Series against the Kansas City Royals. Kansas City rallied for two runs in the ninth inning, thanks to a blown call at first base by Denkinger. Kansas City won Game 6 and a totally demoralized Cardinals team lost Game 7 by a score of 11–0. Umpires in baseball are like regulatory agencies in our business. You cannot let any of their guidelines cause you to have a bad day. You need to pick yourself up, dust yourself off, and try to improve and do better the next day. In any event, I really enjoyed baseball in the 1980s. We had to, because we were losing our football team to Arizona, so it was down to either baseball or hockey for St. Louis fans.

Product Development in the 1980s

In 1984 Kmart was Vi-Jon's biggest account. Wal-Mart carried only one Vi-Jon item, a six-ounce store-brand nail polish remover. Our other customers included Safeway, Kroger, Albertsons, Osco Drugs, Walgreen, Eckerd, Rite Aid, Super Valu, Topco, and others. As for the product lines, we were the kings of mouthwash. We were by far the largest private label producers of mouthwash back in those days. Nail polish remover and petroleum jelly were our other major products.

The 1980s started a frenzied growth that would culminate with some very interesting growing pains in the 1990s. Back then we had six production lines, and we were just coming out of glass and going into plastic bottles of nail polish remover. We were also phasing out cold glue labels and going to pressure sensitive labeling, which was a lot more efficient. The company really started growing because of demand for our mouthwash. We had a production line for Rexall, but Kmart was our biggest customer, about 35 percent of our mouthwash business. We ran out of room in the production area, so we put up a mouthwash line in the warehouse, at the west end of the Etzel Avenue facility. In addition, sales of our baby oil grew with the Wal-Mart business. I tried to make sure that our bottles were up to standard. We grew nonstop, in our own way—the Vi-Jon way—sort of a mix of homegrown and current best practices system. Vi-Jon's sales topped the $22 million mark in 1987 and rose to almost $32 million by 1989.

I guess you could say that by most standards we were more than surviving in a highly competitive industry. Nevertheless, success is almost never a straight-line proposition, and as Warren Buffet, the billionaire tycoon, says, "In the business world, the rearview mirror is always clearer than the windshield." The years to come would test the strength of Vi-Jon's foundations.

Seventy-five Years Young

My father and grandfather really put a great deal of importance on our longevity and consistent mode of operation. I was a bit impatient with the speed at which things moved during the 1980s and planned on moving faster once we hit the 1990s. One thing I did admire and respect were the lengths to which my father went when a major Vi-Jon anniversary was attained. Our seventy-fifth year in existence was a benchmark event and was celebrated with great pomp and circumstance.

In his message to the friends and associates of Vi-Jon, he said that for thirty-five years he had been blessed with friendships connected with Vi-Jon Laboratories. He gave much of the credit for whatever success Vi-Jon had attained through the years to the employees, stockholders, customers, suppliers, and people in government. These folks through their advice, energy, and dedication had helped our company to prosper.

From 1980 to 1983 our corporate sales increased 120 percent. My father communicated that we were planning a 20 percent growth for each of the next five years, with emphasis on quality, service, and increased profitability. He let everyone know that equally important to Vi-Jon's success in his mind, and in some ways even more, had been the family. He especially singled out Mom (Virginia Brunner), who had advised, challenged, supported, and cared for him and our family. Dad always had Mom on his mind, just as my Grandpa John always had Grandma Vi on his mind.

"Ginny" Brunner alongside the men she advised, challenged, and supported over the years.

My father noted to everyone that, as we moved towards our one hundredth anniversary, we should all be more mindful of the precious gifts of friendship and caring that had been so generously received from so many. He challenged everyone to set the goal of Vi-Jon Laboratories to impart our substance and our opportunities, as well as the freedom that we enjoy in this country, to those who come after us and now work with us. He stated that it was his hope and intention that these gifts would be more meaningful, more productive and a little more secure than when they were lovingly and trustingly placed in his hands many years ago.

There are rare moments in one's life when they get to witness benevolence and love such as I saw exhibited during our seventy-fifth Vi-Jon anniversary celebrations. How often does a son get to see his hero demonstrate time and time again those great abilities to move people, motivate, and lead them on to bigger and better accomplishments. Dad was always my hero, and now I have been able to add Grandfather to my personal Legion of Honor. I owe both of them so much, and my heart has been blessed by the legacies bestowed on all of us from both of their lives.

Cover of the 75th Anniversary booklet at Vi-Jon.

Eighth Inning

Looking for That Next Big Opportunity

The 1980s for Vi-Jon was a decade of probing and talking and learning about the many possibilities where we might be able to secure profitable growth and better secure our position as a company to be reckoned with. There were all types of business options available, but we needed to be patient and observant and know when it was right to move. Just like a big poker game, you have to know when to hold on to your cards, and when to throw them in, so you can live to play another day.

One little experience I will share with you is a venture where we chose not to move forward. During 1986 we sold citrate of magnesium (a laxative) throughout our distribution network. There were only two companies that packaged this product. It was a somewhat specialized process, so it was not something one could initiate with just *any* packaging plant. The Smyrna, Tennessee facility was one of the production sites, and they turned our world upside down when they bought the only other U.S. manufacturer of this product. They immediately increased the price, leaving about six companies in the lurch on available options.

To show you how creative our minds had gotten at Vi-Jon, let me describe what we attempted to do with a local soda bottler at this point in time. I had Dr. Bickley get with a local plant, Beverage Concepts, in order to develop a batching, filling, and packaging process for making this citrate of magnesium. The plant manager coincidentally was Ed Lemay. This company had a tunnel pasteurizer, which would have made it an even better process than was being done at the Smryna facility. However, after much investigation it became apparent that processing at the beverage food plant would not work. Other customers at this beverage plant threw up a red flag and the opportunity went by the wayside. I sort of understood why they had a problem with our concept. We were literally looking to process this laxative type material right after runs of cola or other flavored soda products. Not the most palatable idea for the franchises with those other popular flavored soda lines that would have been affected! The franchise literally suggested that the use of the filling line would either service product destined for one end of the consumer or the other, certainly not both. Investigating Vi-Jon production of citrate of magnesium involved a number of key people, and even though it was an innovative product for our company, our team did not bat an eye when asked to pursue this opportunity.

We had also discussed high-speed inline blending and bottling of our mouthwash products, but we were just a bit ahead of our time.

Vi-Jon's Core Strength

I am quite certain that since I have been associated with Vi-Jon, the management team has always been quick to attribute the company's success to the hard work and dedication of the people who make up the Vi-Jon family—and rightfully so! Their unselfish attitudes provide a breath of fresh air in their willingness to ask, "What can I do to help?" They appreciate everything; they are loyal and responsible, and quite frankly, they represent the best that our country has to offer. Whenever I think they have set a new level from which they operate—they go out and set a new and higher standard!

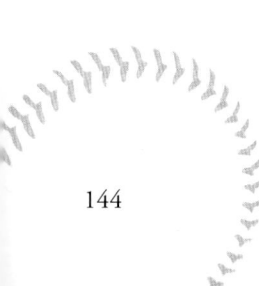

This strength has been seen over the years as our associates continue to go above and beyond for one another to make sure we thrive as a company. Most of those who have worked at Vi-Jon going back through the 1980s, recollect that associates volunteered to work during the annual Christmas parties in order to ship emergency orders "on time and complete" to the customer.

Up until recent years, the inventory process was adjusted to conform to the size and complexity of the company, physical inventory of the Vi-Jon warehouse, and the Page Avenue and Etzel Avenue plants. These inventory checks were undertaken on a designated Saturday during the year by associates who volunteered for the job. Doughnuts and pizza were all that was required to transform the process into a "party"—although it should be noted that the inventory was always completed successfully and accurately. To this day, doughnuts and pizza accompany the spring office cleaning at the Page Avenue facility, also accomplished by volunteers.

Over the years there have been occasions when warehouse moves were required, and each time everyone pitched in to take inventory and pack and ship wherever needed, to help make the move successful. I even recall trying to jump on a forklift a time or two to help. Fortunately, we always seemed to have enough capable forklift drivers around. As usual, food was part of the equation, and everyone from the janitor to the vice presidents could be found in the warehouses doing some type of function.

Speaking of food, and as a special "thank you" to associates for all of their hard work and dedication to Vi-Jon, twice a year I insist that the company hold barbecues—to include food, prizes, and fun—for every Vi-Jon associate from all shifts and all Vi-Jon locations. We need to find every opportunity to let our associates know how much we appreciate their teamwork.

C.O.O. Al Gioia serves up "all beef" brats at one of the many company barbeques.

Sitting at a decorated table, three Vi-Jon employees enjoy the barbeque feast.

Eighth Inning

Associates Prepared to Go to the Mat

I have given many examples of how Vi-Jon associates have gone the extra mile for the company. But here is one instance where one member literally was prepared to go to the mat for country and company. The year was 1989 and the occasion was the Private Label Show in the Rosemont Convention Center in Chicago. Vi-Jon was considering manufacturing products under the "Muhammad Ali" label. Associates learned of the Private Label Show and asked if they could attend to see what it was all about. We made the necessary arrangements for their attendance and I presented to the company's newest associate, Ed Sander, the privilege of escorting Muhammad Ali and his entourage around the trade show floor.

Ed Sander, retired vice president of human resources, gets his shot in at the Private Label Manufacturers Association (PLMA) guest tour in 1989. We don't have the photo of the shot a second later when Ali returns fire.

As you can imagine, his presence caused quite a stir. Ed told me that people recognized Muhammad from at least ten yards away and they shouted, "Muhammad, you are the greatest!" and asked to have their picture taken with him. When Vi-Jon's guests were ready to leave, Ed escorted them to the lobby to wait for their limo. The forty-five-minute wait for the car gave Ed time to talk to Muhammad who told Ed about his farm in Michigan and the work he was doing with disadvantaged kids. Before they left, Ed said that he, too, would like to have his picture taken but didn't want the typical picture standing next to him, smiling as though they were life-long buddies. Ed asked if I could throw a fake punch at him. Ali graciously allowed Ed to pose throwing the punch and then, for the icing on the cake, he gave the widely known Muhammad Ali facial expression.

Lest We Forget

Some of my earliest memories from the time that I joined the company were of special acknowledgements that Dad made sure were received by deserving associates in front of their co-workers. We also have made it customary that when someone receives a promotion, it is acknowledged in front of that person's co-workers. Nothing makes hard work and persistence more worthwhile than receiving that well-deserved round of applause. Congratulations from co-workers for the remainder of that day provide lasting memories to the recipient of the promotion. We even promoted the idea that when a Vi-Jon associate is moving on to another company, we celebrate their work and contributions at Vi-Jon by giving them a cake and congratulations from co-workers. Many of these ceremonies have brought tears to my eyes, and co-workers are affected as well, whenever someone leaves our company.

One of the many celebrations in which cake is the order of the day. Vi-Jon years are so special they are always marked with this nostalgic celebration "lest we forget."

Eighth Inning

This Founder's Day celebration in the Smyrna, Tennessee plant is repeated many times each year at all Vi-Jon installations to mark the accomplishments of the many fine Vi-Jon personnel.

One of the most important celebrations at Vi-Jon is Founder's Day. Every March fourth we celebrate my grandfather's birthday, and his life, and the founding of Vi-Jon. Awards and certificates are given to Vi-Jon associates for their accomplishments during the previous year. We could not imagine a more appropriate way to say "thank you" for his foresight and dedication. We would not be blessed with our current opportunities without his dedication, patience, and fortitude.

I particularly noticed during the 1980s that there was a group of folks who always exceeded expectations. We took great pride in recognizing these individuals with what we called a "Chairman's Award," which recognizes those candidates who have demonstrated the qualities of our founder for integrity, honesty, enthusiasm, and passion to succeed. The award is intended for associates who demonstrate exceptional leadership when encountering daily challenges. We also initiated "Excellence Awards" to be given to associates who exhibit above average qualities in the performance of their job.

We started to see a trend where the same associates were qualifying for the Chairman's Award each year. It was obvious that we had a core group of outstanding Vi-Jon associates who qualified every year for this award. Our managing directors discussed the issue and recommended to me that another tier be developed. Their concept was beautiful—like the Hall of Fame at Cooperstown where all those great Cardinals players had been memorialized over the years. We would put together our own Hall of Fame concept, only we would call it our "Legion of Honor." When any Vi-Jon associate receives a third Chairman's Award, he or she is eligible for Legion of Honor recognition the following year. I'm sure that my father would remember those recipients: Dan Charleville, Nesa Ebenrick, Mona Foster, and Dorothy Harris who unfortunately passed away this past year.

The managing directors insisted that my grandfather and father become the first inductees. Their thoughtfulness in recommending them both for this recognition shows that they really understand what we are all about here at Vi-Jon.

Zekija Karahodizic (center) receives the Chairman's Award from John G. Brunner and Al Gioia at the 2006 Founder's Day ceremony.

Eighth Inning

Farewell to the Soviet Way of Life

We were leaving the 1980s with a Marine's salute to Ronald Reagan for his efforts that culminated in the downfall of the Soviet Union. No one can forget the televised pictures of the Berlin Wall being taken down. The cry of freedom could now be heard in many Slavic countries in Eastern Europe that had not known this way of life for many, many years. The next decade beckoned us and we were listening. We had a newfound pride. Ronald Reagan did that. The military was strong and modern. Our economy was hitting on all cylinders and we were primed for quite a party in the 1990s. President George H. W. Bush appeared to be carrying on the programs of his predecessor, and the only question appeared to be by how much would he be reelected in 1992?

We also saw the United States reach one of the highest levels of world approval as we demonstrated how freedom and free market applications could outlast socialism. We continued to get more deeply involved with the Middle East, which was not something that most considered to be a good thing.

We finished out the 1980s with an awareness that life in St. Louis was never going to be the same. New highways, shopping malls, and transitions at some of the old-line companies of the past would happen at a much greater pace in the 1990s.

Vi-Jon was strong and getting stronger, which would set the table for some moves that I felt would help better secure our place in our very competitive nationwide economic system. Canada and Mexico were entering the market place with their lopsided exchange rates that attracted a lot of manufacturing from the United States. We kept our associates working and intended to expand to insure protection of the values and livelihoods of the many associates at Vi-Jon we called friends. At Vi-Jon we were going to do something substantial, but we needed to assemble the right team to do the work. Without the right team, even under otherwise favorable circumstances, we would be lost. I like to say that we are just a group of ordinary people, who in working together as a team produce extraordinary results.

The joy of the Berlin Wall opening is celebrated in this *Post-Dispatch* front page, dated Friday, November 10, 1989.

III. John Gammon Brunner's Story

9. Ninth Inning: Victory within Our Grasp —A Millennium Milestone

The last decade of the twentieth century would be a very active ten-year span for me, our company, and for our country. I had visions of what this decade could yield, well beyond anything that my grandfather or father might have ever considered. Expansion of the company in a very bold sense would help secure our future in a way that no other process could provide. It had to be done carefully and with great planning, but I was convinced that it could be done. I wanted to be right in the thick of things and I would be there to take any incoming flak.

Times were fast and, as a company and as citizens of the most dynamic country in the world, we had rolled into a most interesting period to be alive. The whole world watched the United States, and the whole company watched me, to get a glimpse of the future. The 1990s would provide events, such as Lech Walesa becoming the first president of Poland, the collapse of the Soviet Union, Iraq's invasion of Kuwait, Operation Desert Storm beginning the first Gulf War, the eruption of the Bosnian civil war, the massive growth of the Internet, Nelson Mandela's election as president of South Africa, and Prince Charles and Princess Diana's divorce. Add to that list Mad Cow Disease in the United

This *St. Louis Post-Dispatch* article on March 14, 1983, details John G. Brunner's drive towards success in the health and beauty aid business.

153

Ninth Inning

Kingdom, Hong Kong's return to China, Princess Diana dying in a car crash in Paris, India and Pakistan testing nuclear weapons, the introduction of the new Euro currency, and President Clinton's scandal at the White House. It certainly compares in volume to any one of the previous decades of the twentieth century, with one big difference. The massive worldwide media—CNN, FOX, and the Internet—made "breaking news" an hourly event. Unfortunately, these media giants became so good at this that they could literally create their own media events, for instance, the O. J. Simpson "circus" coverage. It also made stars out of the announcers and correspondents. Gossip and rumors became a legitimate media style and hit an all time high level of interest with the average viewer.

I spent many more sleepless nights during this decade than any previous period of time. Not because of the fast pace of world events, but about areas that would require flesh and blood responses with boots on the ground. On top of all the actions taking place on a world scale, there were even more causes for concern happening with our business. Many drives home were spent with my mind going ten different directions. I sort of know how Dr. Bickley felt as he drove home in deep meditation. Some of those trips home are now a blur in my memory as well.

I do remember, as if it were yesterday, driving home one evening in 1991. I was listening to KMOX as a live broadcast from Baghdad announced that the cruise missiles had started hitting their primary targets. It was a strange feeling being "in the bleachers" and bearing witness to such a historical event, similar to when I viewed the tragic crash of the *Hindenburg* Zeppelin on the History Channel. As it crashed to the ground the radio broadcaster exclaimed, "Oh the humanity!" and collapsed into tears. Hearing the loud reports of antiaircraft fire over the radio broadcast from Baghdad gave me pause to think of this humanity once again. I actually wrote to the Marine Corps asking if they needed help.

The Cardinals Search for a New Identity

I tried to find time for lighter events, such as keeping up with the Cardinals, but my mind could not stay fixed on this for long. I do remember that 1990 started off on a sour note with the resignation of Whitey Herzog towards the middle of the season. I always really liked the "White Rat" because he seamed like a player's manager. He was a "people person"—and I could identify with that. Whitey was the "White Rat" and I could have been the "White Barracuda," or maybe something else that could swim. Herzog was someone the average ballplayer would be proud to bust a gut for and someone I would like to play for and emulate as a leader. Joe Torre took over but really did not get much support from the Cardinals owners. He was a nice guy who visited hospitals, more often than not with little or

Joe Torre was manager of the St. Louis Cardinals in the early 1990s. After leaving the Cardinals he has gone on to win a few more games in New York and Los Angeles. Oh yes, and a few World Championships.

no fanfare. As it turns out, all Joe needed was a little extra payroll, like $200 million. He also worked well under the bright lights of Broadway as he went on to manage the New York Yankees after being released from being manager of the Cardinals. The Cards started off the decade finishing in last place for the first time since 1918. The Cardinals would go on to finish third or fourth through 1995.

In the fall of 1995, we got a breath of fresh air with the hiring of Tony La Russa as manager. Tony had experience in the American League at Chicago and Oakland and had a World Series win to his credit. I recall that his first win occurred during the "earthquake series." The Cardinals responded to La Russa by winning a division title in 1996 but were ousted by the Milwaukee Braves by losing the last three games of the divisional playoff and being outscored by a combined 32 to 1 run total. There was another noteworthy event with the Cardinals, which involved the acquisition of Mark McGwire from Oakland. In 1998 the Cardinals faithful experienced a season to remember! McGwire hit a record seventy home runs to beat Roger Maris' record and finish ahead of Sammy Sosa of the Chicago Cubs. The Cards finished no better than third place the rest of the decade, but I think everyone immortalized the long ball events of 1998. I know I'll never forget. It was *the* most commonly discussed topic on the floor and in the office and brought genuine camaraderie to everyone. It gave us something that we could all root for, and after all, isn't that what it's all about?

Above: Mark McGwire celebrates his sixty-second home run, breaking Roger Maris' record sixty-one blast back in 1998.

Right: The brain trust of Walt Jocketty and Tony LaRussa has hit pay dirt for one World Series win and some very exciting baseball over the past number of years.

Expansion at a Price

By 1990, my dad was looking to retire in the not-too-distant future. He had worked hard and deserved to reap the rewards of a job well done. However, his set-in-stone values again were at the center of my concerns. He always paid himself last, and his concern for his Vi-Jon family was not going to let his retirement get in the way. But it was my desire to see him walk away with something from a company to which he'd given so much. So in planning for retirement and succession, we both came to the conclusion that the best way would be for me to purchase the business.

From both a personal and a professional standpoint, I wanted, for my sake as well as my dad's, to purchase at full market value. I did not want a special deal. I wanted to assume the entire cost and obligation of purchasing the business and to maintain the objectivity that I felt was really critical, we got multiple appraisals from two different accounting firms and two different law firms. In fact, the head of the major accounting firm that was engaged on one side of the business here said they'd never in their entire career seen more of an arms-length transaction between father and son. And I was glad to hear that, because that's how I wanted it to be.

I effectively bought the business from my father, and by doing that, provided a way for his retirement and made sure he got full credit for all that he had done in the years he was with the business.

The St. Louis, Missouri headquarters for Vi-Jon, Inc., at 8515 Page Avenue was first occupied in 1992.

With the acquisition of the company came a fair amount of debt that would need to be offset by increased sales and production. So, to try to make this work, I began looking around for help. My desire was to bring in more talent and resources to ensure that we could do a good job of managing the debt and being able to handle all the details in terms of meeting my obligations.

I brought in a new president, a certified public accountant. I also hired a new operations manager with big company experience. With the assistance of some well-credentialed people at Vi-Jon, plans were made to purchase the Page Avenue plant, an acquisition that was finalized in 1992. Previously owned by a garment manufacturer, the plant required a sizable infusion of capital to convert it to a facility capable of meeting Vi-Jon's production of mouthwash. A real estate development company called Paric managed this overwhelming project. Within a year, a compounding section was installed, executive offices were moved from the Etzel Avenue facility to the Page Avenue facility, and six production lines were up and running. In 1993 the Page Avenue warehouse was built to accommodate Vi-Jon's increased production.

Vi-Jon had a long tradition as a company that operated "out of its cash drawer"—a tradition that had now come to an end. As I look back on this period of expansion, I have to admit that I was astounded to learn how much money could be borrowed through the power of sophisticated spreadsheets and opportunistic projections, especially with the financial engineer I brought in as president leading this charge. The word *risk* took on new meaning!

The alcohol storage silos in the east parking lot area at the Page Avenue plant were installed in 1992.

Ninth Inning

Getting On Base

Foundation forms outline the west warehouse at the Page Avenue plant during construction in 1992.

Ninth Inning

The massive superstructure of the west warehouse takes shape in 1992.

Ninth Inning

Getting On Base

Construction of the west warehouse at the Page Avenue plant in 1992.

Ninth Inning

In 1992, Vi-Jon was presented with the St. Louis Small Business Award. On hand to receive it are (back row, left to right) Marvin Sinn, board member; John White Brunner; Mark Lee; David Biernbaum; Jim Maxwell, board member; Tom Marren; and John Oeltjen; (front, left to right) Ed Sander; John G. Brunner; and Dennis Hintz.

The Hunt Dilemma

In 1993, with a good team and with the thought of doing great things to complement the production capabilities we were in the process of developing at the Page Avenue plant, we made the decision to purchase a struggling private-label manufacturer named Hunt Products of Dallas, Texas, a company that was experiencing its own brand of chaos.

Mel Turner joined me on the Vi-Jon team at about the same time. He had retired from the United States Air Force having been a wing commander at Scott Air Force Base just over the river in Illinois. I had met Mel, invited him to visit the company, and gave him an offer of employment. Mel joined Vi-Jon as a middle manager in operations. He later became vice-president of operations and led the company during our recovery.

Mel's assessment of the problem with the Hunt Products Inc. line was that of a company that was trying to be all things to all people with products that were virtually unique to them—strawberry shampoos and conditioners and cream and cocoa butter. So as soon as Vi-Jon took over the inventory and accounts, the pressure was intense from these customers to get inventory they had been out of stock on for some time.

We were doing back-flips and somersaults trying to do everything. Production schedules were complicated and burdensome as a result of the hyper-specialization of the Hunt product line. In a purchase such as this we bought the business upside as well as the downside. I must agree with Mel Turner's assessment that the inefficiencies of the Page Avenue plant were aggravated by short-notice runs and line changeovers to satisfy individual customers demanding their Hunt products. One of my old MBA professors would say that it was intuitively obvious, even to the most casual of observers, that this current state of business affairs was yielding diminishing returns. To say that this was an expensive learning process was a gross understatement.

On top of that and compounding all of the other problems, the plant was running on a central software system that was no longer capable of running a company the size Vi-Jon had become. Our attempt to install a more sophisticated resource management system failed under the weight of more pressing problems, leaving the company in a software-challenged state. I swore that when we ever did future ERP systems we would have plenty of the right personnel, include more than ample budgets, and adapt to timelines that were practical and doable.

By 1994, our annual revenues reflected an annual compounded revenue growth rate of 18 percent over a five-year period. In a sales-driven company, the obvious solution to the debt load Vi-Jon was carrying might have been to simply increase sales—easier said than done. Given the inefficiencies of the Page plant, the increase in sales and production only added to the problems. The financial equation could not be ignored. Despite sales of over $70 million, the company was operating at a loss. For the first time in Vi-Jon's history, our normally strong relationships with vendors were strained.

Using the popular three-legged stool illustration, where the debt load (created by rapid sales expansion) was sitting on our stool, one leg was poor plant efficiencies that did not improve as quickly as needed. This was aggravated by the second leg, the Hunt acquisition, and the problems it caused us in the plant and in the office trying to manage it. Finally—the third leg—it diverted attention away from our computer upgrade, which we desperately needed in order to manage and improve the plant. I agree with Mel's assessment that all of the legs broke simultaneously—and the burden of debt came crashing down.

Mel Turner—calling him "Vi-Jon's Guardian Angel" might be a gross understatement.

Ninth Inning

Difficult Times and Even More Difficult Decisions

I must admit that I literally recall seeing my whole life pass before my eyes, sometimes daily. Perhaps at no other point in my career were the core values I received from my family, along with my faith, more important or more tested.

Vi-Jon was experiencing the worst year in its history. All of these things that were supposed to work with a high degree of synergy failed to occur, and all the brilliant people that I'd brought into the company through this process seemed to fall short of meeting the objectives. And in the fall of 1994, it was quickly becoming evident that our tables were being extended, we weren't making the numbers, we were falling short of the budget in terms of revenues, and the efficiency in the new plant did not occur. Probably just about everything that could go wrong went wrong. Perhaps I had been too aggressive in terms of expansion and growth and hiring people that I considered talented to jump in.

As if the problems the company was facing weren't enough, my wife Jan was battling a serious illness the doctors diagnosed as lupus. There is no known cure for lupus and the prognosis was grim. All else shrank in importance to me.

And so between my wife's serious illness, the business, and having three teenage kids at home (I was trying to raise them on my own, because my wife had to move for specialized medical support out to the West Coast), it was some pretty dark days at that point in time.

With the threat of bankruptcy looming ever larger for me and my company, I had to make some very difficult decisions. It was clear that the company would have to be sold to provide some relief from an overwhelming debt load. One thing was certain—if there was even a shred of a possibility that the business my grandfather had founded could be saved, I was going to find a way. If it wasn't for my dad's counsel I don't know what I would have done.

John G. and John W. Brunner enjoy taking in the "100th Anniversary" Navy–Army Football Game in Philadelphia in December 1999.

It was a tough time for me. It was a tough time for everyone. Jan was getting worse, and Vi-Jon was close behind. I actually remember going back to the Etzel Avenue plant and sitting in that old friend of an office and going through the thought process and prayers that were necessary to determine my next move. Like the old friend that it had been for my father and grandfather, inspiration came to me here in this hardwood museum of an office on how to pull this one out.

Once the decision to sell had been made, I was able to call on the good relationships and solid reputation we'd built within the private label industry and the financial community. You know, you really don't know who your friends are until you go through events such as these. I will never forget those people, and I know they will never forget me.

I contacted a couple of competitors who had really wanted to acquire our business over the years and offered to sell them half or two-thirds of our business that I needed to consolidate. Among these was Perrigo Company, the Michigan-based manufacturer of store-brand over-the-counter pharmaceutical and nutritional products. I wanted to hang onto the Vi-Jon name and some portion of the business, any part they did not need or want. I talked to the president of Perrigo and he told me that he had never bought just "part of a business." So I told him my reasoning—that I wanted to save the jobs; I wanted to save the name and the tradition. It was all about what my grandfather had started and what my dad had expanded and maintained. Ultimately, Perrigo was willing to purchase the brand-new Page Avenue plant, along with their choice of about 75 percent of the product line and hire the associates they wanted. And whatever they didn't want, I kept. My motivation there was to hang on to some semblance of the business, with the hope that we'd try to pull together whatever was remaining and start over again. I guess I was a pretty good salesman after all.

I'd like to state that two good friends, my attorney, Don Paule, and my financial advisor, Larry LeGrand, have really helped to save the day.

Vi-Jon Lives to Fight Another Day!

The deal with Perrigo was signed on December 13, 1994, and the transition was completed, at least on paper, by January 13, 1995. Perrigo crews moved in to adapt the Page Avenue plant to meet Perrigo's production needs. Some of our current partners from Tennessee were involved as well.

In conjunction with the negotiations between Vi-Jon and Perrigo, I agreed that Vi-Jon would not compete with Perrigo in certain product areas, specifically mouthwash, baby products, and shampoos, for a period of five years. We honored that agreement and did not venture back into these product areas until we were legally released to reenter the marketplace. Making something out of what at one point in time appeared to be the loose ends of a lost business soon evolved as the core from which to build a new team at Vi-Jon who would soon become nothing less than heroes!

When all was said and done, every vendor stuck with us except one, and that one we were able to replace within twenty-four hours. Every dollar of debt was repaid in full. I remember when this process began, my attorney said, "John, what do you want to sell the business for?" I said, "I want to pay all my bills and have a dollar left." He said, "Well, John, we can get more than that." I said, "We're too close to have any problems. My goal is to pay all the vendors, pay up all our debt. And if we end up with a dollar, I'll feel that we would have succeeded and hit the goals." And we were able to do that.

Ninth Inning

John G. and Jan Brunner.

But then came the hardest part of the job to me—I sat down with almost every associate and told them they had a chance to work with the company that had acquired most of our business or they could work with me. Some were quick to jump to Perrigo, feeling it provided a better opportunity, a case that I myself argued on their behalf. Others professed their loyalty to Vi-Jon despite my protests. Ultimately the conversations would end with the associates saying, "John, I'm going with you." What could I say other than I was humbled by their faith in me.

I'll never forget Sylvia Bray being the first to make the commitment. She was a receptionist, and she had a child who was a few months old. I sat down with her and started telling her she had a choice to work for either Vi-Jon or for this other company, but before I could finish my sentence, she said, "John, I'm working with you."

I said, "Wait a minute, Sylvia, you've got to hear my talk. I have to tell you the opportunities here. I don't know whether there's going to be much of anything left with Vi-Jon, but you need to go where there's going to be a good opportunity. I think it's important for you—and your child—to consider working for this other company."

And she would have nothing to do with it. She said, "No, John, I'm working with you."

There were a number of associates who responded the way Sylvia did, and what can I say, my faith in my Vi-Jon family restored my faith in mankind. I just thought, "Oh my gosh, if Sylvia and her newborn son are going to depend on me, we've got to make this thing work."

We ended up with quite an unusual group of people that decided to take the risk and see whether there was still going to be a Vi-Jon. When the dust settled, almost every person had a job with either

Perrigo or Vi-Jon. We moved the few remaining products that this competitor didn't want back into the old building and pulled together the few associates that wanted to stay with us. We painted and cleaned up the factory and the building. And within eighteen months, we were moving into one of the best years of our company's history.

Around this same time, I was additionally blessed when we were informed that my wife's incurable disease had gone into remission. Sitting next to her in the specialist's office and hearing this news sent my mind into an almost divine state of joy. Nothing else mattered at that moment. Her health was at the very core of my everyday concerns and focus. I had relied on the wonderful team at Vi-Jon to help steer the company ship during the times I needed to be with Jan. With this news came the opportunity for my family to finally start to move towards the better life that we had always planned for, hoped for, and dreamed about during those many challenging days and nights.

A Break in the Clouds

Somehow one product remained under the radar of both Vi-Jon and Perrigo during the negotiations. It was an unintentional oversight that ended up being a blessing to Vi-Jon. In 1994, not long before the sale of the Page plant to Perrigo, we had begun manufacturing antibacterial soap. Designed to compete with the name-brand soaps, the project was still in its infancy and was apparently too small to be of interest to Perrigo. It ended up as a sideline agreement, drawn up in the eleventh hour of negotiations between Vi-Jon and Perrigo. In an odd twist of providence, Perrigo and Vi-Jon agreed that Vi-Jon would keep the antibacterial product line, but Perrigo would continue to manufacture it for Vi-Jon at the Page plant, which Perrigo now owned.

Mel Turner made the comment that we stayed in the antibacterial soap business almost as an afterthought. How right he was—all I know is that we needed every piece of business we could get and I jumped on it. This turned out to be a very good foundation for the future. I like to say that luck is the anonymous catalyst for success, but I really believe that providence had a hand in it. Antibacterial soap became the lead-in to the Germ-X® line, even though it was overlooked by almost everybody. It was one of the key developments that brought the company to where it is today.

The New Vi-Jon Team

I really know how it must have felt back in the company's infancy, for my grandfather to put together a crew of steady, sturdy, and loyal folks to create and nurture something that was literally surviving by the skin of its teeth. I was quick to take responsibility for the decisions that led to Vi-Jon's difficulties in the early 1990s. I was a bit overanxious, but I learned quickly and completely. Those who have worked with me and for me have been very kind in noting that they felt that the principles of the Golden Rule—respect and care—are the foundation for success. I have been told by outside observers of those difficult years in the early 1990s that it was apparent I depended on a couple of senior executives who were not completely aligned with the goals of the company at the time. Perhaps we all must make the decision at some point in our lives to either live with trust, knowing that trust may at times be violated, or live with doubt, suspicion, and distrust. By the grace of God I made that decision, and to this point in time it appears to have yielded positive returns.

Ninth Inning

Back to Square One

I have found that success rarely results from having a preprinted road map. More often than not it comes with a roller coaster ride that, once experienced, delivers you back to more stable ground. Just in time for the next roller coaster ride.

I can truly say that when you have so many problems and so many challenges, you have to rely on something greater than yourself to survive. I am blessed. When I recall those difficult times in both the company and my personal life, I can point to the scripture verses that I pasted to the back of my desk:

"And my God shall supply all your needs according to His riches in glory in Christ Jesus." (Philippians 4:19)

"Do not fear, for I am with you; do not anxiously look about you, for I am your God. I will strengthen you, surely I will help you, surely I will uphold you with My righteous right hand." (Isaiah 41:10)

"The Lord's loving kindnesses indeed never cease, for His compassions never fail. They are new every morning; great is Thy faithfulness." (Lamentations 3:22–23)

And this was the verse that was for Jan when she was very ill:

"But those who hope in the Lord will renew their strength. They will soar on wings like eagles; they will run and not grow weary, they will walk and not be faint." (Isaiah 40:31)

As I look back on these times, I can actually see the silver lining inside the dark clouds. I have in fact ended up with the finest group of associates you could ever wish to engage. All the business schools and consultants can't teach you about things like this. You have to live through it. Here you have a disaster that would have destroyed a lesser group of people. On top of that, you give people a choice of working for a financially solid company or risking their future with an "unstable" company in the inner city, beaten-down roller-coaster-type facility with a couple of stray product categories. You end up with either some incredibly dedicated souls or some awfully crazy people. We were both!

We ended up with an unusual group of people that decided to risk it all and were ready, willing, and able to take the company back to its roots and rebuild. What they would take with them was a vision for the "new" Vi-Jon, a new understanding of what it meant to be a team, and the traditions and values that built the company all the way back to the first time in 1908. They all pulled together, and the camaraderie was just unbelievable. And on that base and foundation, we continued to grow and expand.

Members of that core group of Vi-Jon associates who were ready for the "new" challenge. Left to right: scuba instructor, Kevin Birkner, Dean Swaller, Ed Arndt, and John G. Brunner, taken somewhere around the Cayman Islands.

When the final agreement was reached with Perrigo, the product mix that was left for Vi-Jon to produce was nail polish remover, petroleum jelly products, and men's toiletries, along with selling the antibacterial soap Perrigo manufactured for us. With three-fourths of the company sold to Perrigo, the job at hand was to take eighty-four loyal employees back to the company's roots at the Etzel Avenue plant and start rebuilding. It would not be an easy task. For one thing, other members of the private label industry were predicting that Vi-Jon wouldn't survive six months. The smart money was apparently stacked against us—so thought the experts in our industry. We were all prepared for what was to turn out to be a very humbling experience, sort of a Marine boot camp for everyone, and we would develop new respect for one another, our company, and the customers who relied on us to provide the very important product categories that they depended on. We never lost our focus on the customer. Our standard hours turned out to be 7 a.m. to 7 p.m., that is, except for Mel and a few other brave souls whose projects kept going "after hours."

The front view from Etzel Avenue of the old reliable Etzel plant.

Ninth Inning

    I would describe the next two years as a time of returning to fundamental principles and relying on the core strengths and values of the people who were willing to work hard as a team, the people I refer to as "the true believers."

    I also knew that I was going to need some capital to put the neglected Etzel Avenue plant back into mainstream operation, but my thoughts were inundated with the question of who was going to lend money to a losing team. I then got a call from the president of Southwest Bank, Andrew Baur, and unlike the previous loans that required complex spreadsheets, this loan came by way of a personal meeting with the management team. Within twenty-four hours, proving once again, the value of straight-talk and integrity, we had the "gas in the tank"!

    Back when my wife's illness demanded much of my time and attention, it was necessary for me to rely, more than ever before, on a few key people to get the Etzel Avenue plant back in peak operation. My right arm proved to be Mel Turner. Mel orchestrated the move back to the Etzel Avenue plant. Mel became the operations person in the company. A lion's share of the credit goes to Mel and his disciplined, analytical thinking that helped make that happen.

Arizona is Mel's new home, and while serving with the Arizona Rangers, he continues to provide strategic support to various Vi-Jon projects.

Along with Mel, I depended on Ed Sander to construct a new human resources staff at Vi-Jon. We continued to make staffing decisions based on character and capability. Dan Charleville would be our maintenance superintendent. I always said that if I was marooned on a desert island with only a few people that Mel, Dan, and the best boat builder in the world, would be in the top ten choices. During the time Mel supervised plant operations, it became obvious to him that Dan was the brains and the work ethic behind the mechanical operations. Dan told me he remembered Mel telling him, "Perrigo is very interested in having you on their team, but John is hoping you'll be part of the "new" Vi-Jon." So Dan took less than a second to decide to stay with Vi-Jon, mostly because of the Vi-Jon values. Dan's loyalty is only matched by his generous spirit that has allowed hundreds of mechanics that have reported to him over the years to thrive and contribute to the Vi-Jon success story. One of Dan's first chores was to go down to Cumberland Swan (which was owned by Perrigo at the time) and remove all their petroleum jelly production lines and bring them to the Etzel Avenue plant, thus satisfying one part of the agreement between the two companies.

Ed Sander, who had been with Vi-Jon since 1988, was also given the responsibility of creating office space where none existed. Ed and Dan looked over the old second floor offices at the Etzel Avenue plant and concluded that it was a dump, hardly suitable for occupancy without some major restoration. He and Dan would see areas where tiles were falling in on the ceiling and wires hanging down. The windows were just single pane windows, which meant it was hot in the summer and cold in the winter. For the most part, for these types of things, we would gut everything. The ceilings would be torn out, the windows replaced, the walls stripped down to nothing; everything would be done from the ground up. So they began the restoration and jumped in with both feet to get the new Vi-Jon staff moved out of the Page Avenue plant and back to Etzel Avenue as quickly as possible while providing a suitable and efficient office setting.

Dan Charleville, our maintenance superintendent, who always answered the bell and who retired from Vi-Jon in 2008.

Ninth Inning

Bob Hess, Vi-Jon's chief financial officer, sits patiently between meetings, ready for the next project requiring funds.

Tom Marren, vice president of technical services, sits at his desk contemplating a quality move.

Bob Hess was chosen to run the finance department of the "new Vi-Jon" and has since become the company's chief financial officer (CFO). I knew that Bob was considered as being financially conservative, and along with that we knew he was bright and dependable. If Bob said, "Okay, it looks like we are going to be in the black on the bottom line" then we knew we were going to be in the black. Bob Hess, like other members of the Vi-Jon team, has told me he looks back on those years with a bit of sentimentality contrasted with a lot of pride for a job well done. That first year Bob kept our costs under control and just did a really good job. We went back to the roots. Keeping antibacterial soap was a gift from God and it just skyrocketed. Nail polish remover started taking off, as well as petroleum jelly and men's aftershave. The company thrived. In fact, within two years we had the best bottom line in our company's history. Bob and I had a special phrase—"No surprises"—and the bank loved us!

Tom Marren came on board back in April of 1986 and was deeply involved in operations and logistics. He became our vice-president of procurement in the "new" Vi-Jon. Tom has ended up wearing every hat imaginable for the company. Tom currently fills the position of vice-president of technical services and maintains an overview of ever-increasing challenges that seem to multiply in complexity and required expertise in order to maintain Vi-Jon's compliance with FDA regulations.

Kirk Sanders keeps a close check on the pulse of the company, usually through many phone communications.

Kirk Sanders, a business partner with both my dad and me since 1985 when we collectively owned a company that manufactured plastic bottles, came to work for Vi-Jon in September of 1996. The "new" Vi-Jon had a year and a half under its belt and things were looking good. Kirk recalls this as an exciting time, full of optimism and an abundance of cooperation. If we were behind in the orders or the production folks needed to take a break, office folks would volunteer to run the lines. If we made a promise to deliver product, we'd bust down walls and do whatever it took to keep that promise—our motto was "on time and complete" always.

The folks that we have had working here over the years have never been threatened by organizational charts. Take, for instance, the time Mel Turner and Wright Carter, our maintenance millwright, turned into self-appointed carpenters. The addition of more people in 1996 indicated the need for more space for human resources and computer functions upstairs at the Etzel Avenue plant. We needed to be creative and economical, so Mel and Wright Carter drew up a plan to convert second-floor warehouse space into more office space. Mid-afternoons for several weeks, carpenter Mel changed into construction clothes, grabbed his claw hammer and saw, and worked with Wright to make new office space for MIS and HR. They even added a new lunchroom downstairs which came to be known as "Mel's Diner"—or was it "Microwave Manor"?!

Not everything went as smooth as silk. There was the occasion of an alcohol explosion that we all remember. We had alcohol tanks that were partly below ground level at the Etzel Avenue plant. The trucks would come in and pump alcohol into the tanks. We never understood exactly what happened, but there was an explosion that literally knocked out a section of the Etzel Avenue plant wall, facing and adjacent to what would be the Metro Link line. We evacuated the plant and I joined about thirty or forty people who went out and picked up bricks, walking around in alcohol. Everyone's shoes were ruined but we were picking things up to clean up the place. Dan Charleville had someone come out to board up the building and they not only boarded it up, they painted it the same color as the building so as you drove by, you wouldn't have known that four or five hours ago there had been a hole in the wall. No one was hurt. What a team!

Ninth Inning

Making Etzel a Winner

In addition to modernizing the office space for reoccupancy, we also took a look at the old plant and our three, limited product categories manufactured there, with an eye toward becoming the best we could be in what we did. The men's toiletries looked stable and satisfactorily supported our red and orange lines. But meeting seasonal demands of nail polish remover was always problematic with just the blue line. So our plan was to install another nail polish remover line when we felt financially able—and we did! In the petroleum jelly (PJ), area we had good capability with two lines, the original green line and the newly acquired yellow line from Perrigo. But our capacity for providing jelly to the lines was hopelessly outdated and limited. And we knew it was just a matter of time before we would have to get rid of the rail car storage sitting alongside the plant, rail cars that were now isolated and fixed in place since the rail spur was cut for the future Metro Link rail "people mover." So we drew up a plan for a huge, indoor PJ storage system, a vast network of steam-heated lines, and a sophisticated water-cooling system to bring the liquid jelly down to "jelling temperature" at the fillers. The tank that we purchased from Kansas City was so big (forty by twelve feet in diameter) that it had to go via Oklahoma to avoid road restrictions between Kansas City and St. Louis. It was a great event for the whole company to watch that huge tank being unloaded and slid into place through a back door at the Etzel Avenue plant. It holds about five tanker truckloads of jelly! Never again did we run out of jelly to service the fillers. We became the king of "PJ" bottling.

The new Metro Link rail system that runs on the tracks just to the east of the Etzel Avenue plant.

With rapid growth of sales in our limited product lines, we quickly needed more warehouse space. We solved this by first renting warehouse space across the street from the plant where we stored antibacterial soap brought over from Perrigo and the Page Avenue plant. It soon filled up with overflow from the Etzel Avenue plant, as well as production for our promotions and back-to-school sales. Later, we leased a large warehouse south of the plant and across I-64 on Berthold Street. That gave us a huge warehousing capacity to support the growth curve we were experiencing.

Every year, we planned some capital investment in the old Etzel Avenue plant to keep us moving forward. One sorely needed item was a new label control room down on the manufacturing floor, closer to the lines and big enough to support our newfound growth. The new label room, located just down the ramp from the upper warehouse has been a boon to our productivity and a real joy to the folks that manage and control our label inventory.

The Upside of Tough Times

Before long, Vi-Jon's balance sheet reflected the benefits of real teamwork. In the first year after the sale of the Page Avenue plant, which was to be a test year for Vi-Jon's future at Etzel Avenue, almost $24 million worth of product was sold with a million dollar profit. In 1996, the company made $2 million and in 1997 we made $3 million. Relationships with vendors and customers alike were being mended and renewed. We definitely were back in the game—and celebrated the most profitable year in our history back then.

Though Mel Turner had "officially" retired in 1996 (Mel has, in fact, retired three times from Vi-Jon) he continued to handle some projects for me. In 1997, I prevailed upon our longstanding relationship by asking him to help give the company some direction in the information technology (IT) area. The Etzel Avenue plant had become quite successful and it was time to go back and revisit the PRMS project to update the central software system. I knew that Mel realized the tools hadn't been in place to support the growth in 1992 and 1993. Now that the company was revitalizing, it only made sense to put those tools in place before any more growth occurred. Vi-Jon invested considerable resources in a completely new software system. The hard work of Mel Turner and a team of Vi-Jon associates resulted in sophisticated systems that supported Vi-Jon's operations for ten years.

All Too Familiar Territory

Despite Perrigo's size and reputation as an industry leader, they too encountered problems at the Page Avenue plant. They really hadn't had the facility long enough to make the plant productive. It was not just the Page Avenue plant that proved to be a burden for Perrigo. They closed plants in California as well and exited the mouthwash business completely. This was no business for the meek.

I then did a complete "about-face" from the strategic retreat that had been made in the mid-1990s. I engaged a group of people to evaluate the purchase of the Page Avenue plant. Every time I drove past that location I felt an attraction to somehow revisit that opportunity. I just knew we could be successful. We surely knew what *not* to do at this point in time. I learned that it takes the right team, the right commitment and a lot of hard work to succeed. I know what our team did and could do.

John W. Brunner at the entrance of his "old friend" the Etzel Avenue plant.

We brought in John O'Dwyer, who has been a friend of the company ever since. John has a PhD in organizational behavior and leadership, and thanks to his coaching, we developed strategic goals and objectives and a strategic plan. At the Etzel Avenue facility we were size constrained; we were landlocked, and at that time we thought that the Page Avenue facility was a place we could not outgrow very easily. We knew we'd incur lots of debt. On the plus side, our antibacterial products business was growing like crazy, but all our production was being done through outside contract packers. We knew if we bought the Page plant, we could produce inside. This seemed straightforward enough to me, and I was convinced now to sell the idea to others.

Not everyone was enthusiastic about this decision. After all we'd been there! All we needed was a leader, so Mel Turner came out of retirement to help restore the Page Avenue plant. He told me that there were things about this plant that he didn't like before, and now that we had grown, he knew they were again going to be difficult. However, knowing the determination that I expressed towards the revitalization of Vi-Jon, Mel committed to the project. Mel said he detected a twinkle in my eye and a passion in my voice when I talked about moving back into Page.

We then went ahead and made Perrigo an offer that was low enough for even Bob Hess to be excited about. The key point in our favor concerning our decision to take back the Page Avenue plant was antibacterial soap, a product whose sales were climbing. It was a product that Vi-Jon could begin manufacturing immediately at the Page Avenue plant, with no need to wait for the sales force to line up customers. The only obstacle, and it was a big one, was the absence of tanks big enough to perform the compounding necessary to support the production lines. This wasn't a new problem at the Page Avenue plant, so plans were immediately drawn up to install a ten-thousand-gallon tank right out of the "starting gate."

Resurrecting a Sleeping Giant

Mel, along with Dan Charleville and a fellow whose name you will become more familiar with through this book, Ed Lemay formed a team with Dean Swaller, Rick Miller, Joe Rich, and Wright Carter that jumped into the Page startup project with both feet and came out of the gate running. I can tell you for a fact that the biggest challenge was bringing the lines back in, because Perrigo had literally gutted the production area. The team charged with bringing the plant up and running noted that plumbing was cut, some functional tanks had been taken, key flow meters had been removed, electrical wiring was cut in mid-run and removed from conduit runs, etc. It was a mess, but we got it at a good price. Our planning group concluded that we could get a line installed a lot faster than we would ever be able to begin compounding. So the decision was made to focus on getting two production lines running with product supplied by tanker truck. Had we insisted on compounding first, the first packaging line would have been delayed at least three to six months. The first production line was operational by early fall of 1999 with the second one coming on-line by late fall. Basic compounding was not available until the spring of 2000. I personally watched that first ten-thousand-gallon tank being maneuvered into place.

Ninth Inning

To me it was obvious that when we got it back, the facility was not in good shape. So we rolled up our shirtsleeves and we kept five or six people who had worked for Vi-Jon before to jump in and get the job going. We worked nine months to get the Page Avenue plant in good shape and to get antibacterial soap produced here. Then on January 13, 2000, our non-compete agreement with Perrigo expired, and that opened up mouthwash and baby oil business to us. We then also got into the shampoo business.

Everybody involved in this startup knew that the inefficiencies of the lines at the Page Avenue plant were also at the top of the list of things that needed to be changed to make the second turn successful. It was noted by the team that Dean Swaller (our young dynamic Etzel Avenue plant manager) and Dan Charleville (our head mechanic) had a great deal of success at the Etzel Avenue plant because the lines were greatly condensed and logistically laid out much tighter. Most of the Etzel Avenue plant lines are laid out in a "U" configuration and the lead operator stands in the center so the main touch points are all within two or three steps. When they came into the Page Avenue plant originally, they installed lines that went from one end of the building to another. These lines were fifty to one hundred feet long and the lead operator could hardly see the end of the line, much less operate it. We've done some adaptations since then, but that was one of the first changes we needed to make.

By 2000, Vi-Jon's sales exceeded $90 million. Since then, the company has added 340,000 square feet of warehouse space in the Fountain Lakes facility in St. Charles.

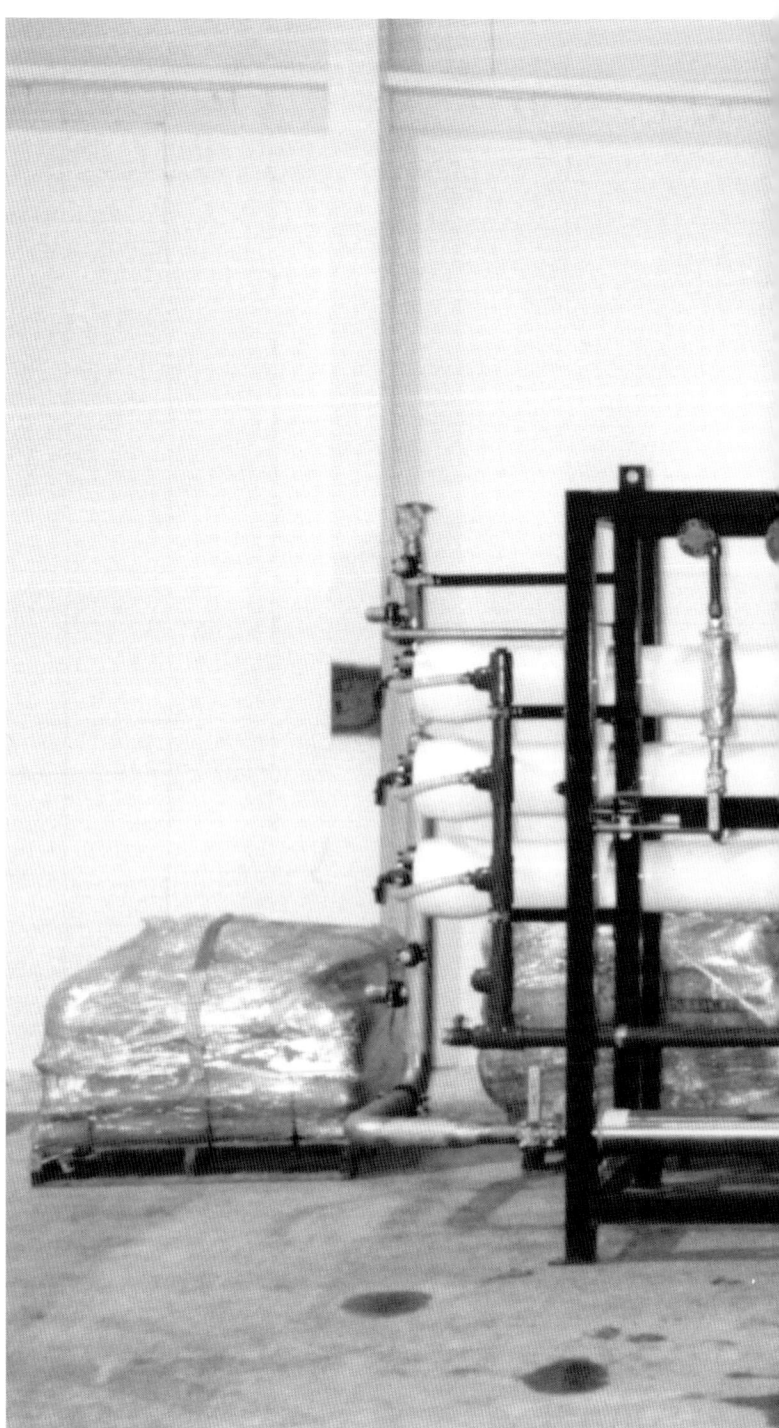

The reverse osmosis system that needed to be refitted for use when Vi-Jon reactivated the Page Avenue plant in 1999.

Ninth Inning

The private label industry has grown dramatically in recent years as consumers continue to demand more value for their money. The consumer has never been smarter and informed about the quality they should expect in the products that they buy. According to an article in the July 5, 2002 edition of the *St. Louis Business Journal*, private label products accounted for 22 to 30 percent of sales, depending on the product category, up from just 3 percent in 1985. In an April 3, 2009 article the *St. Louis Business Journal* reports that as the recession changes buying patterns, companies producing and distributing private label products have experienced revenue increases in the millions. Statistics like these leave little to the imagination as to which way this category is growing.

Still, it is a highly competitive industry that requires a lean and streamlined operation. Many private label companies have gone by the wayside over the years, and it is perhaps our willingness and ability to reinvent ourself that enabled Vi-Jon to survive and prosper. We approached our centennial year with a wide range of capabilities, and we were continuing to do more than talk. After all, procrastination is the thief of time. And doing things faster is a great competitive advantage.

The Brown production line was one of the first production lines to be installed at the Page Avenue plant.

III. John Gammon Brunner's Story

10. Extra Innings: A New Century —Nothing Can Stop Us Now

The Millennium was upon us, and with the Page plant literally expanding every day, we were ready to take on the world. Everything was global now, and most of our competition was shifting outside of the country more and more. In an effort to cut their costs and maintain a competitive edge, were pulling a huge percentage of their products from overseas. When they were buying from domestic suppliers such as Vi-Jon, we had a unique test track on which to compete that included such things as special third party audits, blind internet and telephone auctions, and upgraded quality standards that ended up making some of our products higher in quality than the major brands.

Well, they say that even a journey of a thousand miles starts with a single step. Our single step started with the reacquisition of the Page Avenue facility from Perrigo in the 1999. As I described earlier, we had tried to make a go of it at the Page Avenue facility in the 1990s and had to do a strategic redeployment because of a number of issues. However, I did not think this experience was a complete waste of time and effort. I have always felt that every shortcoming can serve as the seed for future accomplishment; therefore, we would make our experiences at the Page Avenue location an eventual success story.

A Second Day of Infamy

We launched into the new century anticipating that life as we knew it in the next hundred years would be the same. The events of September 11, 2001, made short work of that notion. I often ask people where they were on that fateful day. For me it was a normal day—I got up early, had a light breakfast, glanced at the newspaper, and drove to work—then in utter amazement I saw on the Internet the first ominous descriptions of what was transpiring in New York.

My grandfather described in quite stirring detail how he, my dad, and my grandmother reacted to the infamy and utter devastation of the Pearl Harbor surprise attack and how he remembered every detail of that day. The September 11, 2001 events produced the same feelings of devastation and are etched in my memory forever. Everybody at Vi-Jon knew something had transpired, but we didn't have all the details yet. We actually dashed out, bought a TV, and hurriedly connected it in order to watch the unfolding terror in all its horrible detail and deathly realities.

Extra Innings

The headline says it all about the events of 9/11.

As each eerie moment passed, my blood started to boil and my anger started to surface. The stark reality of helplessness drove a cold shiver through my senses. I endeavored to be calm, collect my thoughts, and do what I prided myself as being able to do. Then I thought of the people, how frightened they must be, and I knew that the best cure for fear is patience and a steady hand. That thought snapped me back into control. I needed to regroup and think about how my grandfather or dad would handle this situation—how to react to the unthinkable, a terrible sneak attack, how to respond to what amounted to a devastation never before witnessed in my generation.

I knew I needed to address the Vi-Jon family. I needed to inform them of what actually happened, fix my eyes on Providence, and remind them that the sky had not really fallen, although to some it may have seemed that way. On more than one occasion, upon learning of bad news, my dad had told me to turn my face to the sun, so the shadows would always fall behind me. We asked all the folks to gather in the middle of the plant. An unsettled hush came over the mass of scared faces as they appeared starved for assurances that things were not as devastating as had been first reported, and that somehow, someway, this had been blown out of proportion and was some type of a news media overkill. I didn't speak to anyone as I made my way to the center of my very good friends. I focused instead on every step and how I needed to convey confidence in a simple stroll through the production area. I looked into the mass of uncertain faces, careful not to focus on just one, cleared my throat, and discovered it was in fact very dry, and delivered one of the more difficult communications of my life. I delivered without editorial comment the worst of what comprised a summary of the day's events. Well, I gave them the bad, the ugly and, eventually, the good. I then shifted gears and verbally performed what was described by one of the associates as the largest "group hug" he had ever participated in. My message was simple and clear, that we as Americans would survive this tragedy and respond tenfold to deal with those responsible for this attack on our way of life. It was as therapeutic for me as it was for them. As I walked back to the solitude of my office, I rediscovered some measure of moisture in my mouth. With the door shut I collapsed in my chair, thanking God for the strength He had somehow temporarily loaned me over the previous fifteen minutes.

Vi-Jon Laboratories, Inc., Reinvents Itself—Again

Well we survived that horrible point in time and we responded to that cowardly terrorist act with our own version of "shock and awe" during Operation Desert Storm. And as we knew we would, as we always will, we gathered ourselves and moved forward. As Vi-Jon celebrates its centennial year in 2008, it is a perfect illustration of the business maxim that says if you're not moving forward then you're moving backward—there is no such thing as standing still. In keeping with its history, Vi-Jon was once again reinventing itself in an industry where ownership of a category sometimes resembles a game of musical chairs. This time, the result was a company that was currently better positioned than it had been at any time in its previous history, to move forward in what has continued to be a highly competitive industry and marketplace. I was determined that we were not going to stand still. I have always felt that in business we are held accountable for not only what we do, but just as often for what we *don't* do. I determined that my future dreams would be about what I did—not about what I didn't do.

Then, we made our move. On July 19, 2006, I teamed up with Berkshire Partners LLC, a Boston-based private equity firm, and announced that together we purchased both Vi-Jon Laboratories, Inc., and Cumberland-Swan. In one moment the size of our company doubled!

I had admired the Cumberland Company over the years, even before I had problems back in 1985. It's an outstanding group, our toughest competitor. I stayed close to the original owners of the business and to that family, to the Perrigo Company that acquired them, and the next group of owners that acquired that company. We spent some time looking at private equity firms and eventually selected Berkshire partners to join with. And together we worked out how to put Vi-Jon and Cumberland together.

I stated in the press release that as a new, larger entity we would have the resources to compete more effectively in the marketplace. With our combined technology, broader distribution, expanded product lines, and our experienced American workforce, we knew we could achieve greater efficiencies and serve our customers even better. It is a merger that has its fair share of ironic twists and yet, when one looks at the histories of both companies, it would appear to be a logical and perfect fit.

The Cumberland Manufacturing Company

Let me take a moment to give some background on the Cumberland Manufacturing Company. It was established in 1898 in Nashville, Tennessee, as a packager of Windsor Brand spices and extracts, Swan Brand drugs, and Cumberland health and beauty aids. Cumberland's "Swan" and "Dr. Lane" product lines have been marketed continuously since that time. Fast forward all the way to 1938, when Isaac "Ike" Goldstein went to work for the company at Cummins Station as Cumberland's vice president of sales. Through the next few years, there were several changes in the management of Cumberland, and the company stumbled just a bit. They entered the 1940s with some pessimism when a petition for bankruptcy was filed on April 27, 1940, and the following July, Ike Goldstein, along with several partners, purchased the assets of Cumberland Manufacturing. This group appeared to be at the right place at the right time. Both the plant and the office were located at 105 Russell Street in Nashville.

The Cumberland Swan front entrance in Smyrna, Tennessee.

Right after the war, in 1946, when building materials were released for private use back home, a manufacturing facility was built in West Nashville at 501 Twenty-fifth Avenue North. When additional facilities were added in 1950, the entire operation moved to the West Nashville address. There appeared to be some pretty good momentum building for the company.

In 1959, with the untimely death of Ike Goldstein, his son, Edward T. Goldstein, purchased the company. The year after, Cumberland Manufacturing Company was formally incorporated under the name CMC, Inc., on July 12 with Edward Goldstein as president. There are some ironic similarities as you follow the rich history of the Cumberland story. But it gets better.

Edward had majored in engineering at Vanderbilt University in Nashville. In addition, he used his advanced skills back in 1942 when he is said to have designed and used 1 x 12s and concrete blocks, in the absence of steel due to the war effort, to build a three-story addition to the old plant at First and Russell. His good friend and longtime colleague, Jack Sheperd, wrote in the *Cumberland Newsletter* in December of 1986, "In 1946, after deciding to go into the Bri-Tex bleach business, he (Edward) designed the manufacturing facilities and built the plant at Twenty-fifth and Felicia in Nashville. Shortly after the initial building was completed, it was decided to move the entire operation to the West Nashville location." Mr. Sheperd captured only the latest in a string of strategic moves initiated in order to grow the company.

A "sell sheet" from the 1970s used by the Cumberland Manufacturing Company.

In the coming years, Cumberland grew through a series of strategically planned acquisitions. In 1970, through a joint venture with Lawrence Pharmaceuticals of Florida, Cumberland purchased International Distributors from Plough, Inc., and that business was moved from Memphis to Smyrna, Tennessee. In 1973, Carroll Chemical Company was purchased from Sperti Drug Products in another joint venture, this time with International Drug. That business was also relocated to Smyrna, Tennessee. In 1976, CMC, Inc., acquired 100 percent ownership of International Drug, Inc., when they bought out Lawrence Pharmaceutical's interest.

From this point, CMC sought to increase its competitive edge and enhance customer service by bringing some of the ancillary aspects of the business under CMC's direct ownership and control. In 1978, they started their own plastic bottle manufacturing operation and in 1981, Cumberland Freight Line was organized as a separate corporation. CMC's operations and corporate offices were moved from Nashville to Smyrna, Tennessee, and in 1985 they started their own pressure sensitive label printing facility.

Just eight years after naming himself chairman of the board and appointing Lonnie L. Smith as president of CMC, Edward Goldstein passed away in April of 1986, leaving behind a legacy of integrity and benevolent leadership. He seems like the type of man with whom I would like to have been associated—very much like my own dad.

In 1987, the CMC, Inc. name was changed to Cumberland-Swan, Inc. In August 1988, ground was broken for a new ninety-five-thousand-square-foot expansion of Cumberland's main facility. The plans included forty-five thousand square feet of manufacturing and packaging space and fifty thousand square feet of shipping and warehouse space. The new facility would include a state-of-the-art solid dosage form granulation, tableting, and packaging operation. As you can see, some real critical strategic planning was used along the way during key periods.

This photo of the first Cumberland truck and driver was taken some time during the 1940s.

This "big rig" was part of the Cumberland Swan Truck Line in the 1980s.

The Perrigo Years

In 1992, Perrigo acquired 100 percent of Cumberland-Swan from the Goldstein and Simon families, ending the company's fifty-two-year run as a family owned and operated business. All of Perrigo's personal care business was consolidated under the entity called Perrigo of Tennessee. This is just three years prior to Perrigo's purchase of Vi-Jon's Page Avenue plant and business.

This is where Vi-Jon and Perrigo's history crossed paths again. In 1999, the fate of both companies changed, as did the names. Both companies represented decades of service and dedication to an ideal, and both companies were revitalized. The same year that Vi-Jon purchased the Page Avenue plant back from Perrigo, C-S Holdings, a group of Nashville investors, acquired Perrigo of Tennessee and reestablished the Cumberland name, this time as Cumberland-Swan, Inc.

Cumberland-Swan was then once more drawn back into the St. Louis theatre of operations. A few years later, Cumberland-Swan went on to acquire Benjamin Ansehl of St. Louis, a manufacturer of store-brand skin-care products. The acquisition of Diamond Products of Tampa, Florida, would follow the next year, adding more first-aid products to their line. This company was not letting the grass grow under its feet! Some of the mechanical folks down at Smyrna still talk about their adventures when they were charged with disassembling equipment, moving it to Tennessee and putting it back together again—some really great stories from some really great guys!

United into an Enterprise

As I stated earlier, it was not my intention to stand still for any length of time. The time appeared right for a major move by way of a merger that would involve Vi-Jon and Cumberland-Swan. My primary concern for everyone affected by this merger was that the two populations, Smyrna and St. Louis, would come together as one unified company. There are fine people at both locations. I did not want to leave one person behind. An integration team was quickly formed in order to achieve this goal, headed up by "Mr. Dependable" Mel Turner (out of retirement for the third time!). Representing both locations, care was taken by this team to ensure that existing managers and leaders facilitated all of the integration initiatives in order to promote buy-in and support for change processes that, under the best of circumstances, could be trying, particularly in light of production demands that had to continue uninterrupted. One of the earliest functional successes was the savings of approximately $15 million realized through the sourcing team's efforts, led by Ed Arndt. They ended up surpassing the savings goals expected by Berkshire from the merger of the two operations. This early success set the pace for the rest of the process. I had no doubts about our capabilities. I knew that we had two excellent companies staffed by great people, all of whom were running excellent operations in supporting our customers. Our approach would be deliberate, thoughtful, and effective, insuring along the way that we wouldn't compromise anything and would not jeopardize our excellent on-time and complete (OTC) customer service record. "OTC" would rule the day—as it had for Vi-Jon for nearly one hundred years.

Ed Arndt, Vi-Jon's vice president of sourcing, inspects some of the new "Inspector Hector."

The Joining of Two Cultures

I realized that it was one thing to integrate processes and quite another to integrate cultures. That process would require patience and take some time. Considering the history of both of these companies and their many similarities, it may be a shorter process than one might imagine. However, we could not count on that. We needed to pay special attention to this dynamic in the integration process.

Both companies had a history of family ownership and a history of "family" that went well beyond the definition of mere ownership. Both of our companies had placed tremendous value on the dedication and hard work of our employees, listening to and valuing their input along the way. There is little wonder that both companies can boast an inordinate number of longstanding and dedicated employees. The work ethic, focus, and attention to customers was also very similar.

We'd heard all the stories about mergers, acquisitions, and companies combining. There are two issues: how long does the integration take, and do you really get the synergies? And generally the integration takes twice as long as what you forecast, and you only gain half of the expected synergies.

But we were able to get the integration done in half the time that we forecasted. And, in terms of the financial synergies, it was twice the financial return that we expected. So we did the opposite of what happens in most companies, and I really attribute that to a great team working together back and forth. I personally bought a nine-passenger plane even before we closed the deal, understanding the importance of people getting back and forth between the two facilities. At the end of the day, it's all about people. And synergies, integration, and creating value are basically how people work together. And when that little nine-passenger airplane was flying daily back and forth between Smyrna, Tennessee, and St. Louis that was probably the best integration tool we ever used to pull people together, to learn about each other's operations and organization structures, and just to unify the company.

To Serve and to Protect

Along the way, another very important facet of a strong company infrastructure has been bolstered. Both Vi-Jon and Cumberland-Swan initiated their safety programs as a direct result of an employee's initiative. In St. Louis, setting safety records was at the top of our list of accomplishments through 2006. As I understand, at Cumberland-Swan, Jerry Casey filled out an employee suggestion form in 1979, expressing his concern over the hazards that might arise from women wearing open-toed shoes. As a result, departments were outfitted with rescue and first-aid supplies and safety programs were launched. Some real foresight was exercised that had a direct bearing on the welfare of the work force.

On the Missouri side, almost forgotten at Vi-Jon in St. Louis, was a lady named Annie Tiernon who worked for Vi-Jon from 1943 to 1993. Annie noticed smoke coming in the back window of the Etzel plant one day shortly after she was hired. At the time, the maintenance man, Walter Stotler and his wife lived in a little house behind the plant. The smoke Annie saw was from the leaves Walter's wife was burning in the yard. That was enough for Carl Mueller, who was vice-president at the time, when he realized the value of Annie's warning. Fire drills were launched and Vi-Jon's safety program was under way. This practice is maintained with a high degree of readiness at all levels today.

The Personal Touch

I am proud to say that both locations published regular newsletters; corporate updates interspersed with notes of congratulations and appreciation, wedding and birth announcements, humor and words of wisdom and inspiration. And whether I talk to people in Smyrna, Tennessee, or St. Louis, Missouri, all will tell you stories of benevolent leadership, of supervisors and managers who are as committed to their employees as the employees are to them.

Extra Innings

Both companies have legacies that longtime employees look back on with great fondness. For the people of Vi-Jon Laboratories, it is the Etzel Avenue plant. My Grandfather and Dad made the Etzel Avenue plant a strong foundation from which to anchor our growth and to guarantee our survival. As we all know, the Etzel Avenue plant served that purpose not more than twelve years ago. For the folks at Cumberland-Swan, it is the plant at 501 Twenty-fifth Avenue North in Nashville. Both served as firm cornerstones to help support the long-term efforts that have sustained both companies.

An article in the 1980 *Cumberland-Swan Newsletter*, written by Rebecca Derseweh, closely paralleled recollections of the plant folks on Christmas celebrations from the past. Hired as the "first girl employed in the office" back in the mid-1940s, Rebecca recalled Eddie Goldstein and his wife, Dorothy, bringing in a spread of kosher delights on the last day before the Christmas holiday, adding touches of their own faith and culture to the Christian traditions. After they enjoyed the corned beef and salami, breads and cheeses, "Mr. Eddie" donned a Santa suit to give out the Christmas presents everyone exchanged.

I recall my grandfather telling similar stories about Grandma Vi coming in with so many treats during the holidays. And my parents always made Christmas at the plant a very special event. Dad had a tradition of reading the Christmas story in the second chapter of Luke from his old Bible that he carried in World War II. These are such pleasant memories for me.

John W. "Jack" Brunner reading the traditional Christmas story at one of the Christmas parties.

Above and Beyond Always

Besides many acts of benevolence from within, both companies have traditions of community service to their credit. Both the company and the people of Vi-Jon have benefited local charities, food pantries, and children's homes, particularly during the Christmas season. In 2004, Vi-Jon sent hefty supplies of Germ-X® to survivors of Hurricane Charley in Florida and to soldiers in Iraq, along with a large number of personal care items sent to soldiers in forty-two different units. Individual acts by company personnel stand out to confirm some of these efforts. Of special note was the trip that two associates made in 2005 to Katrina-devastated New Orleans to help restock a Wal-Mart store in Kenner, Louisiana. Just nine miles west of New Orleans, the Kenner store was the closest one to New Orleans left standing, but it had been stripped of all its merchandise. A call came in from the senior vice president of Wal-Mart, Joe Grady, on a Sunday afternoon just two weeks after Katrina first hit shore, urgently requesting a supply of Germ-X®. Just hours later, Vi-Jon associates Burton Cooper and Kevin Birkner managed to secure a twenty-six-foot truck in which they loaded twelve pallets of Germ-X® and headed southbound on I-55 toward Kenner. Several days later they returned home with the grateful appreciation of Wal-Mart and the people of Kenner, Louisiana. The beauty of this story is that it could have been any two Vi-Jon associates. We have an endless resource of people who are ready, willing, and able to make the sacrifice and go the extra mile to help others.

Left: Grateful American soldiers serving in Iraq send their thanks in return.

Right: More American soldiers expressing their heartfelt thanks to the Vi-Jon team.

A Fresh Start for the New Vi-Jon Family

I will tell you that when you are making the type of decisions that have impact on so many Vi-Jon families, you must treat these actions with a good deal of respect. The decision to move forward with the merger was an agonizing one for me, as I weighed the loss of family-based ownership against the benefits of providing our employees with even greater security and opportunity for the future. As for Vi-Jon's future, my rules for moving forward were very basic and echoed the advice from my grandfather and father. First, you must approach the customer with humility, with the intent of really listening to them. Second, deal with the customer with integrity, and as a team, respond to the customer, with a compelling value proposition. And third, but just as important, maintain an attitude of gratitude for the opportunities we have in America.

One thing that I can say is that after numerous courses, at all kinds of prestigious business schools, although I may have felt well-versed in the complicated theories of the business world, it is all about the basics. It is all about taking care of people—working as a team and sticking with integrity. That simple concept cannot be overstated or over applied. I have always been confounded as to what my appeal is for those who have worked with me, but I think it has a lot to do with common sense, values that have withstood the test of time, and sincerity from the heart. I received these values from my father, who in turn received them from my grandfather. If asked to describe my management style, I might respond that if ever I wrote a book on business the title would be "God, Sweat & Beer," because every worthwhile endeavor begins with something greater than yourself. Then it takes a lot of hard work every day. And finally, every now and then, you get the opportunity to celebrate the small successes. For me and my management team, as these two companies are coming together, the main priority is to continue maintaining the sense of Vi-Jon as more than a team—we're a family.

The Cardinals Keep Pace with Vi-Jon with the 2006 World Series Victory

I am pleased to say that the home baseball team also kept up with us by having a pretty noteworthy performance during this current decade. Tony La Russa kept his Cardinals teams as focused on winning as our team at Vi-Jon. A new clubhouse leader emerged. Albert Pujols launched his star in no small way with eight of the most successful seasons in the history of professional baseball. In 2001 Albert hit .329, with 37 home runs, and 130 rbi's. He was unanimously chosen as the National League Rookie of the year. Albert even appeared on the advertisement of our Germ-X® products. It only makes sense, a winner promoting another winner. The World Series victory in 2006 made the celebration of the Vi-Jon merger complete.

Some of the other highlights of the first decade in the new millennium included Mark McGwire hitting home run number 574 to move to fifth place on the all-time list of homerun hitters. Following that Mark ended a prolific career with his retirement in 2001. Ozzie Smith was elected to the Baseball Hall of Fame in 2002. The Cardinals made good showings through 2008 when Tony consistently worked miracles with other teams' rejects when he and Dave Duncan would reinvent players not regarded as useful prospects. Tony and Dave would fit right into the Vi-Jon team but right now they have their hands full, as do we.

Getting On Base

Right: The patented stance of prolific homerun hitter Mark McGwire, who hit seventy homeruns in 1998, breaking Roger Maris' home run record of sixty-one.

Below: A shot from behind the Cardinal field, boss Tony La Russa and his pitching coach, Dave Duncan, in the dugout at the former Busch Stadium, which was located just north of the current Busch stadium.

Extra Innings

Above: YES!" says it all in an October 2006 *Post-Dispatch* story: "St. Louis Cardinals 2006 World Champions."

Left: Albert Pujols takes a full swing at a fast ball in the new Busch Stadium. Albert's first eight years in the National League have set a new standard for quality, and he has served as a spokesman for our Germ-X brand hand sanitizer. A great combination of winners.

2008—A Year for the Ages

As Vi-Jon celebrates its one hundredth anniversary in 2008, we are proud of a total of three manufacturing facilities: two in St. Louis and one in Smyrna, Tennessee. Fountain Lakes in St. Charles, Missouri, is the distribution center for the Page Avenue and Etzel Avenue plants in St. Louis. Mount Juliet is the distribution center for the Smyrna location. Among the three manufacturing facilities, we run a total of fifty-four production lines, generating annual sales in the neighborhood of $500 million. That's a pretty nice neighborhood. The Peroxide Specialty Company that my grandfather founded in 1908 has been transformed, over this past century, into a company that now produces thousands of products in millions of packages. It is at the apex of one of the more dynamic success stories in our corner of the American free enterprise story.

Still, the strength of Vi-Jon rests, as it always has, in its people. As Babe Ruth once said, "The way a team plays as a whole determines its success. You may have the greatest bunch of individual stars in the world, but if they don't play together, the club won't be worth a dime." The Vi-Jon team consists of approximately six hundred active associates in St. Louis and nearly eight hundred in Smyrna. There are also around two hundred full-time temporary employees, and many of them will eventually join the Vi-Jon team. As we begin our next century, new leaders have joined our team. Roy Rosas, is our new Chief Administrative Officer, and he brings with him years of consumer products company experience. He will be spending part of his time looking for merger and acquisition opportunities. And, Robert Kirby came on board as our new Chief Executive Officer. He also brings with him many years of experience and leadership in various positions with major consumer products companies. I'm confident that Bob will lead the Vi-Jon team to the next level of success. These are the people, along with Vi-Jon's many customers, who are at the forefront of every big decision the company undertakes. When I spoke at the 2000 Founder's Day celebration, I recall saying that the Vi-Jon family will keep going down the same path of teamwork, passion, and pride. And when each of us reaches that personal milestone in our lives, when we pull off to the side of the road to rest, we can cheer for the Vi-Jon team as they continue on. We'll be able to look back with pride and say, I gave it my best, and the very best is yet to be.

The Reality of My Dreams

As I sat in my office, the sun was slowly setting below the warehouse roof across the way, my head was still full of wonderful memories, colorful history, close friends and associates, and a clear perspective on how to finally tell our story. Looking back on our past, I learned the true meaning and impact this little old company has had on so many, and just as important was the fact that I learned what impact this company really had on *me*. How could I have not seen this wonderful mural of our lives?

Now, I see my son, J. B., having the same passion and dedication as my dad to carry on the tradition of this wonderful company. The company is now approaching a billion in sales here, and we have over two thousand associates. J. B., who has grown up along with Vi-Jon, has stepped in here very, very knowledgeable about the business. I remember he came to Vi-Jon when he was only days old. On the way home from the hospital, we stopped over at Vi-Jon, and I carried him up the front stairs in my arms. All the ladies in the office here were eager to meet him. He was highly well received when he was only three days old.

As a child, J. B. would sometimes come on Saturday mornings to help empty the drawers and mess around with pencils and pens, colors, and labels. When he was five or six, I'd walk the factory floor with him and had him practice saying, "Hello Mr. So-And-So. My name is John Brunner." I'd tell him to look them in the eye and give a firm handshake.

That was just the beginning of everything. As he got older, he worked on the production line and in the warehouse during the summers. He's been my right-hand advisor here, somebody who truly understands the strategy and dynamics of the business. He has as much of a grasp, if not more, as anybody in the company.

I think my son's strengths are closer to mine, in that he really does have a strategic insight and vision. He has very good intuitive insight on the business, and his strengths really are more in the marketing aspect, as well as in the strategic acquisition opportunities, understanding the growth and what it takes to get this company going forward.

So I think, for him, the challenge is dependent on what he really wants to do and what opportunities he wants to tackle. There's an opportunity, really, for anybody to become president of the company of this business. And if this is a goal he would like to go after, he has a challenge and opportunity like many of the other people in the organization to continue to make a contribution to the business.

Looking at these four generations of Brunner men in the long history of Vi-Jon, this story links us to our past, helping us to understand the present and allowing us to be better prepared to handle the future.

I'll always remember my father in this office. It is like a direct connection to a wonderful past. The picture of all of us in this old office with its warm and friendly confines will forever be in my mind. I think that I shall revisit this place in my heart and reflect upon it from time to time in the future. Yes, I think that I should like very much to dream here in the days to come. The three of us set forth and nurtured the culture within this company. We established the brand of leadership that continues today. This culture speaks in a very optimistic tongue, with a gentle but direct voice, a voice that has been passed down to each generation of Vi-Jon associates. It is that spirit and company direction that maintain our ability to survive, but more importantly to grow. I have witnessed, since joining the company, a common thread that runs through all four generations of our family. The cornerstone is everyone's concern for, and appreciation of, the people who have been part of the team, whose hard work and dedication have built the company that, in return, has provided well for them. My mission will be to continue that work and to cherish and nurture that culture into the fourth generation.

Speaking of a fourth generation concern, my son J.B. said, "I've been meaning to talk to you Dad, there is something that I am really interested in having the company seriously pursue. It has to do with the new offices that we are starting our planning on. I would like to see this initiative go forward as an open office concept so we become an active part in instilling the culture. The open space is more conducive to improving the face-to-face communication-just like the 'good ol' days. Now, I know what you must be thinking. Don't worry, this old Etzel Avenue office space will go to good use-for training, for safety classes, or just to share new ideas. We can rest assured of that. Earlier my Dad described your new ideas when he first joined Vi-Jon and pushed for some new Vi-Jon thinking." So there you have it from my son J.B., this is another generation, my son's generation, pointing the future and he is encouraging me forward—just like my Dad did with me!

So, in the end, it was another win for the Cardinals, with a lot more of the summer still ahead! And similarly, for Vi-Jon, it's been a century of ups and downs, but we have pulled through in the end. We have entered into the twenty-first century stronger than ever before and look ahead to great things to come. Can it get any better than this? I have to say that in order to top it off even more, we really do need a chance to show the Red Sox a thing or two!

John and Jan Brunner and family in 2007.

John G. Brunner and the first of the new generation of the Brunner legacy, little grandson Christopher James Kline.

A "sales warrior" reflecting at the Private Label Manufacturers Association (PLMA) Show at the Rosemont in Chicago, Illinois.

III. John Gammon Brunner's Story

11. Postgame Wrap-Up from the Heart: A One-Hundred-Year-Old Love Affair

I call this postscript chapter "Postgame Wrap-Up" because it includes the words of some of the many Vi-Jon associates who've had the privilege to work with the Brunners. The stories, comments, and feelings are from the heart and describe a love affair that was cultured by hard work, promoted by respect, and maintained by loyalty and humility. There are very few stories that have survived through the years to give us a true sense of the company's founder, outside of what has been shared in the earlier chapters when John B. Brunner "told his story." Many Vi-Jon associates are fortunate enough to have worked for both his son and grandson. Ask any associate about Vi-Jon's leadership and they will tell you, without exception, about the extraordinary kindness, courtesy, and humility of the Brunners.

Here are some of the testimonials and stories that we would like to share with those who have experienced this wonderful family's love story with their company and associates.

From left to right: John G. Brunner, president of Vi-Jon; Bernard M. Fauber, CEO of the Kmart Corporation; and John W. Brunner, CEO of Vi-Jon in 1987, after being awarded the Exceptional Achievement and Excellence Award from Kmart.

Having been in business with the Brunners before joining Vi-Jon, Kirk Sanders knows well the differences and the similarities between the two men. "The good of John W. has been passed to John G.," he said. "I've seen lots of different characters in business throughout my life. There are those who care about people and those that don't have that capacity. The Brunners care about all people." As for their differences: "Mr. Brunner was always in front of the customer—continually. He just felt at home with the customer, carrying his sample bag, trying to get the order. Mr. Brunner was a salesman and John is a business executive. But I think they lead in similar fashion—by example." Talking to Kirk, as with many Vi-Jon associates, it is sometimes difficult to remember that John W. Brunner passed away in January of 2006. You just have the sense that he will come high-stepping it down the short hall at the Etzel Avenue plant, clasping a new bottle or point of sale (POS) sign, anxiously looking for someone to describe his latest sales idea to. So, it is not uncommon for people to speak of him in the present tense, and it is obvious that he is still very much a presence; very much a part of the culture at Vi-Jon.

Because of his experience in human resources, Ed Sander had a unique observation about the Brunners that indicates an interesting understanding of the challenges both men have faced. "The similarity has to be their interest in the customer and the employees," he said. "The only difference is that John had to take a slightly different approach, just by virtue of regulations and the company's size." Noting how much the business environment has changed since Jack Brunner took over the helm in 1946, Ed said, "Mr. Brunner could do business on the back of an envelope while sitting down with a customer. John has to rely on refined analysis and resources. It's just a different world." Today's approach requires more formal discipline and past techniques took a bit more finesse and grass roots initiative.

Employee Benefits

"In the early years," John W. Brunner acknowledged in an interview several years ago, "we didn't have much in the way of benefits, although if the company had a good year we'd have a Christmas bonus. When we didn't have a good year, I remember my father would buy a bunch of turkeys and give one to each employee. That was all he could do." At the end of the line always was a Brunner. "Daily bread" was always distributed to his friends first.

When John G. Brunner bought the company from his father in 1990, he continued the trend toward enhanced employee benefits. Through the years, benefits have been expanded to include a 401(k) plan, a more formalized bonus arrangement, and improved health care, disability benefits, and life insurance. He has fostered a responsible approach to living and doing business that has been impressed upon all who have worked for his father and him.

Listening and Responding to the Employees

Communication is at the very core of working with people. But it is a two-way street, and it is important that the employees understand that they are equal partners in that equation. At Vi-Jon, the management team not only listens to what the employees say, sometimes they even hear what *isn't* being said. In his 1993 book, *Corporate Dandelions*, author Craig Cantoni tells the story of how John Brunner learned an important lesson just by walking through the employee parking lot. The management and employee parking lots had just been combined and, while touring the plant with Mr. Cantoni, John pointed out a section of sidewalk and explained, "It's raised up because we didn't realize until the employee lots were combined that the walkway filled with water whenever it rained. It took us getting our dress shoes wet to realize that employees had to slosh through water to get to the door. It's amazing what can be learned by coming into contact with the employees."

As Kirk Sanders said, "John Brunner is extremely perceptive. He just has a gift for being able to listen, to learn what it is the individual is really trying to say. He's able then, to help us if we need to modify our behavior; if we're doing something wrong." Sense and some amount of sensibility are not found in any business book at the Harvard Business School. It is, however, found in the hearts of very special individuals.

The Vi-Jon display at the 2002 Trade Show. Jack Brunner passes on some invaluable sales advice to Eduardo Alves.

This emphasis on listening to associates is a tradition at Vi-Jon. When asked what most impressed him about Jack Brunner, Tom Marren replied, "When we had a meeting, everyone truly had input. If a line person didn't agree with something somebody said, we'd stop and discuss it. Everybody had a voice. There was no "caste system" here. Some discussions truly emanated from the bottom up in some instances, because that was where the best ideas often come from. He cared about everybody." Tom also recalled the time when he actually left the company for a couple of months. When he returned to Vi-Jon, John called him on a Sunday night. Tom said, "I thought he was going to chew me out but instead he was nice, complimentary, and said, 'Thanks for coming back. We're glad to have you back' just like I was part of the family, and he meant every word."

Sometimes even the simplest of gestures are the ones remembered most fondly. Dorothy Burns who has been with the company since 1973 said, "Mr. Brunner [John W.] would come down to the line and he knew everybody's name. He'd come by and stop and talk to you or whatever. I was in the label room and I was in charge of the vending machines. I would have to stock them and keep up with the money, and I remember one year that he gave me a little award for doing that. He was great." He simply looked you in the eye and his warm expression made you know that talking to you at that very moment was very important to him. It was also very important to the associates he shared these moments with.

A Culture that Cares

Ed Sander will bear witness to the fact that John G. Brunner has always wanted Vi-Jon to be a company that people referred to as "a family-style company." Bob Hess summed it up candidly by saying: "While you work very hard at Vi-Jon, when you have personal issues of any kind, they are there for you. They understand. As big as this company is, and as busy as John Brunner is, if you are in the hospital, John will take time out and come see you or give you a call. That says a lot about a company." The result of this unique approach to business is a culture of caring in which concern for the individuals and their families extends to everyone, without regard for position or rank.

Dorothy Burns recalled the many acts of kindness they received from John W. Brunner's wife, Virginia. "She would bring us little gifts and she fixed the ladies' bathroom up with mirrors and everything. At Christmastime she would give us chocolates and things. It was nice." While Dorothy is quick to express appreciation for the elegance of the company's more recent Christmas dinners, something in her eyes reveals nostalgia for the days when these annual celebrations meant a box lunch from Kentucky Fried Chicken spread out on tables at the Etzel Avenue plant.

Mona Foster recalls that she and her coworkers in Label Control, Dorothy Burns and Nesa Ebenrick, referred to themselves as the Three Musketeers. "Our motto was 'One for all and all for one' and we all looked out for each other," she said. Her fondest memory, however, was the outpouring of compassion she received when she had a house fire. Many of her co-workers had become friends and gave her things to put her household back together. She recalled, "I cannot tell you how truly touched I was." This was the compassion that the Brunner family reinforced with all who work at Vi-Jon.

Left to right: Wright Carter, Dan Charleville, unidentified, and Terry McBride (deceased in 2007) cook up some brats at one of the barbeques.

Everyone has put the extra effort into critical projects, with one guiding light being that penchant for "getting the job done for Vi-Jon and Mr. Brunner." Even in the darkest of times Vi-Jon associates have risen to the occasion, like the time in New Jersey. This story is told often by a group of mechanics and our engineering group about the "breath strip" challenge some years back, and the team's dedication to getting the job done for John. Some of our Page crew—Dan Charleville, Ronie Hanselman, Rodney Renner, Wright Carter, Ed Lemay, and Farley Roemer—flew out to New Jersey. They were directed by Kirk Sanders to start early and push hard to get as many of the breath strip cutting machines done and out on the production line to package the breath strips. Ronnie and his team recall Kirk cheering on the process with his relentless chant, "One more hour and we'll all get a nice meal." Well, 11:00 p.m. would roll around and the team would pull into the Holiday Inn Restaurant, only to find out the kitchen was closed and cold finger food and a cold beverage would have to do. Kirk even made the cold pizza rolls everybody was devouring taste like rib eye steak. He would try to boost everyone up and compliment each day's efforts. And he would encourage everyone's *future* efforts by quizzing them all on how many machines they might complete before the target date on Saturday, two days from then. Kirk would start the projections with a hearty eight-machine forecast, but he only got a counter-bid from the mechanics of "one or two more machines . . . maybe." Undaunted, Kirk and Tom Marren would continue to pump up the team and pulled on T-shirts the last two days to help kick the effort along. They then arranged on the Friday night before the Saturday departure to have an Italian feast catered in that was fit for kings. The team delivered four machines and surprised themselves, but not Kirk Sanders!

Postgame Wrap-Up

Gil Burgess leads the Vi-Jon Team in a prayer during one of the many Christmas celebrations at Vi-Jon.

Gil Burgess, who has been with the company since 1979, talks about the Brunner family's leadership at Vi-Jon, with the passion of a man who was born to be behind a pulpit. He started working in the Shipping Department and he recalled, "I noticed something right away. I saw people watching each other's backs, taking care of each other. Then I met with the late John W. Brunner and he'd give me words of wisdom. And then I got acquainted with his son when he came on. What makes us number one is that they have a heart for the people. You've got to take your eyes off 'me' and put your eyes on someone else. That's what it's all about, each one helping one another."

Another typical story touching on John's impact came from the nerve-wracking days of the ROSS startup in the fall of 1998. Vi-Jon was in the process of installing this new centralized software system. John Brunner wanted to find a way to help the start-up team but respectfully did not want to get in the way. With a full measure of confidence in the people working on this project, John was satisfied with getting periodic updates and reassurances that all was going well. Coincidentally, a competitor was in the process of installing an even larger and more complex system at the same time Vi-Jon was installing theirs. One day John went to Mel Turner and showed him a press release that this competitor had put out, heralding the news that the installation of their new system had caused serious business interruptions for several weeks and cost them a commensurate amount of sales. John's demeanor changed a bit and Mel recalled John asking a lot more questions in the weeks to come. The decision was made to implement Vi-Jon's new system over a weekend in order to avoid any down time.

Left to right: Kevin Birkner, Bob Hess, Mel Turner, and Mike Luebbers at a 1996 function.

When the long anticipated weekend arrived, John Brunner was present, along with the other key people on the project. Mel recalled, "John would be in his office and come out and ask, 'How are we doing?' I told him the group needed a break; some time for a sandwich and a Coke. John said, 'I'll take care of it.' and hopped in his car." The entire weekend, John provided support by running out for snacks, lunches, anything the group needed to help keep them on track. Finally, late Sunday afternoon they were bringing up the databases, trying to get jobs ready for production when John went to Mel once again and asked, "Where are we?" Mel assured him they'd done all they could, and when John asked if there was anything at all that could be done to assure the successful installation of the new system, Mel said, "John, it's time to pray." Recalling that weekend, Mel said, "John went to his office and I know to the depths of my soul, that's exactly what he did." The plant ran Monday morning; orders were shipped Monday afternoon and invoiced on Tuesday without missing a beat. There's no doubt in Mel Turner's mind but that John's involvement and support was highly encouraging for the six or eight people "who carried the weight of the company on their shoulders that weekend."

Going the Extra Mile

The people at Vi-Jon have any number of stories to tell of occasions where they or someone else have gone "the extra mile" in order to get the job done. When asked the origin of that "extra mile" mentality, Ed Sander replied, "I don't know that you can build that into a company. It has to be a function of the relationship between the people that are running the company and those who are working for the company."

When asked about the "extra mile" tradition, Dorothy Burns' response seemed to suggest there was simply no other way to work: "Well, basically, everybody would. I mean, if they're asked to do something or they need to do something, they just do it. A lot of times they don't have to be told, 'Hey, you need to do this.' Most of the time, they just do it."

Charlie Krebs told a story that took place sometime during the 1980s, when four rows of steel shelves full of heavy rolls of labels toppled over in domino fashion, creating a mass of twisted steel and rolls of labels. No one was injured, but Charlie requested some emergency temporary help to begin sorting all the salvageable labels and restore order. Debbie, who was one of his press operators, volunteered to remain and help supervise the temporary help. They worked through the night and by morning had made enough progress to release the temporary help. By the next evening almost everything was back in place. As Charlie said, "Thanks to the additional help and a willing spirit, all necessary labels were available for normal production on all lines. And the shelves were securely anchored."

The "Legend" of Rudolph

The story of this project made its rounds over the years and has tickled many associates who knew John W. Brunner and his zest for new products to market especially during holidays. As everyone now knows, Rudolph the Red-Nosed Reindeer shampoo bottle was a pet project of John W. Brunner, who had his heart set on producing a reindeer-shaped container filled with bubble bath as a Christmastime promotion. Ed Sander was head of operations at the time and remembers scouring the globe for the perfect container and the perfect cap, only to discover that, once on the line, filling Rudolph proved to be extremely problematic. Apparently, he just wouldn't stand still for it. Rudolph never made it to the store shelves but, as Ed said, "Everybody, out of respect for Mr. Brunner, would just work to try to make it happen." Ask anyone who has worked for Vi-Jon for any length of time and you will get their version of a "Rudolph story"—whether breath strips, robotics, warehouse relocation, new offices, SAP, or packaging and raw material challenges. The team has always had its tradition set by the leadership and motivation from the Brunner family.

The infamous "Rudolph the Red-Nosed Reindeer" shampoo product, which proved to be a much greater challenge to fill with product than originally anticipated.

Faith in God and Country

So what would you see if you dissected this culture of caring; what would stand out as being so special? One might say that it is rooted in some very fundamental beliefs, another tradition in the Brunner family. As Charlie Krebs recalled, "Everyone who knew Jack Brunner was aware of his patriotism and great love for America. Also of intense interest to him was our political process, so much so that during significant campaigns for state offices, he invited candidates from both major political parties to present their views and qualifications for office to Vi-Jon employees. What made these gatherings significant was that they were conducted during regular working hours. Very few business owners would sacrifice profitable production time to impress on everyone the importance of exercising their duty to vote."

The Brunner family is not only respected and honored by their co-workers at Vi-Jon but in the public sector as well. In 2001 Jack Brunner received the National Federation of Republican Assemblies' McDaniel Lewis Lifetime Achievement Award for his years of service to America's founding principles. His father-in-law, Jesse Gammon, had been an active committeeman in Indianapolis and was a tremendous influence on Jack. As far back as 1950, Jack Brunner was serving as precinct captain in the Gravois Township. When presenting the award, Phyllis Schlafly referred to Jack

John W. "Jack" Brunner and his wife Ginny, with forty years of Service Award to add to their collection.

Brunner as "a shining example of what one businessman can and should do if he cares about the future of America"—impressive words and so richly deserved as well.

Evidence of the patriotism of the Brunner family can also be found among the souvenirs Charlie Krebs saved from both his and his father's days in the printshop. From time to time, the printshop was called on to do some work for churches and organizations when production schedules allowed. Among Charlie's souvenirs is a program booklet from a class in "Mothercraft" held by St. John's M.E. Church in 1928 and 1929. Amidst the yearlong schedule of presentations on topics ranging from ancestry to manners, is one to be given by Mrs. J. B. (Viola) Brunner on "Citizenship." She was truly a mother figure to all who had the privilege to know her over the years.

Service to One's Country

When one is at a Vi-Jon facility one does not have to look far to understand what country you're in and how much patriotism resides at those installations. There is always an American Flag respectfully flown, as well as flags for the various branches of the military—just one more legacy from the Brunner family for the country that they love and have defended. One hallway at Vi-Jon's Page Avenue offices is dedicated to photos of Vi-Jon associates who have served in the military, including some of Vi-Jon's management team. Ed Sander (now retired from Vi-Jon) joined the company in 1988 upon his retirement from the United States Air Force, as did Mel Turner in 1993. Joe Streitz, current vice president of distribution, brought his experience from the United States Marine Corps to help improve Vi-Jon's customer service and distribution costs when he retired and joined the company in 1999.

The respect that John G. Brunner had for the military was multiplied after his own experience in the U.S. Marines. What he learned about accountability and leadership there has translated into many of the policies that govern Vi-Jon. "When bonuses are cut, it starts at the top, and when they're reinstated, it starts at the bottom. I learned this in the Marine Corps chow line; the senior officer is the last to eat. You have a tendency not to run out of food that way!"

Corporate Humility

If there was a dictionary that had a description of the makeup of a Brunner it would say: "A humble personification of a spirit rich in appreciation, motivation, and performance." The act of humble appreciation indicates gratitude and honor for something or someone. The motivation and performance relate to a success story that has had sustainability and tenure. In today's business world, more books should be written about this type of success story than about Enron-type failures that describe the very depths of business character and debauchery that predominate our daily business reports and leave us all shaking our heads in disbelief. The Brunners put together a simple formula, told here in this story—the type of story that is far too often neglected in corporate America.

To Those Who Partner Our Load

This book is a tribute to the honor and respect the Brunner family has demonstrated towards their employees over the years, and to their vendors, who also represent a valuable part of this magical business adventure called Vi-Jon.

Recognizing that customer service is a team effort between Vi-Jon and its vendors, awards are given to the companies that have shown outstanding dedication to meeting and exceeding customer service goals throughout the year. Towards the end of each year, Vi-Jon associates nominate companies in different categories. Winners are chosen to receive awards at various levels—"Vendor of the Year," "Outstanding," and "Honorable Mention." These awards are presented at our annual Vi-Jon Vendor Appreciation Awards banquet each February.

The award ceremony is like nothing else seen in the manufacturing industry. John Brunner insists that all presentations be made with all the pomp and circumstance and professionalism that these deserving companies should receive. Each award is given by a presenter who delivers a speech specially prepared, practiced, and nervously—but sincerely—delivered during the night's activities. Various speakers are invited to share a message with the honored guest. The evening concludes with an uplifting message from John G. Brunner, who addresses the guests and defines these very special partnerships. He invites everyone to participate and deliver even greater accomplishments in the coming business year.

A photo of one of the Vendor Appreciation Award Banquets.

About the Author

Edward A. Lemay is a lifelong St. Louisan and director of engineering at Vi-Jon's Missouri operations. He was born at Barnes Hospital—a year before the St. Louis Browns moved to Baltimore—just a stones throw away from Forest Park, site of the 1904 Worlds Fair, and just a short trolley ride down the road from the Vi-Jon Etzel Plant.

Ed credits his penchant for taking on challenging tasks, like writing this book, to a solid upbringing by his mom and dad. Ed's dad, Edward F. Lemay was a bricklayer foreman working throughout the area both on residences and a cadre of other assorted noteworthy landmarks. The serpentine wall at the St. Louis Zoo right down from the "bird cage" was one of his dad's proudest achievements. Ed's mother, Jacquelene, was a beautician/homemaker who managed a family including two brothers (Gerry and Larry) and two sisters (Cheryl and Becky) under a tight rein. He credits his mother with influencing some of his writing habits. She was a prolific letter writer and always amazed him as to how she could be so original in communicating the same piece of news to so many different people in so many different ways.

Ed went to Southern Illinois University at Edwardsville where most of his studies were in fields related to science and engineering with absolutely no concentration in writing. Upon graduation he joined Bardenheier Wine Cellars ultimately becoming master winemaker directing all wine and grape growing operations. His next stop was a senior position helping to direct a contract beverage operation. Ed followed that endeavor by performing consulting roles for a number of prominent soft drink and hair-care customers requiring a fair amount of traveling in Canada, the United States, and Africa.

Ed's first contact with John G. Brunner came in 1986 while looking at a potential contract packing opportunity for Vi-Jon. In 1999 John invited Ed to look at assisting in the Page Plant start-up project and within weeks Mel Turner hired Ed to come in as an assistant project manager. His initial Vi-Jon experience sold Ed on the Vi-Jon culture along with the opportunity to work for a fast-growing company. He subsequently accepted a full-time position managing projects along with other assorted engineering duties. Ed has called his ten years at Vi-Jon the opportunity of a lifetime.

It should also be noted here that Ed's written reports are legendary at Vi-Jon. The first thing that Ed wrote for Vi-Jon was a plant analysis for John Brunner the afternoon following his morning interview with John. It was a seventeen-page, minutely detailed review covering most facets about the new venture. The length of the report was only superseded by his overwhelming interest in getting the position. Writing presentations for the annual Vendors Appreciation Award Banquet was another opportunity for Ed to use his "stradevarian" writing capabilities. The "stradevarian" tag was given after a speech during which Ed used the analogy of the Italian violinmaker with a quality designation in a related story. The tag stuck and Ed has continued to provide entertaining "stradevarian" presentations at recent banquets.

Ed has three children: Edward P., Danielle, and Brett. Ed noted that the degree of their writing talents is still pending and that the three of them literally tiptoed around him during the almost full year that he spent writing the book. Ten months of work yielded this story that can best be described as having developed into a "magnificent obsession" for Ed. He made the statement that, "when you write a story like this you literally become a Brunner, you live the stories and feel the emotions that you are so respectfully trying to communicate to the reader. It has truly been a life changing benchmark for me personally."

Postscript: Next Season

This book is dedicated to all of the members of the Vi-Jon Team—of which I have had the utmost privilege as a player, coach, and owner. But Vi-Jon history continues to be made; to be captured in the next edition—a volume with a story even more compelling. It would be my desire to confer acknowledgement in the next chapter to the next generation who symbolizes the future; specifically a young man, like so many others, who joined our company, with hopes and aspirations, for his turn in getting on base—my son, and namesake of our founder **John Burgess Brunner III.**

Few could possibility know the personal concessions and sacrifices you made growing up as a Brunner in the Vi-Jon family. For you it became "normal" to encounter your father staggering home so late after innumerable exhausting days and months that dragged into years. I brought home the problems and challenges of the business, which crowded out the time for those things most dads do with their sons. And for those years, when your mother was ill, and I was trying to keep the business above water, you and your sisters kept me afloat. Yet in growing up for most of those twenty-eight years, at every waking hour, the kitchen table discussions, and every "working" vacation, you were personally affected by trials and tribulations, obligations, and responsibilities of the Vi-Jon family. Taking care of the Vi-Jon associates was our family focus.

As you matured into a young man I was gratified that you achieved a good classical education. Believing that every person should try to follow their dreams, I wanted you to follow yours. Though encouraged to take different paths, you never relented from your indomitable passion and determination to join the Vi-Jon team; to do what you could to make a contribution.

Over the last few years, you joined other dedicated associates in making a mark at Vi-Jon. Your strategic insight and recommendations in prioritizing the tactical opportunities is constructive and effectual. You are always there to encourage me to stay focused on the important issues, and not let the minor distractions send me off course. Your discernment of people is poignant as we build a team that bleeds Vi-Jon red. Many associates may give me credit for my insight, unaware that the acuity of my vision is facilitated through the distillation of your own perception and intuition. As a member of the Vi-Jon family you are a member of a great team that earned my respect and admiration these past thirty-one years.

I am overwhelmed by your passion for Vi-Jon to be the company it can be. There are so many good associates that believe like you do. The challenge is to "hang in there together" and "fight the good fight" as a team. As Stephen Crane, the American novelist, so clearly stated,

You cannot choose your battlefield, God does that for you;
But you can plant a standard where a standard never flew.

Four generations is unique in the American Dream. But it is not about the Brunner family, Board of Directors, or individual associates. It is about something greater than individual effort and accomplishment. It is about our culture—the personification of providing a better future; with integrity, dedication, and mutual respect. Our vision captures the essence of our culture as we work together to provide *a Value Choice for a Better Life*. It takes a team to live this dream!

—John G. Brunner

Vi-Jon Laboratories, Inc.

Boards of Directors
1966 to 2009

1966

John W. Brunner

R. Walston Chubb

Carl Duhrsen

Jeannette Duhrsen

Carl J. Mueller

H. O. Short

O. A. Zahner

1967

John W. Brunner

Carl Duhrsen

Jeannette Duhrsen

Carl J. Mueller

Howard O. Short

Oscar A. Zahner

1968

John W. Brunner

Carl Duhrsen

Jeannette Duhrsen

Carl J. Mueller

Howard O. Short

Oscar A. Zahner

1969

John W. Brunner

Carl Duhrsen

Jeannette Duhrsen

Carl J. Mueller

Howard O. Short

Oscar A. Zahner

1970

John W. Brunner

Carl Duhrsen

Jeannette Duhrsen

Carl J. Mueller

Howard O. Short

Oscar A. Zahner

1971

John W. Brunner

R. Walston Chubb

Jeannette Duhrsen

Carl J. Mueller

Howard O. Short

Joseph C. Weiler

Oscar A. Zahner

1972

John W. Brunner

R. Walston Chubb

Jeannette Duhrsen

Carl J. Mueller

Howard O. Short

Joseph C. Weiler

Oscar A. Zahner

1973

John W. Brunner

Robert W. Copeland

Jeannette Duhrsen

Carl J. Mueller

Howard O. Short

Joseph C. Weiler

Oscar A. Zahner

1974

John W. Brunner

Robert W. Copeland

Carl J. Mueller

William Schierholz, Jr.

Jeannette Duhrsen Stephenson

Joseph C. Weiler

Louis P. Whiting

1975

John W. Brunner

Robert W. Copeland

Carl J. Mueller

William Schierholz, Jr.

Jeannette Duhrsen Stephenson

Joseph C. Weiler

Lewis P. Whiting

Vi-Jon Board

1976

John W. Brunner

Robert W. Copeland

Carl J. Mueller

Jeannette Duhrsen Stephenson

Joseph C. Weiler

Louis P. Whiting

1977

Cress Auinbauh

John W. Brunner

Carl J. Mueller

David Lupo

Ray Scholin

Charles W. Sunderman

Lewis P. Whiting

1978

John W. Brunner

Robert W. Copeland

Carl J. Mueller

Ray Scholin

Charles W. Sunderman

Lewis P. Whiting

1979

John W. Brunner

Robert W. Copeland

Carl J. Mueller

Ray Scholin

Charles W. Sunderman

Louis P. Whiting

1980

John W. Brunner

Robert W. Copeland

Carl J. Mueller

Ray Scholin

Charles W. Sunderman

Louis P. Whiting

1981

John W. Brunner

Carl J. Mueller

Ray Scholin

Marvin Sinn

John Smith

Charles W. Sunderman

1982

John W. Brunner

Carl J. Mueller

Ray Scholin

Marvin Sinn

John Smith

Charles W. Sunderman

1983

John W. Brunner

Carl J. Mueller

Ray Scholin

Marvin Sinn

Charles W. Sunderman

1984

John W. Brunner

Carl J. Mueller

Ray Scholin

Marvin Sinn

Charles W. Sunderman

1985

John W. Brunner

James W. Maxwell

Carl J. Mueller

Ray Scholin

Marvin Sinn

Charles W. Sunderman

1986

John W. Brunner

James W. Maxwell

Ray Scholin

Marvin Sinn

1987

John G. Brunner

John W. Brunner

James W. Maxwell

Ray Scholin

Marvin J. Sinn

Vi-Jon Board

1988
John G. Brunner

John W. Brunner

James W. Maxwell

Ray Scholin

Marvin J. Sinn

1989
John G. Brunner

John W. Brunner

James Maxwell

Raymond Scholin

Marvin J. Sinn

1990
John G. Brunner

John W. Brunner

James W. Maxwell

Raymond Scholin

Marvin J. Sinn

1991
John G. Brunner

John W. Brunner

James W. Maxwell

Raymond Scholin

Marvin J. Sinn

1992
John G. Brunner

John W. Brunner

James W. Maxwell

Ray A. Scholin

Marvin J. Sinn

1993
John G. Brunner

John W. Brunner

Ralph D. Crowley, Jr.

John Maxwell

Marvin J. Sinn

Ray A. Scholin

1994

John G. Brunner

John W. Brunner

Ralph D. Crowley, Jr.

John Maxwell

Marvin J. Sinn

Ray A. Scholin

1995

John G. Brunner

John W. Brunner

Ralph D. Crowley, Jr.

Lawrence J. LeGrand

Donald W. Paule

1996

John G. Brunner

John W. Brunner

Lawrence J. LeGrand

John Oeltjen

Kirk Sanders

Mel Turner

Gary Watson

1997

John G. Brunner

John W. Brunner

Robert T. Corbett

Ralph D. Crowley, Jr.

Lawrence J. LeGrand

Kirk Sanders

Mel Turner

Gary Watson

1998

John G. Brunner

John W. Brunner

Robert T. Corbett

Ralph D. Crowley, Jr.

Lawrence J. LeGrand

Kirk Sanders

Mel Turner

Gary Watson

Vi-Jon Board

1999

John G. Brunner

John W. Brunner

Robert T. Corbett

Ralph D. Crowley, Jr.

Lawrence J. LeGrand

Kirk Sanders

Mel Turner

Gary Watson

2000

John G. Brunner

John W. Brunner

Robert T. Corbett

Ralph D. Crowley, Jr.

Lawrence J. LeGrand

General Alfred M. Gray, Jr.

Kirk Sanders

Mel Turner

Gary Watson

2001

John G. Brunner

John W. Brunner

Robert T. Corbett

Ralph D. Crowley, Jr.

Lawrence J. LeGrand

General Alfred M. Gray, Jr.

Kirk Sanders

Gary Watson

2002

John G. Brunner

John W. Brunner

Robert T. Corbett

Ralph D. Crowley, Jr.

Lawrence J. LeGrand

General Alfred M. Gray, Jr.

Gary Watson

2003

John G. Brunner

John W. Brunner

Robert T. Corbett

Ralph D. Crowley, Jr.

Lawrence J. LeGrand

General Alfred M. Gray, Jr.

Gary Watson

2004

John G. Brunner

John W. Brunner

Robert T. Corbett

Ralph D. Crowley, Jr.

Lawrence J. LeGrand

General Alfred M. Gray, Jr.

John Scherer

2005

John G. Brunner

John W. Brunner

Robert T. Corbett

Ralph D. Crowley, Jr.

Lawrence J. LeGrand

General Alfred M. Gray, Jr.

John Scherer

2006

John G. Brunner

Robert T. Corbett

Ralph D. Crowley, Jr.

Lawrence J. LeGrand

General Alfred M. Gray, Jr.

John Scherer

2007

John G. Brunner

Ralph D. Crowley, Jr.

Lawrence J. LeGrand

Joshua Lutzker

Randy Peeler

Jane Brock-Wilson

2008

John G. Brunner

Ralph D. Crowley, Jr.

Greg Delaney

Lawrence J. LeGrand

Joshua Lutzker

Randy Peeler

Jane Brock-Wilson

2009

John G. Brunner

Ralph D. Crowley, Jr.

Greg Delaney

Lawrence J. LeGrand

Joshua Lutzker

Randy Peeler

Jane Brock-Wilson

Robert E. Kirby

Awards Presented to Vi-Jon

1987
Kmart Presents Vi-Jon with Award of Recognition
for Many Years of Service

1990
"REX" (Retail Excellence) Award Presented to Vi-Jon
for Outstanding Performance in Creating New Marketing Opportunities
in the Drug Chain Industry

1992
Vi-Jon Receives St. Louis Small Business Award

1993
Vi-Jon Receives Kmart Private Label Supplier of the Year Award

1997
Wal-Mart Presents Vendor/Partner Award of Excellence to Vi-Jon

1998
Wal-Mart Honors Vi-Jon with Vendor Award of Excellence
for Second Quarter of 1998

2000
Vi-Jon Received St. Louis Economic Council's
Business Expansion Award for 1999

2000
Vi-Jon Congratulated by Wal-Mart for Achieving
Outstanding Results in Co-Managed Vendor Program
Week Ending March 17, 2000

2001
Rite Aid Presents Vi-Jon the 2000 Supplier of the Year

2001
Wal-Mart Presents First Quarter Supplier Award of Excellence

2002

Wal-Mart Honors Vi-Jon as a 2001 Vendor of the Year

2002

Target Presents Vi-Jon with 2001 Vendor Award of Excellence

2002

Wal-Mart Department 26 Awards Vi-Jon Best New Supplier Award

2003

Wal-Mart Department 46 Awards Vi-Jon Excellence
in Asset Management and Best Improved in Gross Margin Return on Investment

2003

Wal-Mart Presents Vi-Jon with Supplier Award of Excellence Second Quarter

2003

Wal-Mart Presents the Cost Savings Got It Done Award

2005

Sam's Club Honors Vi-Jon with Supplier Award of Excellence Third Quarter

2005

Sam's Club Awards Vi-Jon Outstanding Supplier of the Year

2006

Brooks-Eckerd Honors Vi-Jon as Private Label Vendor of the Year

2007

Wal-Mart Presents Vi-Jon with Pyramid Power Award

2008

Kroger Presents Vi-Jon with 2007 Outstanding Supplier of the Year

2009

Wal-Mart Presents Vi-Jon with the 2008 Private Label Supplier of the Year

Chairman's Award Winners over the Years

James Adams	2007	Jim Childree	2006, 2007
Sue Alexander	2008	Wyatt Clark	2007
Greg Alvarado	2000	Pam Collins	2007
Ed Arndt	1995	Burton Cooper	2001
Cindy Arnold	2007	Patrick Creamer	2007
Lisa Banger	2001	Pam Davis	2004
Ibrahim Bektic	2006	Nurija Delic	2005, 2008
Gloria Bell	2008	Khansing Dengsot	2007
Kevin Birkner	1998	Allen Donaldson	2007
Ronnie Breece	2006, 2007, 2008	Kate Duffin	2003, 2007
Darrion Brown	2004, 2006	John Dukes	2004
Susan Brown	2006	Osman Dulic	2003, 2006, 2008
Dorothy Burns	1993	Nesa Ebenrick	1994, 1999, 2000
Kim Byrn	2007	Legion of Honor-2005	
Cindy Carlon	2006, 2007	Debbie Edwards	2006, 2007, 2008
Wright Carter	2001, 2004	Nicole Edwards	2007
Dave Cash	2008	Al Evans	2001
Don Cato	2006	Lorraine Fierro	2000
Dan Charlville	1996, 1999, 2005	Mona Foster	1998, 2000, 2003
Legion of Honor-2006		Legion of Honor-2005	
Debbie Chenoweth	2006	Andre Fuller	2003
		Pat Galland	2006

Doug Glacken 2007, 2008

Terrance Godfrey................................... 2002

Moysey Gorelik 2001

Mary Habert 2002

Cheryl Ham 2001

Jay Hampton.. 2006

Mike Hannibal....................................... 2008

Ronie Hanselman................................... 2000

Audie Hariri 2007

Dorothy Harris 1995, 2002, 2004,
    Legion of Honor-2005

John Hayes.. 2003

Dwayne Henderson............................... 2006

Lanny Hendrix, Jr. 2002, 2004, 2007

Jim Heyden 2006

Jackie Hofius 2005, 2006

Sharon Hoffmeister 2007

Kyle Hooper... 2007

Alonzo Hudgins 2007

Nate Hudson.. 1996

Karen Jackson.. 2008

Marquita Johnson 2001, 2007

Sky Johnson 2007

Martin Judd 2007

Sanela Jugovic 2006

Pat Jurgensmeyer................................... 1991

Zekija Karahodzic 2005

Carla Kinder 2007

Geralyn Kras-Wrinkle 2005

Anita Lane... 2008

Jeff Lenk.. 1999

Tom Lewandowski 1993

Patty Lorenz.. 1992

Shawn Luesse 2007

Patricia Macon 2008

Tom Marren... 1997

Ramo Memisevic 2007

Debbie Moore.. 2002

Saliha Mujanovic................................... 2007

Dave Mullins... 2002

Patsy Mummel 2007, 2008

Pasa Murselovic 2002

Aijka Mustafic....................................... 2005

Barry Nichols 2006

Chariman's Award

Tyler O'Neil	2001	Debbie Ursery		2005
Gloria Patterson	2007	Tony Utley		2008
Andy Peercy	2007	Steve Van Buren		2006
Boualine Phosarath	2007	Demetric Vaughn		2007
Dijana Ramic	2003	Rabbit Victory	2006,	2007
Jerry Reams	2004	Annetta Walton		2005
Rodney Renner	2002, 2005	Rita Weir	2007,	2008
Farley Roemer	2006, 2008	Ken Westhoelter	2004, 2007,	2008
Ed Sander	1991	Ernestine Williams		1997
William Scott	2006	Michael Willis		2007
Tracey Sherrill	2006	Ted Willis		2006
Timothy Singleton	2006, 2008	Gary Wilson		2008
Debbie Sizemore	2006, 2007	Margie Wilson		2001
Stanley Smitty	2008	Kellee Wright		2008
Laura Snow	2007			
Missy Stack	2007			
Karole Stout	2007			
Ralph Swoape	2007			
Slavica Tambic	2007			
Tammy Taylor	2007			
Nell Tillman	2005			
Glenn Thompson	2006, 2007, 2008			
Charlie Underwood	2007			

The Eighty-One
Charter Associates of Vi-Jon's New Beginning in 1995

Gregory Acoff	Ollie Floyd
Jill Alexander	Virginia Foens
Eduardo Alves	Walter Gaal
Edward Arndt	Gretchen Gannon
Kevin Birkner	Ronald Gibson
Sylvia Bray	Leonid Golynskiy
John G. Brunner	Steward Griffin
John W. Brunner	Bob Ham
Gil Burgess	Cheryl Ham
Leon Chapman	Jacqueline Hamilton
Daniel Charleville	John Hancock
Shensheng Chen	Lawanda Hardges
Bill Clemens	Dorothy Harris
Dana Bradford Cooper	Golda Helton
Leo Cunningham	David Henderson
Nesa Ebenrick	Lanny Hendrix, Sr.
Armenta Edelen	Lanny Hendrix, Jr.
Daniel Ehrhard	Robert Hess
Theodore Ewald	Jacalyn Hofius
Anna Farmer	Janice Winston Holland

The Eighty-One

Nathaniel Hudson	Julie Hawkins Oligschaeger
Sharon Jackson	Christopher Palazzolo
Mark Janes	Tracy Parker
Alvin Jones	Janette Peters
Carla Kinder	Beverly Pleasant
Lisa King	Mona Foster Roberts
Timothy Kobermann	Edward Sander
James Koesterer	Elizabeth Brown Simmons
Jean Landwehr	Dorothy Springer
Sandra Lay	Anthony Starzyk
Jeffrey Lenk	Sidney Stewart
Patricia Lorenz	Joni Sweet
Michael Luebbers	Melvin Turner
Thomas Marren	James Upchurch
Dorothy Boyd Moore	Deborah Ursery
James Moss	Gary Watson
Diane Mueller	Deborah Williams
Nga Nguyen	Ernestine Williams
Jon Nowotny	Margie Wilson
Brenda Odom	Pamela Wilson
William Odom	

Veterans Working at Vi-Jon

St. Louis, Missouri

Zachary Adams

Henry Braswell

Sylvia J. Bray-Thomas

Kames E. Broom

John G. Brunner

Terry Carter

Burton P. Cooper

Richard A. Cooper

Gregory Crosby

Sarah Darrow

Gary Depew

Thomas Eddings

Albert L. Evans

Claude M. Feathers

Jorge Fernandez

James Hagar

Matthew Hanson

Donald R. Hand

Georgia A. Handy

Brooke Hostmeyer

David P. Hughes

Barbara Jones

Tewana M. Jones

Elizabeth Lafargue

Raymond Laugh

Darryl McCoo

Mark Menteer

Wayne Meyer

Charles Mooney

James V. Nickelson

David Nihart

Richard Riley

Farley Roemer

Lee R. Rush

Glen Sammons

Edward F. Sander

Steve R. Santoyo

Jesse Sharp

Eugene Smith

Joseph J. Streitz

David Sweeso

Amos Thomas

Melvin L. Turner

Paul C. Ward

Kenneth Wells

Veterans at Vi-Jon

Karl Williams

Reginald Winston

Gary G. Wunderle

Kenneth Yeske

Smyrna, Tennessee

Cedric L. Aaron

Dennis A. Adams

Chirvougha P. Alexander

Ben C. Anderson

Buel N. Arbuckle

William T. Austin

Allen F. Bales

Thomas H. Barr, Jr.

Leslie J. Batson

Vincent S. Berry

Timothy J. Bittner

Angelo Q. Breland

Tony M. Butler

John J. Camaratta

Hershel Carpenter, Jr.

Gary W. Carr

Michael A. Casey

William D. Clegg

Lewis M. Clevenger

Gerald Cloyd

Sherrie L. Cowan

Richard A. Cunningham, Jr.

Vincent T. Davies

Glenn Davis

Nathan A. Davis

Wallace T. Dobbs

Michael K. Dougan

Mack A. Douglas

Cecil W. Duke

Richard D. Edens

Deborah K. Edwards

Carl T. Eick

Ronald G. Eisinger

Melvin L. Farless

Rafael J. Felix, Jr.

Larry D. Foster

Michael J. Garcia

Richard W. Gibbs

Richard L. Grissom

Michael D. Groomes

Tim A. Haddock

Timothy R. Handley

Paul B. Haradon

Norris B. Higdon

Jon K. Holland

Phyllis A. Housley

Getting On Base

Charles D. Jackson	William R. Murphy
Karen S. Jackson	Luther J. Myers
Ronnie G. Jett	Thomas Overton, Jr.
Daryle L. Johnson	Weston A. Pedigo
Kent L. Kelch	Michael P. Rabalais
Kerry W. Kimbrough	Benny S. Robson
James S. Kitchens	Ronnie L. Rutley
Terri A. Kitchens	Jose R. Sanchez
Victor R. Kraw	James E. Smith
Miliam C. Lafon	Donnie D. Sparkman
Bobby W. Lanius	Andrew G. Stevenson
Kevin L. Larson	Frank B. Sullens
Donald R. Lemons	Charles E. Taylor, Jr.
Roger B. Lewis	Edward D. Thompson
Geoffrey S. Lindsey	Rick P. Tomlin
Louis S. Lopez III	Charles R. Underwood
Larry W. Marshall	Jeffery E. Van Dyke
Robert E. Mason	Larry W. Ward
Sarah N. McAllister	Larry E. White
William D. McElroy	Rodney E. Whitington
John C. McGlothlin	Phillip D. Wilkerson
Stephen M. McKenzie	Randall W. Willis
Raymond J. McMullen	Jack M. Wilson
Jeffrey S. Michaels	Donald L. Wittwer
Robert L. Miller	
Thomas J. Moss IV	

Vendor of the Year Recipients

Accurate Mechanical	Emerson Transportation
Action Plus	Form Consultants
Advanced Distribution Services	Freedom Freightways
Advertising Artist	GK Packaging, Inc.
Arnold Electric	Handicraft
Averitt Express	Handwriting Labs
Berje, Inc.	Harbison Walker, Inc.
BKD, LLP	Harcros Chemicals, Inc.
Boone Center, Inc.	Holmes Freight Line
Boxes, Inc.	Hyman Freightways
C.A.P.S.	Illini Environmental, Inc.
Central Transport	Impression Label Company
Certified Packaging Corporation	In Transportation, Inc.
Chemcentral Corporation	Inland Paperboard and Packaging
Chemia Corporation	Intermodal Sales Corporation
Chemisphere Corporation	Jacobson Companies
Chemrite Industries, LLC	Javo-Mex Corporation
City Electric Supply	Keystone Container, LLC
CompuCom	KPMG Peat Marwick
Conrad Consulting, Inc.	Laciny Brothers, Inc.
Continental Glass	Laub\Hunt Packaging Systems
Cowan Benefit Services, Inc.	LithoFlex Corporation
E. M. Shaw, Inc.	Lyondell Basell

M K Packaging, Inc.

Mahurin Industries

McIntyre Group, Ltd.

Metropolitan Electric

MGP Ingredients Inc.

Mike Shell Chemical

Nehmen Advertising

Northwestern Bottle Company

Paule, Camazine & Blumenthal, P.C.

Penreco Corporate

Plastic Container Corporation

Polster, Lieder, Woodruff & Lucchesi, L.C.

Poly-Seal

Prime Package & Label

Roadway Express

Silgan Plastics Corporation

Southwest Bank of St. Louis

St. Elmo Plastics

Stone Container Corporation

Templock Corporation

Transportation Associates

Travelplex American Express

Trio Drayage

United Freight Company

Univar USA Inc.

Unlimited Services

Varian

Witte Brothers Exchange Inc.

Epilogue: The "Perfect Game" *by Mel Turner (Retired, finally!)*
Adapted from a homily (message) by Joe Griffin, Pastor of Grace Church, St. Louis, MO

For the Vi-Jon "old-timer," current associate or business partner, this book may have brought back personal memories of where we were and how far we have come. For those with a business interest but no prior Vi-Jon association, I hope you have gained an appreciation for the kind of company we were and hope to remain, one dedicated to the well being of our associates and committed to serving our customers. Some of you may have read these pages, more interested in the thread of baseball history that we have woven through this Vi-Jon history. So, let me reference baseball one more time as I leave you with a final, enduring, and oh so important thought.

You probably know the term *no-hitter* in baseball. An official no-hit game occurs when a pitcher holds the opposing team hitless during the entire course of a game that consists of at least nine innings. But in a no-hit game, a batter may reach base via a walk, an error, hit by a pitch, a passed ball or a wild pitch on strike three, or a catcher's interference. If you are a baseball fan, you probably have been lucky enough to have seen a no-hitter. But how many of you know what a *perfect* game is or have seen one?

An official *perfect* game occurs when a pitcher retires each batter on the opposing team during the entire course of a game that consists of at least nine innings. In a perfect game, the victimized team never gets a runner on base. Perfect games are so rare that, since 1900, there have been over two hundred thousand major league games played, but only fifteen perfect games. Here they are:

Cy Young (May 5, 1904); Addie Joss (October 2, 1908); Charlie Robertson (April 30, 1922); Don Larsen (October 8, 1956, World Series, Game 5); Jim Bunning (June 21, 1964); Sandy Koufax (September 9, 1965); Jim Hunter (May 8, 1968); Len Barker (May 15, 1981); Mike Witt (September 30, 1984); Tom Browning (September 16, 1988); Dennis Martinez (July 28, 1991); Kenny Rogers (July 28, 1994); David Wells (May 17, 1998); David Cone (July 18, 1999); and Randy Johnson (May 18, 2004).

Interestingly, nearly half—seven of the fifteen—occurred in the last twenty-five years. Note the long drought of over thirty years from 1922 until Don Larsen pitched perhaps the most remembered perfect game during the 1956 World Series. Many of the pitchers' names are familiar to the baseball fan because some of our greatest pitchers accomplished the feat—although no one did it more than once. To call a perfect game a rare event is an understatement. With that setting, let me tell you about the perfect game that almost was—but wasn't.

In June 1917, a young pitcher named George Herman Ruth—yes the Babe—started on the mound for the Boston Red Sox against Washington, and quickly walked Ray Morgan, Washington's first batter. The Babe was so incensed at the called fourth ball that he rushed the plate and confronted Brick Owens, the home plate umpire, threatening to punch him. Babe Ruth was ejected and immediately took a swing at Owens, landing a glancing blow. And that was the end of Ruth's day. In came Ernie Shore to pitch for Boston—without any warm-up—and what he did on June 23, 1917, caused a baseball controversy for years! Remember, up to that date, there had been only two perfect games.

Not only was Ray Morgan thrown out trying to steal second base, but Ernie Shore retired the next twenty-six batters in order without a single batter reaching first base. The controversy began! Should Ernie Shore be credited with a perfect game? He certainly pitched perfectly—to twenty-six batters—and the Red Sox retired the Babe's walked batter trying to steal second, Shore as the pitcher of record being credited with the out. All twenty-seven batters were thus retired. And a debate on this game raged for over fifty years.

Some felt Ernie Shore, whose performance was perfect, should be credited with a perfect game. However, baseball purists argued that the game itself was not a perfect game, because it had two pitchers, and a runner actually reached first base. The purists finally won out and the game is listed under the category of "No-hit games of nine or more innings." Of course, Ernie Shore could do nothing about the situation into which he came to pitch. He inherited Ruth's base runner, Ray Morgan. The "sin" committed by Ruth of placing a man on first was transferred to Ernie Shore and he had to live with it.

This strange baseball story has some parallels in life. Ernie Shore inherited the Babe's "sin" of Ray Morgan; he had no choice. And so it goes for us at birth. We inherit Adam's original sin and have no choice. We are born physically alive but spiritually dead because of that one sin.

Just as through one man [Adam], sin [the sinful nature] entered into the world and so spiritual death through the sin [of Adam], consequently spiritual death spread to all *men because* all *sinned when Adam sinned.* (Romans 5:12)

So what do we do about it? Ernie Shore cannot come in and pick up the pieces. Even if he could, it would not restore you to sinless perfection in God's eyes. We are born with Ray Morgan on first and need a savior. God provided the solution to this imputed sin, this loss of perfection, this Ray Morgan standing over there on first base. He gave us his Son.

Believe on the Lord Jesus and you shall be saved. (Acts 16:31a)

For by grace you have been saved through faith; and that salvation is not of yourselves, it is the gift of God; not of works, so that no one may boast. (Ephesians 2:8-9)

Salvation for eternity is available for those who simply believe on our Lord and Savior. A simple act of faith is all that is required. When all is said and done, what we leave behind are the fruits of our integrity. What we have going forward is the promise of our faith.

And so, we wrap up the first hundred years of this great adventure named Vi-Jon, hopeful that we will be remembered by our associates, our customers, our suppliers, and the consumer for our integrity as a company. We, the Vi-Jon family, have been blessed as a company beyond our wildest expectations. Our wish is that the faith that brought us here will sustain Vi-Jon for years to come.

Prayer

God of our fathers, whose almighty hand hath made and preserved our nation, grant that our people may understand what it is they celebrate tomorrow.

May they remember how bitterly our freedom was won, the down-payment that was made for it, the installments that have been made since this Republic was born, and the price that must be paid for liberty.

May freedom be seen not as the right to do as we please, but as the opportunity to please to do what is right.

May it ever be understood that our liberty is under God and can be found nowhere else.

May our faith be something that is not merely stamped upon our coins, but expressed in our lives.

Thursday, July 3, 1947
Source: Prayers by the Chaplain, Senate of the United States, Reverend Peter Marshall

This was a personal favorite of John W. Brunner.

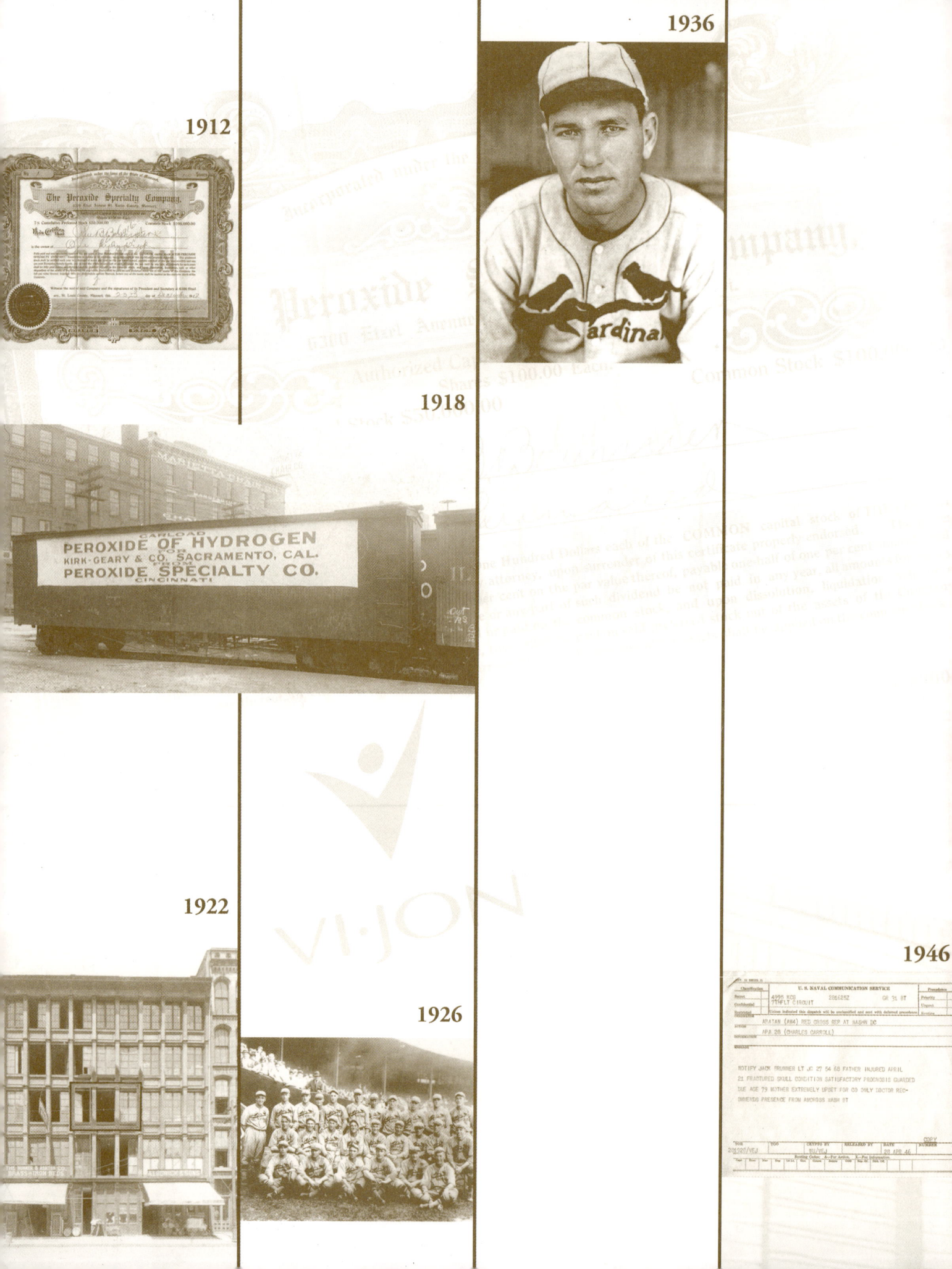